MW01615242

Published by
California Chamber of Commerce
P.O. Box 1736
Sacramento, CA 95812-1736

1-57997-925-4

5 4 3 2 1

The information compiled in this handbook is being provided by CalChamber as a service to the business community. Although every effort has been made to ensure the accuracy and completeness of this information, CalChamber, the contributors and the reviewers of this publication cannot be responsible for any errors or omissions, nor any court/agency's interpretations, applications and/or changes of the laws/regulations described herein.

This publication is designed to provide authoritative information in a highly summarized manner with regard to the subject matter covered. It is sold with the understanding that the publisher and others associated with this publication are not engaged in rendering legal, technical or other professional services. If legal and other expert assistance is required, the services of competent professionals should be sought.

This publication is available from:

CalChamber
P.O. Box 1736
Sacramento, CA 95812-1736
(800) 331-8877
store.calchamber.com

Table of Contents

Chapter 3

Chapter 4

Chapter 5

Chapter 6

Chapter 7

Chapter 8

Chapter 9

What's New for 2020?

This preface lists additions and changes to the *2020 HR Quick Guide for California Employers*, detailed in chapter order.

Hiring Employees

- In 2018, California passed the California Consumer Privacy Act (CCPA), which changed the rules around how consumer data is collected. Effective January 1, 2020, employee data is exempted from the CCPA. However, an employer is still required to make a disclosure to applicants and employees under the CCPA. See "Complete the Appropriate Paperwork" in Chapter 2, page 28.

- A 2019 Ninth Circuit decision clarified that the Fair Credit Reporting Act's (FCRA) requirement that the disclosure document can consist only of the FRCA disclosure means that it can't include any additional information, including disclosures required under state law. For more information, see "Credit Checks" in Chapter 2, page 39.

- Effective January 1, 2020, most employers must satisfy a strict test to properly classify workers as independent contractors. For more information, see "Properly Classifying the Individual as an Independent Contractor" in Chapter 2, page 56.

- Effective January 1, 2020, California law bans mandatory arbitration agreements entered into between employers and employees. See "Employment Contracts" in Chapter 2, page 61.

Leaves of Absence

- Effective January 1, 2020, airline employees will be eligible for California Family Rights Act leave if they meet certain requirements. See "Eligibility Requirements" in Chapter 3, page 82.

- In 2019, a federal Department of Labor opinion letter stated that employers are prohibited from delaying designations related to the Family and Medical Leave Act. See "Designating Family and Medical Leave" in Chapter 3, page 86.

Providing Benefits

- Beginning July 1, 2020, the maximum duration of Paid Family Leave (PFL) benefits individuals may receive will be extended from six to eight weeks. See "Paid Family Leave Benefits" in Chapter 4, page 136.

- Beginning January 1, 2021, the PFL wage replacement program will be expanded so that employees can collect PFL benefits if they take time off for activities related to the covered active duty status of a family member. See "Paid Family Leave Benefits" in Chapter 4, page 136.

- Effective January 1, 2020, employers must notify employees who participate in flexible spending accounts of any deadline to withdraw funds before the plan year's end in two different ways. For more information, see "Health Insurance and Other Benefits" in Chapter 4, page 150.

Paying Employees

- Effective January 1, 2020, employers with 26 or more employees must pay a minimum wage of $13 per hour, and employers with 25 or fewer employees must pay a minimum wage of $12 per hour. See "California Minimum Wage" in Chapter 5, page 166.

- The minimum salary threshold for the executive, administrative and professional exemptions have increased for 2020. See "Executive, Administrative and Professional Exemptions" in Chapter 5, page 168.

- Hourly rates for the computer professional exemption increased effective January 1, 2020. See "Computer Professional Exemption" in Chapter 5, page 170.

- The hourly rate for the licensed physician or surgeon exemption increased effective January 1, 2020. See "Licensed Physicians and Surgeons" in Chapter 5, page 171.

- A 2019 California Court of Appeal decision determined that "regular rate of compensation" means an employee's base hourly rate for missed meal and rest break premiums. See "Missed Meal or Rest Break" in Chapter 5, page 179.

- Starting January 1, 2020, employers with 26 or more employees must pay agricultural employees overtime when they work more than 9.5 hours per day and 50.5 hours per week. "Overtime and Agricultural Employees" in Chapter 5, page 190.

- Effective January 1, 2020, employees now have two ways to bring a private action against an employer for failing to pay wages, and the Labor Commissioner may issue citations and recover amounts owed by an employer who has paid less than the wages set by contract. See "Failing to Pay Wages Due" in Chapter 5, page 206.

Ensuring Workplace Safety

- In 2019, California passed an emergency regulation to protect outdoor workers from the harmful effects of wildfire smoke, under which, affected employers must take steps to protect workers who could be exposed to wildfire smoke. See "Wildfire Smoke Regulation" in Chapter 6, page 235.

- Effective January 1, 2020, the definitions of "serious injury" and "serious exposure" were changed to align with the federal Occupational Safety and Health Administration standards. See ""Serious" Injury, Exposure Defined" in Chapter 6, page 241.

- Effective January 1, 2020, California employers must immediately report a serious occupational injury, illness or death to the Department of Industrial Relations (DIR) either by telephone or through an online portal created by the DIR. See "Reporting an Incident" in Chapter 6, page 241.

Preventing Discrimination

- In July 2019, California expanded the domestic partnership criteria to let any opposite sex couple register as domestic partners. See "Marital Status" in Chapter 7, page 270.

- Effective January 1, 2020, California law expands lactation accommodation requirements, and limits its undue hardship exemption to employers with fewer than 50 employees. See "Lactation Accommodation - Expressing Breast Milk at Work" in Chapter 7, page 272.

Preventing Harassment

- Prior to January 1, 2021, virtually all California employers must provide sexual harassment prevention training to all employees. For more information, see "Harassment-Prevention Training" in Chapter 8, page 296.

- Starting January 1, 2020, the statute of limitations to file a complaint with the Department of Fair Employment and Housing extends to three years. See "Time Limits for Filing Sexual Harassment Claims" on page 302.

Chapter 1

Getting Started

This book is designed to make it easy for you to quickly find the information you need.

Icons

These icons identify important information:

Table 1. *HR Quick Guide for California Employers* **Formatting**

❶	Identifies information you should pay close attention to
TIP	Identifies definitions of terms and helpful advice
New	Identifies new laws, regulations and court decisions for 2020

Does This Employment Law Apply to Me?

Use the chart on the next two pages to determine if a particular employment law applies to your company. For more information about each law, see the Index, which refers you to material throughout this book.

Law/Requirement	All	2 or more	4 or more	5 or more	15 or more	16 or more	20 or more	25 or more	50 or more	75 or more	100 or more
Affirmative Action									✓	✓	✓
Alcohol and Drug Rehabilitation								✓	✓	✓	✓
Americans with Disabilities Act (ADA)					✓	✓	✓	✓	✓	✓	✓
Ban-the-Box				✓	✓	✓	✓	✓	✓	✓	✓
Cal-COBRA (2–19 employees only) (*pg. 4)		✓	✓								
Child Labor		✓	✓	✓	✓	✓	✓	✓	✓	✓	✓
Civil Air Patrol Leave						✓	✓	✓	✓	✓	✓
COBRA (health insurance continuation)							✓	✓	✓	✓	✓
Crime Victims' Leave	✓	✓	✓	✓	✓	✓	✓	✓	✓	✓	✓
Disability Insurance	✓	✓	✓	✓	✓	✓	✓	✓	✓	✓	✓
Discrimination and Immigrant Workers			✓	✓	✓	✓	✓	✓	✓	✓	✓
Discrimination Laws (State)				✓	✓	✓	✓	✓	✓	✓	✓
Discrimination Laws (Federal)					✓	✓	✓	✓	✓	✓	✓
Domestic Violence, Sexual Assault and Stalking Victims' Leave: Legal Proceedings/Reasonable Accommodation		✓	✓	✓	✓	✓	✓	✓	✓	✓	✓
Domestic Violence, Sexual Assault and Stalking Victims' Leave: Medical Treatment								✓	✓	✓	✓
Employee Safety	✓	✓	✓	✓	✓	✓	✓	✓	✓	✓	✓
Equal Employment Opportunity (EEO) Reporting (**pg. 4)											✓
Fair Employment and Housing Act (FEHA)	✓	✓	✓	✓	✓	✓	✓	✓	✓	✓	✓
Family and Medical Leave (FMLA and CFRA)								✓	✓	✓	✓
Illiteracy Accommodation								✓	✓	✓	✓
Immigration Reform and Control Act (IRCA)	✓	✓	✓	✓	✓	✓	✓	✓	✓	✓	✓
Independent Contractors	✓	✓	✓	✓	✓	✓	✓	✓	✓	✓	✓

Law/Requirement	All	2 or more	4 or more	5 or more	15 or more	16 or more	20 or more	25 or more	50 or more	75 or more	100 or more
Injury and Illness Prevention Program (IIPP)	✓	✓	✓	✓	✓	✓	✓	✓	✓	✓	✓
Jury Duty Time Off	✓	✓	✓	✓	✓	✓	✓	✓	✓	✓	✓
Mandatory Paid Sick Leave	✓	✓	✓	✓	✓	✓	✓	✓	✓	✓	✓
Mandatory Sexual Harassment Training				✓	✓	✓	✓	✓	✓	✓	✓
Military Leave (USERRA)	✓	✓	✓	✓	✓	✓	✓	✓	✓	✓	✓
Military Spouse Leave								✓	✓	✓	✓
New Employee Reporting	✓	✓	✓	✓	✓	✓	✓	✓	✓	✓	✓
New Parent Leave Act							✓	✓	✓	✓	✓
Organ and Bone Marrow Donor's Leave					✓	✓	✓	✓	✓	✓	✓
Paid Family Leave (PFL)	✓	✓	✓	✓	✓	✓	✓	✓	✓	✓	✓
Pay and Scheduling	✓	✓	✓	✓	✓	✓	✓	✓	✓	✓	✓
Posters and Notices	✓	✓	✓	✓	✓	✓	✓	✓	✓	✓	✓
Pregnancy Disability Laws				✓	✓	✓	✓	✓	✓	✓	✓
Prior Salary Ban	✓	✓	✓	✓	✓	✓	✓	✓	✓	✓	✓
Privacy	✓	✓	✓	✓	✓	✓	✓	✓	✓	✓	✓
School Activities Leave (***pg. 4)								✓	✓	✓	✓
School Appearance Leave	✓	✓	✓	✓	✓	✓	✓	✓	✓	✓	✓
Smoking in the Workplace	✓	✓	✓	✓	✓	✓	✓	✓	✓	✓	✓
Unemployment Insurance (UI)	✓	✓	✓	✓	✓	✓	✓	✓	✓	✓	✓
Volunteer Civil Service Leave	✓	✓	✓	✓	✓	✓	✓	✓	✓	✓	✓
Volunteer Civil Service Training Leave									✓	✓	✓
WARN Act (plant closings)										✓	✓
Workers' Compensation	✓	✓	✓	✓	✓	✓	✓	✓	✓	✓	✓

Cal-COBRA, EEO Reporting, School Activities Leave

*Cal-COBRA covers employers with 2-19 employees who offer health insurance benefits to employees. Cal-COBRA covers employers with 20 or more employees when the employee loses COBRA coverage, if the COBRA coverage was for less than 36 months.

**EEO reporting also applies to employers covered by Title VII who have fewer than 100 employees if the organization is owned or affiliated with another organization or there is centralized ownership, control or management (such as central control of personnel policies and labor relations) so that the group legally constitutes a single enterprise, and the entire enterprise employs a total of 100 or more employees.

***A covered employer must employ 25 or more employees working at the same location.

Required Posters and Revisions

The information in the following charts is current as of this book's publication date.

Table 2. Required Posters

Federal Law			
Title	**Who Must Post?**	**Source**	**Version/Date**
Employee Polygraph Protection Act	All employers.	U.S. Department of Labor.	WH1462 Rev 07/16 WH1462 SPA Rev 07/16
Equal Employment Opportunity is the Law	All employers.	Equal Employment Opportunity Commission.	EEOC-P/E-1 Revised 11/09 Includes GINA
Federal Family and Medical Leave Act Poster	Employers of 50 or more employees and all "public agencies."	U.S. Department of Labor.	WH1420 Rev 04/16
Federal Family and Medical Leave Act Poster - Spanish	Employers of 50 or more employees and all "public agencies."	U.S. Department of Labor.	WH1420 SPA Rev 04/16

Table 2. Required Posters

Federal Law			
Title	**Who Must Post?**	**Source**	**Version/Date**
Federal Minimum Wage	All employers must post the federal and state minimum wage notices.	U.S. Department of Labor.	WH1088 Rev 07/16 WH1088 SPA Rev 07/16
Your Rights Under USERRA (Veterans Benefits)	All employers.	U.S. Department of Labor.	Publication Date — April 2017

California Law			
Title	**Who Must Post?**	**Source**	**Version/Date**
California Minimum Wage	All employers must post the state and federal minimum wage notices.	Industrial Welfare Commission.	MW-2019
California Wage Orders	All employers must post the industry-specific Wage Order for their business.	Department of Industrial Relations.	There are 17 Wage Orders with various dates
Discrimination and Harassment in Employment are Prohibited by Law	All employers.	Department of Fair Employment and Housing.	DFEH-E07P-ENG December 2018 DFEH-E07P-SP/ December 2018
Emergency Phone Numbers	All employers.	Department of Industrial Relations/Division of Occupational Safety & Health.	S-500 March 1990
Family Care and Medical Leave and Pregnancy Disability Leave notice	California employers with 20 or more employees subject to the NPLA, CFRA or FMLA.	Department of Fair Employment and Housing.	DFEH-100-21ENG/ (March 2019) DFEH-100-21SP/ (March 2019)

California Law			
Title	**Who Must Post?**	**Source**	**Version/Date**
Healthy Workplaces/ Healthy Families Act of 2014 Paid Sick Leave Poster	All employers. This poster advises employees of their sick leave rights under the law.	Division of Labor Standards Enforcement.	11/2014
Notice to Employees - Injuries Caused by Work	All employers.	Division of Workers' Compensation.	DWC 7 (1/1/2016)
Notice to Employees - UI, SDI, PFL	All employers. EDD posting DE 1857D gives employees notice of their rights under the Unemployment Insurance program. It's intended for use by employers not subject to SDI/PFL. CalChamber includes the DE 1857A because it contains not only the UI information, but the SDI/PFL information as well.	Employment Development Department.	DE 1857A Rev. 43 (5/18) DE 1857A/S Rev. 43 (5/18)
Pay Day Notice	All employers.	Department of Industrial Relations.	DLSE 8 (Rev 06/02)
Pregnancy Disability Leave Notice	All employers with 5 or more employees. Covered employers must provide notice to employees of the right to request pregnancy disability leave in a conspicuous place where employees tend to congregate.	Department of Fair Employment and Housing.	DFEH-E09P-ENG/ June 2017 DFEH-E09P-SP/ Junio 2017
Safety and Health Protection on the Job (Cal/ OSHA)	All employers.	Department of Industrial Relations/Division of Occupational Safety & Health.	No version number August 2019
Time Off for Voting	All employers. Must be posted for 10 days preceding statewide election.	California Secretary of State.	No version number (No date)

California Law			
Title	**Who Must Post?**	**Source**	**Version/Date**
Transgender Rights in the Workplace	All employers.	Department of Fair Employment and Housing	DFEH-E04P-ENG November 2017 DFEH-E04P-SP November 2017
Whistle-blower Protections	All employers.	Department of Industrial Relations.	CalChamber created (1/1/2016)

Required Local Employment Posters

Employers should be aware of posting requirements relating to local minimum wage ordinances or other local employment laws, which may vary by city and county. Employers should check with their local governments to determine whether any specific ordinances apply, or consult with legal counsel. For more information, see "Local Minimum Wage Ordinances" in Chapter 5, page 167.

Log 300 and *300A* Notices

Some employers must comply with Cal/OSHA's *Form/Log 300* recordkeeping requirements.

CalChamber members can use the ***Log 300 Wizard*** in HRCalifornia's Forms & Tools section to determine whether they are required to record workplace injuries and illnesses.

If you are **not** exempt from these requirements, download and post the *Log 300* notices. Note: the *Log 300A* is not a year-round poster — it must be posted in February, March and April.

Table 3. Posters Required with Special Circumstances

Title	Who Must Post?	Source	Version/Date
Log of Work-Related Injuries and Illnesses (Log 300)	High hazard employers of 10 or more employees	Department of Industrial Relations/Division of Occupational Safety & Health	Form 300 (Rev. 7/2007)
Summary of Work-Related Injuries and Illnesses (Log 300A)	High hazard employers of 10 or more employees	Department of Industrial Relations/Division of Occupational Safety & Health	Form 300A (Rev. 7/2007)

Other Required Posting Information

Unique posters and notices may be required depending on certain circumstances, such as the use of heavy equipment or forklifts in the workplace, the use of chemicals in the workplace and whether your business works on government contracts. Following are two of the industry-specific required postings, but there may be more depending on your industry. Visit ***https://hrcalifornia.calchamber.com/hr-library/posters-pamphlets*** for more information.

Hair Salons/Nail Salons

Any establishment that is licensed by the Board of Barbering and Cosmetology (BBC) (e.g., hair salons, nail salons, estheticians, etc.) must post a notice regarding workplace rights and wage-and-hour laws. The BBC is required to inspect for compliance with the posting requirement; failure to post the notice will result in a fine.

Human Trafficking Disclosure Notice

State law requires some retail sellers and manufacturers doing business in California to post on their website a link to the company's efforts to eradicate slavery and human trafficking from its direct supply chain.

In addition, California law requires specified businesses to post a notice that contains information about organizations that provide services to eliminate slavery and human trafficking, including a number for those who wish to send text messages.

The notice must be posted near the public entrance or another conspicuous location where the public and employees may view the notice. The California Department of Justice is responsible for developing the model notice and making it available for download on its website. The required posting and a full list of covered businesses can be found on the California Department of Justice's website at ***https://oag.ca.gov/ human-trafficking***.

Businesses covered by the law include specified transportation businesses, such as airports, and public premises with alcohol licenses; and hotels, motels and bed and breakfast inns.

Failure to comply with the notice posting may result in a civil penalty of $500 to $1,000 per offense.

Online Forms

Throughout this book, you'll find references to many forms and checklists. Because regulations can change throughout the year, accessing your forms online ensures that you will always have the most current version of each form.

Be sure to check ***https://www.calchamber.com/customer-service/Pages/Forms-Downloads.aspx*** occasionally for updates to forms and descriptions of important midyear regulatory changes.

To download the forms mentioned in this book:

1. Open a web browser and go to ***https://www.calchamber.com/customer-service/Pages/Forms-Downloads.aspx***.

2. Click ***HR Quick Guide for California Employers*** in the 2020 Product Forms list.

3. Open your copy of the ***HR Quick Guide for California*** to the inside front or back cover to find the forms access code.

4. Enter the forms access code (exactly as it appears) into the input field and click "Submit."

5. On the ***2020 HR Quick Guide for California Employers*** page, click "All ESB2020 Forms" to download the .zip folder containing all of the available forms. To download a specific form, use the "Find by Name" feature to locate the form by its name.

Working With the ESB2020.zip Folder

Double-click the ESB2020.zip folder when the download is complete. A window will open automatically in your computer's File Explorer. Click "Extract All" to extract the forms from the .zip folder, then choose the folder on your computer to which to extract the forms. The forms will be stored in that folder.

CalChamber Resources

CalChamber produces books, websites, newsletters and online products to help employers comply with California's complex employment laws. For more information on CalChamber products, visit **store.calchamber.com**.

Below is a brief sample of our products:

- **HRCalifornia.com** is a comprehensive website designed to help California human resources supervisors deal with everyday issues. It's intuitive to navigate, great for powerful searches and contains dozens of user-friendly, time-saving features. It's included with CalChamber membership.

- **2020 California Labor Law Digest.**

- **Employee Handbook Creator** (English or Spanish policies).

- **2020 Required Notices Kit** (English or Spanish), includes the **California and Federal Labor Law Poster.**

- **California Employer Update** newsletter.

- **HRCalifornia Extra** is a free electronic newsletter that gives you employment law updates every two weeks. Register at **www.calchamber.com/enewsletters.**

- **HRWatchdog** is CalChamber's employment law blog.

Chapter 2

Hiring Employees

Recruiting and hiring a new employee is a difficult process that involves significant legal risks. If employers don't properly handle the hiring process, they can open themselves to allegations of discriminatory hiring practices.

Continually review your policies, procedures and practices to make sure you follow the overall hiring process. If your policy states that you open all new positions to existing employees before looking outside the company and you fail to do so, you could open yourself up to an employee complaint and even legal action against you.

If you determine that your current process is satisfactory, be sure to reassess it frequently.

This chapter will provide answers to questions about:

- Lawful hiring and recruiting practices.

- Credit and background checks for applicants.

- Independent contractors.

- Required and recommended forms.

- Other hiring related issues.

Hiring Process

You give yourself the best opportunity to create a smooth hiring experience and avoid litigation over your hiring practices if you establish and follow a sound hiring process.

A sound hiring process helps you:

- Find the best candidate for the open position.

- Meet extensive requirements for documentation associated with a new hire.

- Avoid violating complex discrimination laws.

- Avoid creating oral or written employment contracts that can create the potential for litigation.

Your hiring procedures should address important steps, such as creating job descriptions, conducting interviews, making the hiring decision and properly training new employees.

Sticking to an established process can help you comply with legal requirements throughout hiring a new employee. Use the *Pre-Hire Checklist* and the *Hiring Checklist*, described in Table 12 on page 65, to organize the steps you will follow to recruit, interview and hire new employees.

This section will help you:

1. "Define Job Requirements" on page 12.

2. "Create Job Descriptions" on page 13.

3. "Determine Which Type of Worker to Hire" on page 15.

4. "Properly Classify Workers" on page 18.

5. "Recruit for the Position" on page 19.

6. "Evaluate Potential Candidates" on page 20.

7. "Conduct Background Checks" on page 25.

8. "Make the Hiring Decision" on page 26.

9. "Complete the Appropriate Paperwork" on page 28.

10. "Welcome New Employees" on page 30.

Define Job Requirements

It's vital that you start the hiring process with up-to-date information about the job requirements. To do that, you must understand and identify the job to be performed. If you don't have this information, the recruiter or manager wastes time and money in the recruiting process. Worse, the selected applicant may be ill-equipped for the job, require extended training and/or have a greater likelihood of failure.

If you're filling an existing position, locate the existing job description and make sure that it's accurate. If you're creating a new position, write a new job description that clearly outlines the job's "essential functions."

 Essential functions are the position's fundamental job requirements or the reason the job exists. For guidance on documenting the job's essential functions in the job requirements, please see "Essential Functions" in Chapter 7, page 280.

Make sure the job description doesn't use any language that might create an employment contract. For more information, see "Employment Contracts" on page 61.

Create Job Descriptions

While no specific state or federal law requires you to create job descriptions or specifies what they should contain or how they should be formatted, it's a best practice that every position in your organization have a job description.

The requirements listed in the job description must support the essential functions and serve as the primary criteria for selecting/rejecting candidates. Remember that under the Americans with Disabilities Act (ADA) and California's Fair Employment and Housing Act (FEHA), you can't refuse to hire a qualified candidate with a disability who meets the requirements and whose disability can be reasonably accommodated.

Job descriptions clearly set forth job duties and expectations by:

- Clarifying the job's role and the expectations for the person performing the job.
- Taking the uncertainty out of differentiating between the expectations and requirements of various jobs.
- Minimizing employee discontent associated with pay differentials between jobs.
- Guiding initial training and helping management and employees agree on that training's expected outcomes.
- Supporting the performance evaluation process.
- Supporting the employee's proper classification as exempt or nonexempt.
- Guiding the interactive process and reasonable accommodations for disabled employees.

Consider including the following key elements in your job descriptions.

Table 4. Job Description Elements

Element	Description
Job Title	If it's difficult to create a job title for a position, reviewing the essential functions of the job may guide you to selecting an appropriate job title. If you add a new function to an existing job, the new job title may match a previous job title, but designate the job at a higher level, such as "Clerk II" or "Senior Mechanic."
Summary	This should be a one- or two-paragraph summary of the job's essential functions and reporting relationships.
Essential Functions	This component serves as the heart of the job description. To identify a job's essential functions, first identify the job's purpose and the importance of actual job activities to achieve this purpose. For more information, see "Essential Functions" in Chapter 7, page 280. When evaluating the importance of a job's functions, consider the following questions: • How frequently is the function performed? • Does the job exist to perform this function? • Who else is available to perform this function? • What level of expertise or skill is required to perform this function? • What is the experience of previous or current employees in this job? • What is the amount of time spent performing this function? • What are the consequences of failing to perform this function? • What is stated in the job description and employment advertisements?
Physical Requirements	Identify the job's essential physical requirements and describe them in terms of physical activity and degree of strength, flexibility and agility required, and frequency and duration of effort that must be exerted.
Knowledge, skills, experience	List all knowledge, skills and experience necessary to perform the job. You may wish to divide these components into requirements and preferences. Certain attributes may be absolutely required for a particular job. Other attributes may be desirable but not necessary.
Reporting relationship	Each job occupies an important place in the organization, and it's important that the employee and others in contact with the employee thoroughly understand that place. The job description should identify the position's place in the organization's chain of command, including the position(s) to which it reports and the position(s) reporting to it.

Table 4. Job Description Elements *(continued)*

Element	Description
Financial responsibility	If the position includes responsibility for a profit or cost center, some companies prefer to quantify the extent of that responsibility. This aids the recruiter in evaluating the candidate's previous level of responsibility and clearly defines the expectations for the candidate or employee.
Compensation category	The information gathered for the job description aids in evaluating whether the position is likely to be exempt or nonexempt, but it is not determinative. This decision should be confirmed by further analysis using the information provided in Chapter 5, "Paying Employees."

Determine Which Type of Worker to Hire

The next task in the hiring process is to figure out what kind of help you need and determine what type of employee will meet that need:

- Do you need a full-time employee?
- Do you need a part-time employee?
- Would an independent contractor or a temporary employee better suit your needs?

Table 5. Types of Workers

Type	Definition
Full Time	A full-time employee works the number of hours that you designate as "full time." You can define "full time" as 40 hours or more per week, 32 hours or more per week or any other number of hours. You should define the number of hours that constitute full-time employment in your employee handbook or other policy documents.
Part Time	A part-time employee works less than the number of hours that you designate as full time. You should define the number of hours that constitute part-time employment in your employee handbook or other policy document. Part-time employees may or may not receive the same level of benefits as full-time employees.
Regular	A regular employee is someone who is not employed on a temporary or casual basis. Regular employees may be either full-time or part-time employees, depending on the number of hours they work.

Table 5. Types of Workers *(continued)*

Type	Definition
Temporary	Temporary employees are hired for specific assignments of limited duration. They may work full time or part time, but the length of their employment is usually specified. You should reserve the right to extend the duration of temporary employment without implying such employees' rights to benefits during the extension. Benefits established by law, such as Workers' Compensation, State Disability Insurance and Unemployment Insurance, generally apply to temporary employees who otherwise qualify.
Independent Contractor	An independent contractor is not an employee. In general, an independent contractor works for another entity under a verbal or written contract, usually for a specific length of time. Independent contractors are responsible for only their own work and are generally responsible for their own schedule. The independent contractor must also be responsible for how the work is completed. Calling a worker an "independent contractor" doesn't not make that person an independent contractor in the legal sense. Mislabeling a worker as an independent contractor creates potential liability for employment taxes and penalties. For a complete discussion of this employment relationship and the penalties associated with misclassifying a worker, see "Independent Contractors" on page 55.
Contingent workers	This category includes employees who are part time, temporary or seasonal; secured through temporary agencies; or are under employee leasing arrangements. Contingent workers may be treated differently than permanent workers under some California and federal labor laws. Employers may be held liable for its staffing agency's or labor contractor's wage and-hour violations if an agency or contractor fail to properly pay workers or provide workers' compensation coverage. Contact legal counsel to determine how you can limit your exposure to liability for a labor contractor's wage-and-hour violations or failure to secure workers' compensation coverage.

Table 5. Types of Workers *(continued)*

Type	Definition
Casual (on call, per diem, irregular)	Casual workers perform intermittent service on an as-needed basis. For example, a retail establishment might have an employee who floats between departments as needed, or a preschool might bring in an additional teacher for a week to make sure state teacher/child ratios are met during attendance peaks, but the teacher isn't on staff all the time.
Interns	Whether a worker is an intern or employee depends upon which party is the relationship's primary beneficiary — the employer or the individual. Employers must weigh the following seven factors to determine who is the primary beneficiary. No single factor is determinative, and each intern classification is evaluated individually. **1.** The intern and the employer clearly understand that there is no expectation of compensation. Any promise of compensation, express or implied, suggests that the intern is an employee — and vice versa. **2.** The internship provides training similar to that given in an educational environment, including the clinical and other hands-on training provided by educational institutions. **3.** The internship is tied to the intern's formal education program by integrated coursework or the receipt of academic credit. **4.** The internship accommodates the intern's academic commitments by corresponding to the academic calendar. **5.** The internship's duration is limited to the period in which the internship provides the intern with beneficial learning. **6.** The intern's work complements, rather than displaces, the work of paid employees while providing significant educational benefits to the intern. **7.** The intern and the employer understand that the internship is conducted without entitlement to a paid job at the conclusion of the internship. ❗ Employers shouldn't treat internships lightly. Always use caution when adding individuals seeking training or "internship programs" to your workforce. Always consult with employment law counsel when using interns.

Properly Classify Workers

Certain employees are exempt from wage and hour requirements. Because it is highly litigated, understanding the distinction between exempt and nonexempt employees is critical.

For a complete discussion of determining whether an employee is exempt or nonexempt, see "Exempt and Nonexempt Employees" on page 53.

 Always assume employees are nonexempt unless they clearly meet the standards for an exemption. For more information, see "Exempt Employees" in Chapter 5, page 168.

If you're not experienced in determining exempt and nonexempt status or if you're unsure about a particular position's status, ask your employment law counsel to review your determination.

Table 6. Worker Classifications

Type	Definition
Exempt Employee	An exempt employee is not subject to any of the laws pertaining to overtime and meal and rest periods.
	Generally, exempt employees are your key personnel, such as executive, administrative or professional employees, who possess management and decision-making responsibilities. Other exempt employee types include some inside and outside salespeople and some computer software employees.
Nonexempt Employee	All other employees generally fall under the nonexempt category. A nonexempt employee is subject to all Wage Order rules and federal and state wage-and-hour laws, including requirements that you: • Pay the applicable minimum wage based upon where the employee works. For more information, see "California Minimum Wage" in Chapter 5, page 166 and "Local Minimum Wage Ordinances" in Chapter 5, page 167. • Pay nonexempt employees overtime for working more than eight hours in one day or more than 40 in one workweek; • Provide required meal and rest breaks to nonexempt employees; and • Track and record all hours worked by nonexempt employees and also the hourly rate of pay associated with each hour worked.

Recruit for the Position

Advertise in general interest venues or a wide range of special interest venues rather than recruiting from one source that doesn't yield a diversity of applicants so as to avoid the appearance of the intent to discriminate.

You can use a variety of methods to let potential candidates know about the position:

- Advertising in magazines, newspapers or trade publications.

- Posting job announcements on the Internet.

- Recruiting in person at trade shows and job fairs.

- Sending a job request to a staffing agency, California's Employment Development Department or schools.

Make sure the language in your recruiting efforts doesn't:

- Imply a secure employment contract, which overrides employment "at-will." At-will is a legal concept, created by California law, that assures both employer and employee that either party can terminate the relationship at any time, for any reason or for no reason. Although California is an at-will state, courts have ruled that various factors, including employment advertisements and applications, can create an implied employment contract. For more information, see "Employment Contracts" on page 61.

  - Avoid advertisements that seem to guarantee future employment by using language such as "secure position," "looking for candidates willing to make a long-term commitment to the company," or "looking for someone who can grow with the company."

  - Make sure that recruiters know they don't have the authority to promise job security to applicants.

- Violate state and federal discrimination laws that prohibit limiting or excluding someone from employment because they have, or you think they have, certain characteristics. See "Discrimination" in Chapter 7, page 257, for a more complete definition. Make sure to avoid words and phrases that single out characteristics that could belong to a protected class.

Bona Fide Occupational Qualifications in Hiring

A "bona fide occupational qualification" (BFOQ) is a protected characteristic employers are allowed to consider when making hiring decisions, even though these characteristics would be considered unlawfully discriminatory in other contexts. For example, a religious school can require that teachers be members of the school's religion.

A BFOQ based on a protected class is extremely rare. Consult legal counsel before ever listing a protected class, such as sex or religion, as a job requirement.

California law prohibits discrimination based on gender expression or gender identity, whether or not stereotypically associated with the person's assigned sex at birth, making the use of sex as a BFOQ even rarer. So, advertising for a male model for a men's clothing photo shoot may no longer qualify as a BFOQ. For more information, see "Gender" in Chapter 7, page 264.

Salary History Questions Prohibited

Employers are banned from asking about a job applicant's current or prior salary, including information on compensation and benefits. Additionally, employers may not seek this information through an agent, such as a third-party recruiter.

While applicants may voluntarily disclose salary information without any prompting, employers are prohibited from relying on salary history information as a factor in determining whether to hire or how much to pay the applicant. Employers may, however, ask applicants about their "salary expectation" for the position they've applied for.

An employer must also provide a job applicant, upon reasonable request, with the pay scale for the position. A "reasonable request" for a pay scale is defined as a request made after an applicant has completed an initial interview and "pay scale" is defined as the salary or hourly wage range for the job.

The salary history ban applies only to individuals seeking employment with an employer for which they haven't worked or don't work in any capacity or position.

Both California's salary history ban and California's Fair Pay Act also state that, with the exception of current employees, prior salary can never justify a pay disparity.

Compensation decisions based on a *current* employee's existing salary, such as for giving raises or bonuses, may be permissible if justified by such factors as a seniority or merit system.

Evaluate Potential Candidates

Thoroughly examining potential candidates gives you the best chance of finding an employee who matches what your company wants. This person should have the necessary skills to do the job, but you should also find out about the individual's work style, history and employment-related interests. Consider all this information to make sure the employment relationship will be a good fit for both of you.

Review Résumés

Applicants submit résumés that provide helpful information about their personal education, skills, past work experience and accomplishments. A résumé is the candidate's marketing tool and should be treated as such. It doesn't contain all of the information you should gather about a potential candidate, but it can give you a way to preview the person before beginning the application process.

You are not required to keep unsolicited résumés. You can send them back to the applicant along with a note explaining that no openings currently exist for the position sought, or keep the unsolicited résumés to use as a pool of potential employees.

Review Applications

The questions you ask in your employment application also supply information about applicants. A good employment application should gather a broad range of standardized information to help you evaluate all applicants more equally.

 Employers may not use job applications that ask applicants about their criminal history. For more information, see "Criminal Background Checks" on page 32.

An employment application should request that applicants provide information about their:

- Availability;

- Experience and skills, including related military experience;

- Licensing and/or certification;

- Employment history; and

- Specialized knowledge or training, such as proficiency in a language other than English (if necessary for the job).

Compare the information in an applicant's résumé to the information the applicant supplied when completing your employment application to make sure that the information matches. For more guidance on correct note-taking techniques, see "Taking Notes" on page 24.

 To reduce the possibility of liability for discrimination, compare your own application with the provided sample *Employment Application – Short Form* and review your application using the *Guide for Pre-Employment Inquiries*, both described in Table 12 on page 65.

Employers should use caution with provisions and disclaimers for applications used in multiple states.

 Job applicants might not notice certain provisions in "one-size-fits-all" applications, and applicants in California might answer questions that California law prohibits employers from asking. This could create potential liability for employers.

You should include the following "damage-control" provisions in the application and require the applicant to separately initial each provision:

Table 7. Application Provisions

What	Why
An "authorization to check all references" listed by the applicant.	Since you may be liable for "negligent hiring" if you fail to check an applicant's references, this provision will help protect you from a claim that you invaded the applicant's privacy by checking that individual's references without permission. It's also easier to gain information from former employers if they know that their former employee authorized disclosure to you. This authorization won't protect you against claims of intentional misconduct or employment discrimination if you ask an applicant about protected information, such as an applicant's medical history.
A "statement that all answers given by the applicant are true," and any omissions or false information are grounds for rejecting the application or for termination.	Courts allow employers to use an applicant's placement of false information on a job application as evidence in wrongful termination lawsuits, even if the employer did not discover the information was false until after the employee was terminated.
A "statement that employment is at will."	This helps applicants understand that employment is at-will. State that for any contrary representations to be binding, they must be in writing.

Screen Candidates with a Phone Interview

A phone interview presents an informal way to screen a potential employee before interviewing the applicant in person. A phone interview gives you a chance to talk over points of the résumé or employment application and get more details on anything you want to know about the applicant.

CalChamber®

As in all conversations, be careful not to create an implied contract or to open yourself to a discrimination charge. You might consider developing a script for the person conducting the phone interview:

- Use the *Guide for Pre-Employment Inquiries*, described in Table 12 on page 65, to make sure your script doesn't contain any illegal questions.

- See the *Employment Interview Checklist* described in Table 12 on page 65, for a series of questions you can ask. You can find these forms in your forms download, described in detail in "Online Forms" on page 9.

For tips on steering clear of implied contracts, see "Employment Contracts" on page 61.

Interview Candidates

Interviewing candidates is your opportunity to learn more about your applicants and to determine which applicant is best for you, based on the candidates':

- Skills;

- Suitability for the position;

- Work style; and

- Employment-related interests.

 You will probably only select a small fraction of the candidates for interviews and/or background checks.

Be careful of questions that can put you at risk for a discrimination lawsuit. In general, don't ask questions about:

- Marital status or children;

- Age;

- Disabilities; or

- Hobbies and outside activities that might indicate race, religion, age, etc.

The *Guide for Pre-Employment Inquiries*, described in Table 12 on page 65, can guide you in asking appropriate questions.

Also be careful of statements that can establish employment contracts or violate your policies. Read "Employment Contracts" on page 61 and the *Employment Interview Checklist*, described in Table 12 on page 65, for more information.

Taking Notes

It's usually necessary to take notes during interviews so you can review the notes when making a final decision. However, it is important to ensure that you record interview information in a manner that won't cause you problems in court. Take brief, clear and legible notes that pertain only to the candidate's answers. Don't use abbreviations or a coded rating system that could be misinterpreted at a later date.

Keep objective records of why an applicant was or was not hired to avoid any inference of discriminatory motives. Consider the following examples.

Table 8. Taking Notes During Interviews

Job or Business	Do Note	Do Not Note
Alarm Installer	Did not possess experience with necessary equipment.	Not impressed with his attitude.
Retail Store	Did not have enough customer service experience.	Was not right for the job

In addition, be sure that your interview notes evaluate criteria actually necessary to perform the job. For instance, when interviewing for a telemarketer, your notes should:

- Reflect **impartial items**, such as "Good interpersonal skills; types 75 WPM."

- Not reflect **personal observations**, such as "Did not like the way he talked."

Interview Tips

When conducting your interviews, consider these pointers:

Table 9. Tips for Conducting Interviews

What?	Create a script of questions to ask each applicant, using "Employment Contracts" on page 61 and the *Employment Interview Checklist*, described in Table 12 on page 65. Make sure other interviewing managers understand the guidelines for interviewing.
Where?	Invite candidates to visit your office for the interview. This is their chance to learn more about your company and work environment, and to meet potential co-workers. Additionally, it's a professional way to receive applicants and allows you to select a quiet place for talking with the candidate without distractions.
When?	It's up to you to decide whether to interview all applicants, maybe throughout a workweek, or interview candidates one-by-one until you fill the position.

Table 9. Tips for Conducting Interviews *(continued)*

How long?	Interviews generally last between 30 and 60 minutes, depending on the job requirements and the candidate's experience. Tell the candidate at the beginning how long the interview will last, and allow time to answer any of the candidate's questions.
Notes?	You may take notes during the interview, but you must exercise caution in how you phrase your written comments because the notes could be used in a legal claim.

Conduct Background Checks

Before selecting a new employee, it's advisable to check the applicant's references and/or background to evaluate the candidate's job-related abilities.

As part of a background check, you might examine each candidate's:

- Credit history and/or investigative consumer reports.

- References.

- Educational background.

- Drug/alcohol screening results (post-offer).

- Physical health (post-offer).

Federal and California laws place specific procedural requirements on employers who perform background checks. For a complete discussion, see "Investigative Consumer Reports" on page 41. Also, federal, California and local laws place strict restrictions on employers' use of criminal background checks and credit history checks in the hiring process. For example, criminal background checks can be conducted only after a conditional offer of employment has been made to the applicant. For a complete discussion, see "Criminal Background Checks" on page 32 and "Credit Checks" on page 39.

CalChamber members can visit HRCalifornia's Local Ordinances section, at ***https://hrcalifornia.calchamber.com/hr-library/local-ordinances***, for detailed information on local employment-related ordinances in California, including criminal background ordinances.

Improperly researching an applicant's background may expose you to legal liability in the form of a lawsuit alleging that you invaded the applicant's privacy. This includes investigating an applicant's online activities in various social media websites, such as Facebook or Twitter. For more information, please see "Checking Online Activities" on page 43.

The law doesn't specifically require you to check an applicant's references and background, but researching an applicant's background can provide you with valuable information and make costly litigation far less likely. A court could hold you liable for negligent hiring if you don't perform a background check and the employee commits an offense that you could've predicted had you made a reasonable effort to research that person. A reasonable effort, even if former employers don't cooperate, can protect you from negligent hiring claims.

It's considered negligent to hire someone whose documented past presents an unreasonable risk of harm to others; specifically, to co-workers and customers.

For example, if an employee with a record of violent behavior assaults someone in your office, the victim of the assault may bring a negligent hiring suit against you, alleging that you should have known about the employee's violent past and not hired the person.

Records related to a credit check must be kept separate from the employee's regular personnel file. It's a best practice to keep these records confidential.

Make the Hiring Decision

Once you've reviewed résumés and applications and screened and interviewed candidates, it's time to make your hiring decision. Make all hiring decisions carefully. To prevent claims of unfair hiring practices:

- Be sure you have valid reasons for making the hiring decision, based on the person's:

  - Qualifications;

  - Experience;

  - Skills;

  - Knowledge; and

  - Education.

- Document the reasons why one person was selected over other candidates.

- Review documents from hiring supervisors to ensure decisions were based on valid reasons, and that no applicant was rejected for a discriminatory reason.

Make the Offer

Once you select a candidate, send an employment offer letter to him/her. The offer letter clarifies the terms of employment, such as:

- The start date.

- "At-will" employment status.

- Exempt or nonexempt status (see "Exempt and Nonexempt Employees" on page 53).

- Wage or salary: If the employee will be exempt, phrase the pay rate in terms of dollars weekly, biweekly or monthly. If the employee will be nonexempt, phrase the pay rate in terms of dollars per hour.

- Whether the offer depends on the applicant passing a medical exam, drug test, or reference or background check. For more information, see "Medical Exams and Inquiries" on page 42.

 If you send an offer letter, be sure that the salary for an exempt employee meets the minimum salary requirements for an employee to be exempt. See "Exempt Employees" in Chapter 5, page 168.

You are not required to send the successful candidate an offer letter, but many employees won't want to leave their current jobs until they have something in writing confirming the new job.

 Be careful that you don't create an employment contract in your letter, overriding employment at-will status. See "Employment Contracts" on page 61. To see a sample letter that contains no contractual language, read the *Employment Letter*, described in Table 12 on page 65.

How Do I Handle Unsuccessful Applicants?

Although you are not required to do so, you might consider sending a letter to all applicants not hired letting them know that they are no longer under consideration for the position. This is a courtesy to the applicants that pursued employment with your company. You can send a standard letter to all unsuccessful applicants. To see a sample letter, read the *Letter to Applicants Not Hired*, described in Table 12 on page 65.

Complete the Appropriate Paperwork

In 2018, California passed the California Consumer Privacy Act (CCPA), which changed the rules around how consumer data is collected. Effective January 1, 2020, employee data — information collected and used within the context of a person's employment or application for employment— is exempted from the CCPA. This exemption is good for only one year.

Employers subject to the CCPA must still comply with the act's requirement to disclose, at or before the time of collection, the categories of personal information collected about an applicant or employee and the purposes for which the information will be used.

Employers should consult with legal counsel on how to amend employee privacy notices or otherwise comply with their obligations under the CCPA.

The paperwork involved with hiring a new employee is extensive. You can use the *Hiring Checklist* to help keep track of which forms/notifications you provided to your new employee and subsequently processed. This checklist is described in Table 12 on page 65.

Use the following forms throughout the hiring process:

- Employment applications (see "Review Applications" on page 21).

- Forms for checking background (see "Background Checks and Testing" on page 31).

- Forms for special types of workers:

  – Minors: see "Hiring Minors" on page 58 for more information.

  – Independent contractors: see "Independent Contractors" on page 55.

Fill Out or Provide These Forms on the Employee's First Day of Work

- Information and pamphlets about employee rights and benefits, such as:

  – *Sexual Harassment Hurts Everyone* pamphlet (available in the ***2020 Required Notices Kit*** at ***store.calchamber.com***)

  – *Your Rights to Workers' Compensation Benefits and How to Obtain Them* pamphlet (see "Workers' Compensation" on page 142).

  – *Paid Family Leave* pamphlet (see "Paid Family Leave Benefits" in Chapter 4, page 136).

- *Disability Insurance Provisions* pamphlet (see "Required and Optional Benefits" in Chapter 4, page 135).

- *New Health Insurance Marketplace Coverage Options and Your Health Coverage* (required if an employer is covered by the Fair Labor Standards Act; there are separate forms for employers who do/do not offer a health plan).

- COBRA and Cal-COBRA rights notifications (if you offer health benefits).

- *Notice of Victims' Rights - Domestic Violence, Sexual Assault and Stalking.*

• Safety information, such as:

- *Emergency Information* form.

- *Initial Safety Training Certificate* (see Table 74 in Chapter 6, page 250).

• Government forms, such as:

- *W-4 - Employee's Withholding Allowance Certificate.*

- *DE4 - California Employee's Withholding Certificate.*

- *Form I-9 - Employment Eligibility Verification.*

• The required written wage information (if the new employee is a nonexempt employee). Use the *Wage and Employment Notice to Employees (Labor Code section 2810.5)* form.

- Employers must use the *Wage and Employment Notice*, which contains information regarding the mandatory paid sick leave law (Healthy Workplaces, Healthy Families Act of 2014). You can find this notice in Table 12 on page 65. For more information on this form, see "Notifying Employees About Paydays" in Chapter 5, page 194.

- *New Employees Report - Form DE34.*

• An employee handbook.

• A copy of the company's Injury and Illness Prevention Program (IIPP) (see "Injury and Illness Prevention Program" in Chapter 6, page 218).

TIP   You can find these forms in your forms download, described in detail in "Online Forms" on page 9. CalChamber's **Required Notices Kit** includes pamphlets on Unemployment Insurance, State Disability Insurance, Paid Family Leave, Sexual Harassment Prevention and Workers' Compensation.

Welcome New Employees

The first day of a new job is the ideal point in the employment relationship to make sure new employees understand your policies and work rules; are informed of their legal rights and obligations; and receive the necessary training to do their jobs safely and efficiently.

Document all training and orientation. Proper records can help protect you from lawsuits. Use the *Employee Orientation Checklist*, described in Table 12 on page 65, and keep it in the employee's personnel file.

 You might be tempted to designate the first few weeks or months of work as a "probationary" period, but this could be understood as a promise that, when the probationary period is over, the employee will have permanent status.

Employee Orientation

Verify that employees:

- Tour the building/facilities and learn the exits' locations;

- Meet managers and other employees;

- Understand information on company processes and resources; and

- Get a chance to ask questions about anything they don't completely understand.

Employee Training

You must provide all employees with the necessary knowledge and training to complete their tasks safely. If an employee gets hurt because you didn't take the time to make sure that the individual understood how to operate a machine properly, you will be liable. See "Safety Training" in Chapter 6, page 238.

 Remember, time spent on orientation and training must be paid.

 A new law that took effect on August 30, 2019, requires virtually all California employers to provide sexual harassment prevention training to all employees. Specifically, by January 1, 2021, employers with five or more employees must provide one hour of sexual harassment prevention training to nonsupervisory employees and two hours of such training to supervisors. Temporary and seasonal employees will be required to be trained within 30 days of hire or 100 hours worked, whichever is earlier. For more information, see "Harassment-Prevention Training" in Chapter 8, page 296.

Verifying Social Security Numbers

Though not required by law for most employers, you may choose to verify the Social Security number (SSN) of newly hired employees. The Social Security Number Verification Service (SSNVS) allows registered users (employers and certain third-party submitters) to verify employees' names and SSNs against Social Security Administration (SSA) records.

This service can only be used for wage reporting purposes. With SSNVS, you may:

- Verify up to 10 names and SSNs online and receive immediate results. You may use the SSNVS website an unlimited number of times per session.

- Upload electronic files of up to 250,000 names and SSNs, and usually receive results the next government business day.

Employers can register to use the free SSNVS through the SSA's Business Services Online website at **www.ssa.gov/employer/ssnv.htm**.

The use of the SSNVS should be implemented and utilized in a nondiscriminatory manner. Employers should specify, through policy, what classifications of employees will be submitted to the SSNVS system. The SSA emphasizes that such verifications can only occur after an employee has been hired and that the use of SSNVS is applied to employees consistently.

Background Checks and Testing

Poor selection practices could potentially lead to claims of negligent hiring. You must exercise reasonable care in determining a candidate's fitness for employment and continued employment.

Reference checks are a part of good selection practices. Other types of background checks or pre-employment testing may also be necessary, depending on the position involved.

Table 10. Types of Checks and Testing

What	Why
Criminal Background Check	Per the ban-the-box law, which applies to employers with five or more employees in most industries, strict rules govern when you can obtain criminal history information and how it can be used. For full details, see "Criminal Background Checks" on page 32.

Table 10. Types of Checks and Testing *(continued)*

What	Why
Credit Checks	Employers may not use a consumer credit report for employment purposes except in certain circumstances, and if such information is used for employment purposes, employers must complete certain actions. For full details, see "Credit Checks" on page 39.
Investigative Consumer Reports	These help employers discover information about an applicant's character and general reputation, and is typically obtained through personal interviews. Certain requirements apply when obtaining and using these reports. For full details, see "Investigative Consumer Reports" on page 41.
Drug Testing	In most cases, drug testing is not a legal requirement, but those wishing to test should follow specific guidelines. For more information, see "Drug Testing" on page 42.
Medical Exams and Inquiries	Employers may not conduct physical examinations prior to making an offer of employment. For more information, see "Medical Exams and Inquiries" on page 42.
Reference Check	You're not required to check your future employee's references, but doing so can protect you from liability. For more information, see "Reference Checks" on page 43.
Education Check	This is not required, but verifying an applicant's transcript and a university's accreditation can save headaches later.
Checking Online Activity	Exercise caution if you use social media in the hiring process. For full details, see "Checking Online Activities" on page 43.

Criminal Background Checks

Employers with five or more employees cannot ask applicants any criminal history questions or use criminal history information **until after** a conditional offer of employment has been made. Employers also must follow set processes before making any employment decision based on criminal history information.

Moreover, all employers need to make sure that any consideration of criminal history information does not disparately impact individuals in a protected class, such as race, national origin or other characteristic protected by law.

Strict rules govern when you can obtain criminal history information and how it can be used. Local ordinances may also apply.

Conducting Criminal Background Checks When Hiring

Covered employers are prohibited from asking about criminal history information on job applications and from inquiring about or considering criminal history *at any time before a conditional offer of employment has been made*.

This type of law is commonly referred to as a "ban-the-box" law, as it eliminates the frequently used criminal history check box found on many employment applications. This law is part of California's FEHA, under which an applicant may sue for a violation.

 The Department of Fair Employment and Housing (DFEH) also passed criminal history regulations in 2017. To the extent that the ban-the-box law conflicts with those earlier regulations, the ban-the-box law takes precedence.

Coverage

5+ The ban-the-box law applies to employers with **five or more employees**. It does not apply to the following types of jobs:

- Positions for which a state or local government agency is required by law to conduct a conviction history background check;

- Positions with a criminal justice agency;

- Farm labor contractors (as defined in Labor Code sec. 1685); and

- Positions in which an employer is required by any state, federal or local law (including the Securities Exchange Act) to check criminal background for employment purposes, or to restrict employment based on criminal history.

 Employers who must conduct criminal background checks to comply with federal or state laws should consult with legal counsel.

If you have fewer than five employees, limitations on what criminal history you can consider when making employment decisions still exist; see "Other Rules Limiting Use of Criminal History in Employment Decisions" on page 36.

Prohibited Inquiries Before a Conditional Offer

Covered employers cannot do either of the following:

- Include on a job application any question that seeks the disclosure of the applicant's conviction history at any time before a conditional offer of employment has been made.

- Inquire into or consider the conviction history of an applicant until after a conditional offer of employment has been made.

Do not use job applications that contain a criminal history "check box" or that automatically disqualify applicants because of a criminal record.

Restrictions After a Conditional Offer

Once you've made a conditional offer of employment, you may seek criminal history information *if you follow the process and notice requirements described below.*

However, some criminal history information is always off limits. While conducting a criminal background check in connection with a job application, you cannot consider, distribute or disseminate information about any of the following:

- An arrest not followed by a conviction, except when the applicant is out on bail or on the individual's own recognizance pending trial and except for jobs at specified health facilities;

- A referral to or participation in a pre-trial or post-trial diversion program; or

- A conviction that has been sealed, dismissed, expunged or statutorily eradicated pursuant to law.

An employer may only consider sealed or expunged convictions in circumstances where a particular conviction would legally prohibit someone from holding that job, such as where a bank teller has a conviction related to a bank robbery, even if sealed or expunged.

The Labor Code also prohibits employers from inquiring into an applicant's juvenile criminal history information and from using such information as a factor in determining any condition of employment, such as hiring or termination. For more information, see "Juvenile Criminal History Information" on page 37.

Individualized Assessment

If you are considering denying an applicant the job due solely or in part to the applicant's prior convictions, you must first conduct an "individualized assessment" to determine whether the conviction has a direct and adverse relationship with the specific job duties that justifies denying employment.

You must consider all of the following factors in making this individualized assessment:

- The nature and gravity of the offense or conduct;

- The time that has passed since the offense or conduct and completion of the sentence; and

- The nature of the job held or sought.

You can put the assessment results in writing, but you are not required to do so.

Notice Requirements

If you decide against hiring someone because of a criminal conviction, two separate written notices will be required.

First, any preliminary decision not to hire an applicant because of a conviction history requires a written notice to the applicant, who must be given the opportunity to respond.

The written notice to the applicant must contain all of the following:

- The disqualifying conviction(s) upon which the preliminary decision to rescind the conditional job offer are based. You have the option, but are not required, to provide an explanation for your preliminary decision.

- A copy of the conviction history report, if any.

- An explanation of the applicant's right to respond to the notice before a final decision is made.

- The deadline for the applicant's response (must provide at least five business days).

- An explanation informing the applicant that the response can include evidence challenging the accuracy of the conviction history report and/or evidence of rehabilitation or mitigating circumstances.

The applicant has **at least five business days** to respond to the written notice before you can make a final decision. If within the five business days the applicant notifies you in writing that the applicant disputes the conviction history's accuracy and is taking steps to obtain evidence, then you must give the applicant an additional five business days to respond.

 You are required to consider information submitted by the applicant before making a final decision about whether to hire the applicant.

Second, if you make a final decision not to hire the applicant based in whole or in part on the conviction history, you must again give written notice to the applicant. The employer's final determination notice must include:

- The final denial or disqualification. You may provide an explanation for your final decision, but it is not required.

- Any existing procedure the employer has for the applicant to challenge the decision or request reconsideration.

- The applicant's right to file a complaint with the DFEH.

 Employers must carefully follow the fair chance process outlined by this new state law.

Other Rules Limiting Use of Criminal History in Employment Decisions

The new ban-the box law deals with considering criminal history during hiring, but other restrictions on criminal background checks also exist.

Under California's Labor Code, certain types of criminal history information can never be sought or used as a factor in determining any condition of employment, including decisions related to promotion, training, discipline, layoff and termination. These rules apply to all California employers.

When making decisions about any condition of employment, you cannot seek or use information about:

- Arrests or detentions not resulting in conviction (except when the employee is out on bail or out on the individual's own recognizance pending trial).

- Information concerning a referral to or participation in a pre-trial or post-trial criminal diversion program.

- Convictions for most marijuana possession offenses more than two years old.

- Convictions that have been judicially dismissed or ordered sealed, expunged or statutorily eradicated pursuant to law.

- Juvenile criminal history information.

The ban on using conviction history to make employment decisions has limited exceptions for jobs where the employer is required by law to obtain the information, as well as for other jobs such as peace officers, health care employees, and people with access to drugs and medication.

Juvenile Criminal History Information

All employers are prohibited from inquiring into an applicant's juvenile criminal history information and from using such information as a factor in determining any condition of employment, such as hiring or termination.

Health care facilities can inquire into an applicant's juvenile criminal history if a juvenile court found that the applicant committed felony or misdemeanor sexual offenses or certain controlled substance crimes within five years before applying for the job. Sealed juvenile criminal records are still off limits. This exception applies to health facilities as defined in Health and Safety Code sec. 1250.

If you are a health facility seeking disclosure of this history, you must provide the applicant with a list describing the specific offenses you want disclosed.

Criminal History Information and Discrimination

To avoid liability under state and federal anti-discrimination laws, employers also must be careful that any use of criminal history information does not result in discrimination.

California FEHA regulations prohibit employers from considering criminal information in employment decisions if doing so would have an "adverse impact" on a protected class — unless the employer can prove the information is job-related and consistent with business necessity.

The FEHA regulations emphasize that consideration of criminal history information has the potential to adversely impact individuals in a protected class, such as individuals of a particular race, national origin or gender. The regulations are similar to federal EEOC Guidance that also discusses how an employer's use of an individual's criminal history in making employment decisions could violate prohibitions against employment discrimination.

California's criminal history regulations became effective July 1, 2017. They apply to all employment decisions and contain a detailed process that must be followed if criminal convictions are going to be considered during employment decisions. Unfortunately, the interaction between these FEHA regulations and the 2018 ban-the-box law may cause confusion for employers.

To the extent the 2018 ban-the-box law conflicts with the 2017 criminal history regulations, follow the rules of the ban-the-box law.

Regardless, keep in mind that under both state and federal law, you have a better chance of defending any type of criminal background check policy or practice if you can demonstrate that the practice is job-related and consistent with business necessity. Look at whether your policy or practice bears a demonstrable relationship to successful performance in both the job and the workplace, and measure the person's fitness for the specific position at issue. A policy or practice that excludes everyone with a criminal record will not be job-related and consistent with business necessity.

Also, determine if a less discriminatory alternative can help you achieve your goals. Are there better predictors of risk or job qualifications than a criminal background check?

Again, some employers must comply with federal or state laws prohibiting employment of individuals with certain criminal records in particular jobs. Or a criminal background check may be legally mandated for certain positions or occupational licenses. Examples include peace officers and those in health care facilities with regular access to patients or controlled substances. In these situations, employers that must comply with a federal or state law generally can use the compliance mandate to defend themselves against any adverse impact claim.

Compare your criminal background process with the *Criminal Background Check Checklist*, described in Table 12 on page 65.

Local Ban-the-Box Ordinances

Some local governments, such as San Francisco and Los Angeles, also have enacted ban-the-box laws that impose various prohibitions and requirements related to obtaining and using criminal background information. The new statewide ban-the-box law does not affect the rights under these local ordinances; employers covered by a local ban-the-box ordinance will need to comply with both state and local law.

Credit Checks

Employers may not use a consumer credit report for employment purposes unless the position of the applicant or employee will be:

1. A managerial position (as defined in the executive exemption of Wage Order 4).

2. A position in the state Department of Justice.

3. That of a sworn peace officer or other law enforcement position.

4. A position for which the information in the report is required by law to be disclosed or obtained.

5. A position that involves regular access (for any purpose other than routine solicitation and processing of credit card applications in a retail establishment) to all of the following types of information of any one person:
   - Bank or credit card account information;
   - SSN; and
   - Date of birth.

6. A position in which the person is, or would be, any of the following:
   - A named signatory on the bank or credit card account of the employer;
   - Authorized to transfer money on behalf of the employer; or
   - Authorized to enter into financial contracts on behalf of the employer.

7. A position that involves access to confidential or proprietary information.

8. A position that involves regular access to cash totaling $10,000 or more of the employer, a customer or client, during the workday

If one of the exceptions applies and you're able to obtain and use the report, there are still restrictions on how you go about obtaining the report. The federal Fair Credit Reporting Act (FCRA) and the California Investigative Consumer Reporting Agencies Act (ICRAA) place additional restrictions on your ability to use credit reports for employment purposes.

If information from a credit report is used for employment purposes, you must complete the following actions:

1. Written disclosure: Before the report is obtained, make a clear and conspicuous written disclosure to the applicant in a document consisting solely of the disclosure, and get the applicant's written authorization.

    A 2019 Ninth Circuit decision clarified that FCRA's requirement that the disclosure document can consist only of the FRCA disclosure means that it can't include any additional information, including disclosures required under state law. As a result, you must provide separate disclosure documents under the FCRA and the ICRAA.

    You can use the *Disclosure and Authorization to Obtain Consumer Credit Report – California* and the *Disclosure and Authorization to Obtain Consumer Credit Report – Federal,* described in Table 12 on page 65.

2. Provide a separate notice: Give the applicant a copy of the *Fair Credit Reporting Act - Summary of Your Rights* when you tell the applicant of your intent to obtain a report.

3. Certification to a consumer credit reporting agency (CRA): Provide the agency with written certification that you made the disclosure and obtained authorization, and that the information will not be used in violation of any federal or state law. You must also certify that if you take any adverse action based on the credit report, you will provide a copy of the report and a summary of the FCRA rights to the person. You can use the *Certification to Consumer Credit Reporting Agency*, described in Table 12 on page 65.

4. Employee/applicant request: If the employee or applicant requests a report, the employer must request that a copy be provided to the employee at the time the employer requests the report from the CRA. The report must be at no charge to the employee, and must be given at the same time as the employer's report.

5. Pre-Adverse Action Notice: Before taking adverse action based on the credit report, provide the applicant with a copy of the *Pre-Adverse Action Disclosure*, a copy of the credit report and a summary of FCRA rights. You can use the *Pre-Adverse Action Disclosure*, described in Table 12 on page 65, when preparing the notice.

6. Adverse Action Notice: You must also notify the applicant after you take any adverse action based at least in part on information contained in a credit report. You can use the *Adverse Action Notice*, described in Table 12 on page 65, when preparing the notice.

The credit-check process requires many mandatory forms, which you can find in your forms download (described in detail in "Online Forms" on page 9).

Investigative Consumer Reports

These reports help you discover information about an applicant's character, general reputation, personal characteristics and mode of living. The information is typically obtained through personal interviews. Like with credit reports, you must comply with FCRA and ICRAA requirements and California law when obtaining and using these reports. If you intend to obtain such a report, you must disclose this intention to the person being investigated and state the report's purpose. You should also provide a "Summary of Rights" under the FCRA. You must provide the following:

1. **Written disclosure:** Before the report is obtained, make a clear and conspicuous written disclosure to the applicant in a document consisting solely of the disclosure, and get the applicant's written authorization. You can use the *Disclosure and Authorization to Obtain Investigative Consumer Report*, described in Table 12 on page 65.

2. Certification to the consumer reporting agency: Provide the agency with written certification that you made proper disclosure to the applicant.

3. **Additional requested disclosure:** Before taking adverse action based on an investigative consumer report, you must provide the applicant with a copy of the *Pre-Adverse Action Disclosure*, and include a copy of the consumer report that you relied on. This gives the person an opportunity to explain any negative information. You must also provide a copy of the FCRA notice, a *Summary of Your Rights Under the Fair Credit Reporting Act*. If you deny employment after obtaining an investigative consumer report, before taking the action, advise the applicant facing the adverse action. Use the *Adverse Action Notice*.

The FCRA prohibits consumer reporting agencies from providing consumer reports that contain medical information for employment purposes or in conjunction with credit or insurance transactions, without the specific prior consent of the applicant.

It's prudent to limit the scope of these investigations to specifically job-related information, because investigative reports that aren't job-related may violate federal and state civil rights laws if they create an unequal impact on minority applicants. See "Discrimination" in Chapter 7, page 257 for details.

Investigative consumer reports must include the Internet address of the investigative consumer reporting agency. If the agency has no Internet address, the report must include the agency's telephone number.

Drug Testing

In most circumstances, the law doesn't require drug testing. If you wish to require drug testing for applicants, you should follow these guidelines:

- Be consistent. Decide whether drug testing is required for all positions or just those with potential safety concerns.

- Determine what levels of what substances will be considered "passing" levels.

- Obtain the applicant's signed authorization.

- Use an independent testing facility.

Certain transportation employees must pass drug tests, and certain companies with state or federal contracts must maintain drug-free workplace programs. See "Where Do I Go For More Information?" on page 78 for helpful resources.

Be aware that the law limits drug testing employees. If you want to perform any drug testing, it must happen in the application phase after a job offer is made. If you make your offer contingent on successfully passing a drug test, make that clear in the offer letter; it should state that the offer is contingent on passing the drug test. Don't let the applicant start working until you receive the results of the drug test. If an applicant refuses to take a drug test, you can refuse to hire the applicant.

Medical Exams and Inquiries

Employers may not conduct physical examinations prior to making an offer of employment.

The position may require job-related physical fitness, such as being able to lift a certain amount of weight. You may test only for necessary physical qualifications, and only after you have made an offer of employment. You may not test for an individual's HIV status.

An employer may withdraw an offer of employment based on the results of an examination only if the applicant is unable to perform the job's essential duties with or without reasonable accommodation.

Disability discrimination laws restrict your right to require medical exams or to ask applicants and employees about disabilities. Untimely or unnecessary inquiries about health issues or disabilities put you in a vulnerable position if you later take adverse action against the applicant or employee.

Reference Checks

Though you're not required to check your future employee's references, doing so can protect you from liability. See "Conduct Background Checks" on page 25.

When contacting your applicant's listed references, stick to questions that directly relate to job performance to avoid liability for invasion of privacy. But remember to avoid salary inquiries, as employers are banned from asking about a job applicant's salary history. That would include seeking information about prior salary through a reference check. For more information, see "Salary History Questions Prohibited" on page 20.

Checking Online Activities

Employers are prohibited from requiring or requesting applicants to disclose information regarding their personal social media accounts, including their passwords, as part of the hiring process. These same prohibitions also apply if you are interviewing to promote a current employee to an open position.

Social media accounts can include Facebook, LinkedIn or Twitter accounts, as well as personal email accounts.

Employers can't retaliate against, discipline, discharge or threaten to discharge an applicant for not complying with an employer's request or demand to reveal personal social media information in violation of this law.

While California law prohibits employers from requesting applicants to divulge password protected social media information, employers still have access to a vast array of information many individuals choose to share on publicly available social media accounts.

 Exercise caution if you use social media in the hiring process. Searching online media sites may reveal information about applicants that you can't consider in the hiring process, such as the applicant's race, gender, disability, age, etc.

Example: An applicant uses her public Facebook account to announce that she's pregnant. Now, despite your efforts to limit your interview to legally neutral questions, you suddenly know that the applicant belongs to a protected class. If your social media searches reveal an applicant's membership in a protected class, you risk the possibility of a discrimination lawsuit if you then decide not to hire the applicant.

Verify the Employee's Authorization to Work

The Immigration Reform and Control Act (IRCA) of 1986 imposes compliance obligations and responsibilities on every employer regardless of size.

You must verify that an individual you hire is either a U.S. citizen or is authorized to be employed in the United States. You may not knowingly hire, contract for labor, recruit, retain or refer for a fee for employment an individual unauthorized to work in the United States.

Completing the *Form I-9*

You must verify that every new hire is either a U.S. citizen or authorized to work in the United States within three business days after the employee's first day of work for pay. You must use the *Form I-9 Employment Eligibility Verification* to do so.

Make sure that you use the most recent version of the *Form I-9* because the federal government regularly updates the form. Check the revision date, which is located in the form's lower left-hand corner.

In July 2017, the federal government approved a revised *Form I-9 Employment Eligibility Verification*. As of September 18, 2017, employers must use only the new version of the *Form I-9*, dated 07/17/17 N. At the time of publication, employers were still instructed to use this version.

 Visit the U.S. Citizenship and Immigration Services (USCIS) I-9 Central website at ***https://www.uscis.gov/i-9-central*** for a comprehensive selection of *Form I-9* resources, including the *Handbook for Employers, Instructions for Completing the Form I-9 (M-274)*, which employers can consult for additional information on completing the *Form I-9*.

The *Form I-9* is made up of three sections.

Employee Completes Section 1

Employees may complete Section 1 of the *Form I-9* any time between accepting a job offer and their first day of work for pay. USCIS provides detailed instructions on completing the *Form I-9*. See the *Form I-9 - Employment Eligibility Verification - Instructions*. Use the *Form I-9 - Employment Eligibility Verification - Supplement - Section 1* if the employee needs to document that more than one preparer and/or translator assisted in completing Section 1.

Employees must be allowed to choose which document(s) they want to present from the lists of acceptable documents to verify their identity and employment authorization when completing the *Form I-9*:

- "List A" documents show identity and employment authorization.

- "List B" documents show identity only.

- "List C" documents show employment authorization only.

All documents used by the employee for *Form I-9* verification must be unexpired.

 Persons may use one document from "List A" to verify their identity and employment authorization or one item from "List B" *and* one item from "List C."

Example: Persons who present a California driver's license to establish identity must also present a valid document that establishes their right to work in the United States.

 You may not require more or different identity and work authorization documents than specified by the USCIS on the *Form I-9*, and you may not specify which documents an employee must provide. For more information, see ""Document Abuse" and Completing the Form I-9" on page 48.

Employees are not obliged to provide their SSN in Section 1 of the *Form I-9* unless they're employed by an employer who participates in the E-Verify program. For more information on this program, see "E-Verify" on page 49.

Employer Completes Section 2

You must fill out Section 2 and examine evidence of identity and employment eligibility within three business days of the employee's first day of work for pay. If you hire a person for fewer than three business days, both sections 1 and 2 of the *Form I-9* must be fully completed by the employee's first day of work for pay.

USCIS provides detailed instructions on completing the *Form I-9*. See the *Form I-9 - Employment Eligibility Verification - Instructions* for Section 2.

An employer may designate an authorized representative, including personnel officers, foremen or agents, to fill out a *Form I-9* on behalf of the company. If you designate someone else to fill out a *Form I-9* on your behalf, that person must carry out all responsibilities for completing and signing Section 2 of the *Form I-9*. The employer is still liable for any violations in connection with the verification process.

You must examine one document from "List A" OR a combination of one from "List B" and one from "List C." You must examine the original document(s) the employee presents and then fully complete Section 2 of the *Form I-9*. Follow the specific instructions in Section 2 of the form.

The *Form I-9* lists the acceptable documents. The USCIS provides photographic examples of List A, B and C documents on its website: ***www.uscis.gov/i-9-central***.

Do not file the *Form I-9* with U.S. Immigrations and Customs Enforcement (ICE) or USCIS. You must keep the *Form I-9* for either three years after the date of hire or one year after employment is terminated, whichever is later.

You must make the form available for inspection or audit within three days after receiving a request from authorized U.S. government officials (e.g., ICE, U.S. Department of Labor). It's recommended that *Forms I-9* are kept together in a file separate from individual personnel files for easier access.

The Spanish version of *Form I-9* may be filled out by employers and employees in Puerto Rico ONLY. Spanish-speaking employers and employees in the 50 states and other U.S. territories may print this for their reference, but may only complete the form in English to meet employment eligibility verification requirements.

For a non-citizen, make sure you re-verify expiring work authorization documents before the expiration date noted in Section 1 of the *Form I-9*. For more information about hiring non-U.S. citizens, see "What Should I Know About Employing Non-U.S. Citizens?" on page 51.

Receipts

Sometimes, an employee may need to present, in lieu of a List A, List B or List C document, an acceptable receipt, valid for a short period of time, for completion of Section 2 or Section 3 (reverification) of *Form I-9*. Presenting a receipt only temporarily satisfies the requirements of Section 2. See Section 2 of the *I-9 - Employment Eligibility Verification - Instructions* for an explanation of when a receipt can be acceptable and how to record it on the *Form I-9*.

Employers cannot accept receipts if employment will last less than three business days. The USCIS has more information about acceptable receipts at ***www.uscis.gov/i-9-central***.

Electronic Storage of *Form I-9*

Employers may use a paper system, an electronic system, or a combination of paper and electronic systems to store *Forms I-9*.

The federal regulations set standards for employers who want to retain *Forms I-9* electronically. Employers must retain copies in a system that includes:

- Reasonable controls to ensure the integrity, accuracy and reliability of the electronic generation or storage system;

- Reasonable controls designed to prevent and detect the unauthorized or accidental creation of, addition to, alteration of, deletion of or deterioration of an electronically completed or stored *Form I-9*;

- An inspection and quality assurance program evidenced by regular evaluations of the electronic generation or storage system, including periodic checks of electronically stored *Form I-9*;

- In the case of electronically retained *Forms I-9*, a retrieval system that includes an indexing system that permits searches consistent with the requirements of the federal regulations; and

- The ability to reproduce legible and readable hardcopies.

For more detailed information about the requirements for electronic generation and retention of *Forms I-9*, see USCIS Handbook for Employers, Guidance for Completing the Form I-9 (M-274) at ***www.uscis.gov/i-9-central/handbook-employers-m-274***.

According to the USCIS *Form I-9 Instructions*, *Forms I-9* cannot be electronically signed. The form can be filled out on a computer, but a hard copy of the form must still be printed out, and the employee and employer representative must sign and date the form by hand. An employer then has the option of scanning the form for I-9 electronic storage purposes.

Employers may choose between paper and electronic systems, but should apply consistent policies and procedures to all employees to avoid claims of discrimination. Providing an electronic version does not eliminate the employer's obligation to examine documentation provided by the employee prior to completing the *Form I-9*.

 Whether the *Form I-9* gets filled out manually or electronically, an employer representative must still physically examine required identification and work eligibility documentation, and the employee and employer must sign a hard copy of the form by hand.

"Document Abuse" and Completing the *Form I-9*

"Document abuse" is one form of discrimination that can occur during the I-9 process. Document abuse occurs "when employers treat individuals differently on the basis of national origin or citizenship status in the *Form I-9* process," according to the USCIS.

Employers can't specify which document(s) they will accept for verification, as long as they are on the list of acceptable documents included on the *Form I-9*. Instead, employees may choose which document(s) they wish to present from the lists of acceptable documents.

Limiting the types of documents an employee can present can be an unfair immigration-related employment practice in violation of the anti-discrimination provision of the Immigration and Nationality Act (INA), according to USCIS. The INA prohibits discrimination during the I-9 process and it is enforced by the DOJ.

This type of conduct is unlawful under state law, as well. Under California law, the Labor Commissioner can order employers that violated the law to pay a penalty of up to $10,000, as well as issue orders to stop further violations. California law may provide an easier remedy than federal law for workers who believe that their rights were violated.

 The INA's document abuse prohibitions cover employers with four or more employees.

The USCIS considers four broad categories of conduct as document abuse:

1. Improperly requesting that an employee produce more documents than the *Form I-9* requires to establish the employee's identity and employment authorization;

2. Improperly requesting that employees present a particular document, such as a "green card," to establish identity and/or employment authorization;

3. Improperly rejecting documents that reasonably appear to be genuine and to relate to the employee presenting them; and

4. Improperly treating groups of applicants differently when completing the *Form I-9*, such as requiring certain groups of employees who look or sound "foreign" to present particular documents that the employer doesn't require other employees to present.

California Driver's License

The California Department of Motor Vehicles (DMV) issues an original driver's license (known as an AB 60 driver's license) to undocumented persons who are unable to submit satisfactory proof that their presence in the United States is authorized under federal law if they:

- Meet all other qualifications for holding a license; and

- Provide satisfactory proof to the DMV of their identity and California residency.

You may not discriminate against individuals because they hold or present a license issued under AB 60. The California Vehicle Code and the Government Code provide that it is a violation of FEHA as a national origin discrimination for an employer to discriminate against individuals because they hold or present an AB 60 driver's license. For more information, see "Immigration Status" in Chapter 7, page 267.

You may not require applicants or employees to hold or present a driver's license unless:

- Holding a driver's license is required by law for a particular job; or

- You have a legitimate business reason for requiring drivers' licenses and you apply the reason uniformly.

For employers who hire commercial drivers, AB 60 states that its provisions don't authorize individuals to apply for, or be issued, a commercial driver's license without submitting their SSN with their application.

What If the Documents I'm Shown Aren't Valid?

You aren't liable for accepting documents that appear reasonably authentic, unless you know or have reason to know that the documents are false. You may not refuse to honor documents that appear valid on their face.

E-Verify

E-Verify is an Internet-based system operated by the U.S. Department of Homeland Security (DHS) and the SSA that allows employers to electronically verify the employment eligibility of newly hired employees.

Federal contractors and subcontractors are required to use the E-Verify system to verify eligibility of employees to work in the United States.

Some important points regarding E-Verify include:

- Federal contractors and subcontractors must enroll in E-Verify if and when awarded a federal contract or subcontract that requires participation in E-Verify as a term of the contract.

- California employers' participation in E-Verify is voluntary (unless you are a federal contractor or subcontractor).

- E-Verify must be used for new hires only. It can't be used to verify the employment eligibility of current employees.

- E-Verify must be used for all new hires regardless of national origin or citizenship status. It may not be used selectively.

- E-Verify must be used only after hire and after completion of the *Form I-9*. Employers may not pre-screen applicants through E-Verify.

- The program is currently free to employers.

Employers who use the E-Verify system to determine employment eligibility must display the English and Spanish notices supplied by the DHS in a prominent place clearly visible to prospective employees. The notices, *E-Verify Participation Poster* and *E-Verify Right to Work Poster*, can be found on the DHS website.

The forms download associated with the **HR Quick Guide for California Employers** also contains the forms, in English and Spanish versions. To find out more or to sign up for E-Verify, visit the DHS' website at **www.dhs.gov/e-verify**.

Unless required by federal law, employers cannot be required to use E-Verify as a condition of receiving a government contract, applying for or maintaining a business license, or as a penalty for violating licensing or other similar laws. "Employers" does not include the state, a city, county, city and county or special district.

Unlawful Use of E-Verify

California employers may not use E-Verify to check the employment authorization status of an existing employee or an applicant who hasn't received an employment offer, unless the employers are required to do so by federal law or by a condition of receiving federal funds. Employers who use the E-Verify system for applicants after an offer of employment has been made must provide the affected employee with any notification issued by the SSA or the DHS that contains information specific to the employee's E-Verify case or to any tentative non-confirmation notice.

 Employers who use E-Verify unlawfully are liable for a $10,000 penalty, per violation.

What Should I Know About Employing Non-U.S. Citizens?

If employees have valid documents of their employment eligibility, you may not discriminate against them on the basis of:

- National origin;

- Citizenship status; or

- Future expiration date of verifying documents.

Employers are prohibited from engaging in "unfair immigration-related practices" when an employee asserts protected rights under the Labor Code. For more information, see "Immigration Status" in Chapter 7, page 267.

Worksite Immigration Enforcement and Protections

The 2018 Immigrant Worker Protection Act (IWPA), provides California workers with protection from immigration enforcement while on the job.

Employers cannot:

- Provide a federal immigration enforcement agent access to nonpublic areas of a business without a judicial warrant; or

- Provide agents access to employee records without a subpoena or judicial warrant. (This prohibition does not apply to *Form I-9* or other documents for which a Notice of Inspection was provided to the employer. However, employers must follow specific requirements related to *Form I-9* inspections.)

 Recent legal challenges from the U.S. Department of Justice put these two provisions of the law on hold. A federal district judge granted a preliminary injunction blocking the state from fining employers who voluntarily grant ICE access to their worksite or employee records. This is only a preliminary injunction and future appeals are likely. Employers should monitor this area for further developments.

Notice Requirements

Employers that receive a notice from a federal immigration agency of a *Form I-9* inspection must act quickly, as the law imposes strict notice requirements. Once an employer receives a notice of inspection, it must:

- Post a notice to all current employees informing them of any federal immigration agency's inspections of *Forms I-9* or other employment records **within 72 hours** of receiving the Notice of Inspection. The notice must be posted in the language normally used to communicate employment-related information, and must also be given to the collective bargaining representative, if any. The notice must include the following information:

    - The name of the immigration agency conducting the inspection;

    - The date the employer received notice;

    - The nature of the inspection, if known;

    - A copy of the Notice of Inspection of I-9 Employment Eligibility Verification forms (Notice of Inspection); and

    - The Labor Commissioner's model notice, the ***Notice to Employee: Government Inspection of Employment Eligibility Records***.

- Provide, upon reasonable request, a copy of the federal Notice of Inspection to an employee.

- Give, within 72 hours of receiving the inspection results, each current affected employee and the employee's collective bargaining representative a copy of the inspection results and a written notice of the employer's and employee's obligations arising from the inspection. Specific information must be included. An "affected employee" is an employee identified by the inspection results as potentially lacking work authorization or having document deficiencies.

 Create and document processes to meet all notice requirements. The 72-hour time frames are short, and standardized posting and notice processes will help you meet your compliance obligations. Consult a labor or immigration attorney with any questions or concerns.

An employer that fails to follow this law's requirements can be fined between $2,000 to $5,000 for a first violation and $5,000 to $10,000 for each subsequent violation.

Penalties for Not Complying with Worker Authorization Requirements

You may be subject to the following penalties and fines for failing to comply with worker authorization requirements:

- Failing to properly complete, retain and/or make the forms available for inspection carries a fine ranging from $220 to $2,191 per violation.

- Knowingly hiring or continuing to employ workers who are not authorized carries civil penalties ranging from $548 to $21,916 per violation, depending on whether it's a first or subsequent offense.

- Engaging in unfair immigration-related employment practices carries a penalty of $452 to $9,054 per violation, depending on whether it's a first or subsequent offense.

- Document abuse (requiring employees to carry more or different documentation than the law requires) carries a minimum fine of $181 to $1,811 per violation.

- Document fraud can carry penalties from $382 to $7,635 per document, depending on the type of fraud and whether it's a first or subsequent offense.

- Engaging in a pattern or practice of knowingly hiring or continuing to employ unauthorized workers carries criminal penalties up to $3,000 per unauthorized worker and/or six months of imprisonment.

It is unlawful for California employers to reverify the employment eligibility of current employees in a time or manner not allowed by federal employment eligibility verification laws. Federal law already prohibits unlawful reverification practices, such as reverification of unexpired documentation. However, California adds an additional civil penalty of up to $10,000.

Exempt and Nonexempt Employees

Federal and state laws exempt certain employees from wage and hour requirements, especially overtime pay and meal- and rest-break requirements. If you have a problem distinguishing between exempt and nonexempt employees in your company, you are not alone. Some of the largest multimillion-dollar awards of back pay by the courts stem from employers' misclassification of nonexempt employees as exempt from overtime.

Nonexempt Employees

Nonexempt employees are subject to numerous wage and hour laws. For example, nonexempt employees:

- Earn overtime pay (see "Overtime" in Chapter 5, page 164).

- Receive payment of at least minimum wage (see "Other Compensation" in Chapter 5, page 172).

- Must take meal and rest periods (see "Meal and Rest Breaks" in Chapter 5, page 176).

 Don't pay nonexempt employees a salary. This doesn't make them exempt. You must track and document all hours worked by nonexempt employees and the hourly rate of pay for each hour worked. See Chapter 5, "Paying Employees," for more information.

Exempt Employees

Federal and state laws exempt certain employees from wage and hour requirements, including overtime pay and meal- and rest-break requirements. Whether you can classify an employee as exempt depends on the employee's duties and responsibilities, and how the employee is paid.

Exempt employees, such as executive, administrative or professional employees, possess management and decision-making responsibilities. Exempt employees assume responsibility for getting their job duties done regardless of the time it takes to complete their duties. However, employers need to be wary of creating situations in which "managers" also perform nonexempt duties.

For example, a manager supervises other employees but simultaneously performs routine tasks, such as stocking shelves, cashiering or bagging groceries. In this scenario, the manager is not primarily engaged in performing exempt work if more than half of that individual's time is spent performing nonexempt tasks. This employee should be classified as a nonexempt employee. If the employer misclassified the "manager" in this scenario as exempt, the employer could face a lawsuit and might have to pay substantial penalties to the employee.

Employment laws create five major types of exempt positions:

- Administrative.

- Executive/managerial.

- Professional.

- Computer software professional.

- Outside salesperson/commissioned inside salesperson.

For California employees to be exempt, they must generally meet strict job-duties tests particular to each exemption and be paid a minimum salary. Use the *Exempt Analysis Worksheets* (described in Table 12 on page 65) to help you decide how to classify your employee and whether your employee meets the applicable duties and salary tests.

You can find these in your forms download, described in detail in "Online Forms" in Chapter 1, page 9. For more information on classifying exempt employees, see "Exempt Employees" in Chapter 5, page 168.

Independent Contractors

Many employers may be tempted to classify workers as independent contractors instead of direct employees, but doing so is risky.

Effective January 1, 2020, most employers must satisfy a strict test to properly classify workers as independent contractors. The law also extended the test's application so that it now applies both under the Industrial Welfare Commission (IWC) Wage Orders and to the Labor and Unemployment Insurance Codes. For more information, see "Properly Classifying the Individual as an Independent Contractor" on page 56.

California labor law defines an independent contractor as "any person who renders service for a specified recompense for a specified result, under the control of his principal as to the result of his work only and not as to the means by which such result is accomplished."

An independent contractor works for another entity under a verbal or written contract, usually for a specific length of time. Independent contractors are responsible for only their own work, and are generally responsible for their own schedule. Independent contractors must also be responsible for how the work is completed.

Use caution when classifying a worker as an independent contractor. Simply labeling a worker as an independent contractor does not mean the worker is truly an independent contractor in the eyes of the law. Courts and government agencies use many factors to determine whether a worker is an independent contractor and not an employee.

Misclassifying a worker as an independent contractor, rather than an employee, creates potential liability for employment taxes and penalties, and liability for failure to fulfill the many legal obligations owed to an employee, such as wage and hour requirements.

California law prohibits any person or employer from willfully misclassifying an individual as an independent contractor:

- The civil penalty for violation of this law ranges from $5,000 to $25,000 for each violation.

- Other remedies include requiring the employer to display on its website or in the workplace a notice of the serious violation of misclassifying an independent contractor; a statement that the employer has changed its business practices in order to comply with the law; and information on how to contact the Labor and Workforce Development Agency to report misclassification. The notice must be posted for one year, and signed by an officer of the employer.

- These civil penalties are in addition to any fines or taxes owed to the IRS and the EDD. Misclassification can also result in denial of workers' compensation coverage, penalties for failure to provide workers' compensation, and payment of workers' compensation premiums from the date of hire of the independent contractor(s).

The law also prohibits employers from charging a misclassified independent contractor for goods, materials, space, rental, services, government licenses, repairs, equipment maintenance or fines that arise from the individual's employment, if the charges would have violated the law if the person had been an employee.

 Consult legal counsel to ensure proper classification of independent contractors.

Properly Classifying the Individual as an Independent Contractor

No set definition of the term "independent contractor" applies for all purposes. Various state and federal agencies use their own tests to determine whether an individual meets the criteria to be classified as an independent contractor.

 In 2019, California adopted as law the California Supreme Court's "ABC test" to determine whether a worker is an employee or an independent contractor. While the Court only applied this test for purposes of California's IWC Wage Orders, the new California law mandates that the test also is applied to the Labor and Unemployment Insurance Codes.

Under the ABC test, a worker is presumed to be an employee unless the company can prove all of the following:

- Part A: That the worker is free from control and direction of the hiring entity in connection with the performance of the work, both under the contract for the performance of the work and in actually performing the work;

- Part B: That the worker performs work that is outside the usual course of the hiring entity's business; and

- Part C: That the worker is customarily engaged in an independently established trade, occupation or business of the same nature as the work performed.

If a company can't show that the worker meets **all** three criteria, the worker is an employee, not an independent contractor.

Several exceptions from the ABC test are carved out for various industries, in which case the more flexible common law "Borello test" typically applies. Even if an exception seems clearly applicable, businesses using independent contractors should consult with legal counsel regarding their circumstances given the new law's complexity.

Independent Contractor Common-Law Principles (Borello Test)

Under other circumstances where the ABC test does not apply, including the aforementioned exceptions detailed in the new law, California courts and administrative agencies generally apply common-law principles to determine independent contractor status. One of the key factors is whether the worker has the right to direct and control the manner and means of performing the work. But the right to control is just one factor government agencies and courts use to assess an independent contractor classification.

When assessing whether a worker is properly classified, courts and agencies balance a variety of factors, including whether:

- The employer has the right to terminate the contract and pays by job, not by time.

- Both parties believe they're creating an independent contractor relationship.

- The worker:

  - Engages in a distinct occupational business.

  - Possesses significant skills or education required for the particular occupation.

  - Supplies the instruments and tools for performing the work.

  - Performs services over a short or specified period of time.

- – Has opportunity for profit or loss, depending upon the worker's own managerial skills.

- – Employs additional help at the worker's own expense.

- The work:

  - – Usually occurs under the employer's general direction.

  - – Is performed by a specialist, without employer supervision.

  - – Is not part of the employer's regular business.

 Employers should consult with legal counsel and re-evaluate workers currently treated as independent contractors to determine whether reclassification may be necessary under the ABC test's newly expanded application.

Forms Related to Independent Contractors

Each independent contractor you hire needs to sign a contract, approved by your legal counsel, that includes the scope of work and the terms of the agreement.

You must also report independent contractors to the EDD's New Employee Registry within 20 days of the start-of-work date. Use the *Independent Contractors Report - DE542*, described in Table 12 on page 65, and in your forms download, described in detail in "Online Forms" on page 9.

 Be careful in making your decision. It isn't enough that the two parties agree to an independent contractor relationship. You can classify an individual as an independent contractor only if the individual meets the requirements. Each case is unique, and the penalties for making a mistake can be costly. We recommend you consult legal counsel to help you determine an individual's status.

Hiring Minors

When you employ a minor, you must comply with child labor laws designed to help young people acquire work experience and income while safeguarding their scholastic advancement and physical well-being. You can use the *Employing Minors Checklist* as a guide, described in Table 12 on page 65.

 A **minor** is any person under the age of 18 required to attend school, or any person under the age of six.

To employ a minor, you must have a work permit on file year-round, even when school is not in session. You must have the permit on file the day the minor begins work. You can get the permit from the minor's local school district office, even if the student attends a charter school.

This applies to any minor, even:

- High-school dropouts;

- Emancipated minors (those minors who declare independence from their parents for tax purposes), although they can apply for a work permit without their parent's permission;

- Minors who are not state residents, such as children who live out of state with one parent during the school year and visit the other parent in California during the summer; and

- Children who work for their parents.

A **work permit** sets limits on the maximum number of days and hours of work, as well as the spread of hours allowed for that minor. It may also contain limitations on other aspects of the minor's work.

Obtaining a Work Permit

1. Complete a *Statement of Intent to Employ a Minor and Request for a Work Permit - Form B1-1*, described in Table 12 on page 65. The minor's supervisor and parent/ guardian must both sign the form.

2. File *Form B1-1* with the minor's school district.

3. The minor's school district completes and issues a *Permit to Employ and Work - Form B1-4*, described in Table 12 on page 65.

You must keep the work permit on file the entire length of employment. For more information on handling these forms, see Table 12 on page 65.

Circumstances That Don't Require a Work Permit

Direct all questions regarding the need for work permits to the minor's school district (or to the school district in which the minor would go to school if the minor doesn't currently attend, or if the minor attends a private school). You don't need a work permit for minors who:

- Graduated from high school, though in certain hazardous occupations even these minors need a work permit unless they completed a certificate program for that industry;

- Work irregularly at odd jobs, such as yard work and babysitting, in private homes;

- Participate in any horseback riding exhibition, contest or event;

- Are self-employed;

- Are at least 14 years of age and deliver newspapers to consumers; or

- Work for a parent or guardian in connection with property the parent or guardian owns, operates or controls for agriculture, horticulture, viticulture or domestic labor.

Penalties for Incorrectly Employing Minors

Violations of child labor laws carry serious penalties. California law provides civil penalties for violations of child labor laws.

Under California law:

- Treble damages are allowed if individuals are discriminated or retaliated against because they filed a claim or civil action alleging a violation of employment laws that occurred while they were minors.

- The statute of limitations for claims that arise from violations of employment laws is tolled, in other words, delayed or suspended, until the minor is 18 years of age.

- Employers face a penalty of $25,000 to $50,000 for Class A violations involving minors 12 years of age or younger.

Employment Contracts

One of the most significant hiring missteps is accidentally creating an employment contract; this may lead to a wrongful termination lawsuit at the end of the employment relationship.

Employment in California is presumed to be at-will. In brief, this means that you can hire, demote, amend an employee's job description or schedule, or terminate an employee whenever you want as long as you don't break a law or violate a specified public policy when you make those employment decisions.

At-will employment also means that workers can accept or leave employment whenever they want. To emphasize the at-will nature of employment, you should use an employment agreement that outlines the terms and conditions of employment and re-states the definition of at-will employment.

However, if you create employment that is not at-will, you create an employment "contract" that overrides the presumption of at-will employment. A simple statement that seems to guarantee future employment, such as, "Do a good job and you'll always have work here," is enough to create an employment contract.

An employment contract can create explicit limitations on when and under what circumstances you can terminate the employment relationship because contracts usually create a promise that you will only terminate an employee for just cause.

Just cause means a fair and honest cause or reason, acted on in good faith by the employer.

Remember, contracts can be written, oral or implied. An implied covenant exists in every employment relationship. This covenant requires you to exercise "good faith and fair dealing" in the employment relationship.

Good faith and fair dealing means that you make decisions in a fair manner and treat employees who are similarly situated in like manner.

Table 11. Types of Contracts

Type	What Do I Need To Know?
Written Contracts	These are the most obvious. An employee with a written and signed contract has the right to have that contract honored. Written contracts can work to your benefit if the contract clearly states how and why employment may be terminated. You should also consider adding these provisions to the contract: • Specify the duration of the contract and the time period required for notice for termination of the contract. • State that the contract can be renewed at the option of the company. • State that the written document constitutes the entire agreement, that no representations or promises other than those documented can be relied upon, and that the contract can be modified only in writing signed by a corporate officer. Written contracts do carry disadvantages; they are less flexible and any inadvertent omissions or ambiguities in the contract will be interpreted in the employee's favor. All employment agreements entered into, modified or extended on or after January 1, 2017, cannot require an employee who primarily works and resides in California: • To agree to adjudicate a claim in another state when the claim arises in California; or • To agree to apply another state's law to a controversy that arises in California. ❶ Be sure to consult legal counsel if you decide to use employment contracts.

Table 11. Types of Contracts *(continued)*

Type	What Do I Need To Know?
Oral Contracts	Though oral contracts — based on conversations between employer and employee — are less obvious, they're just as binding as signed, written contracts. Watch what you say to an employee in every phase of the employment relationship. For details, see "Employment Contracts" on page 61 for details. Provide training on this topic to managers and supervisors.
Implied Contracts	These are based upon the length of employment and indicators of job security that an employee receives. The courts determine whether an implied contract exists on a case-by-case basis. The best defense against an implied contract claim is a signed, at-will employment agreement. You should also maintain an explicit at-will employment policy in your employee handbook.

 Effective January 1, 2020, California law bans mandatory arbitration agreements entered into between employers and employees. Specifically, an employer is prohibited from requiring an applicant or employee to waive any right, forum or procedure for any employer violations of the FEHA and the Labor Code.

Discrimination in Hiring

Another important misstep to be aware of is making an employment decision or acting in any way that may lead to a discrimination lawsuit. Federal and state laws require that you treat all qualified candidates equally.

You can't make hiring decisions based (in whole or in part) on an applicant's race, religion, color, national origin, ancestry, physical disability, mental disability, medical condition, genetic information, marital status, sex, gender, gender identity, gender expression, age, sexual orientation, union activity, past bankruptcy or status as an authorized immigrant or a veteran.

California laws create stricter protections for applicants than do federal laws. The definition of disability is broader, and more classes are included as protected.

If a person files a discrimination lawsuit against you, your burden is to prove that you acted on legitimate, nondiscriminatory reasons for not hiring that individual. This might be tougher than it sounds. Any documents or notes on documents can be used to prove your case, or to prove discrimination accusations against you. Only constant vigilance and consistent behavior will protect you.

For guidelines on non-discriminatory employment decisions, see "Discrimination and Employment Practices" in Chapter 7, page 259.

Minimum Compliance Elements

1. Hang your **2020 *California and Federal Labor Law Poster*** (available from ***store.calchamber.com***), which includes mandatory postings that all employees and applicants must be able to see, in a prominent place (such as a break room).

    If you have employees working in a city or county with a local minimum wage and/or paid sick leave ordinance, you may also need to post required local ordinances and provide additional notices to employees at the time of hire.

2. Use the *Hiring Checklist* to make sure you fill out all the required paperwork for every new hire. See Table 12 on page 65.

3. Look at all candidates objectively, in terms of their ability to do the job. See "Interview Candidates" on page 23.

4. Make sure you classify workers properly. See "Exempt and Nonexempt Employees" on page 53.

5. Make sure you don't control your independent contractors as if they were employees. See "Properly Classifying the Individual as an Independent Contractor" on page 56.

Forms and Checklists

The following tables describe required and recommended forms associated with the hiring process.

 TIP You can find these forms in your forms download, described in detail in "Online Forms" on page 9.

Table 12. Forms and Checklists

Notice or Form	What Do I Use It For?	When Do I Use It?	Who Fills It Out?	Where Does It Go?
Adverse Action Notice	To take adverse action (such as not hiring an applicant or terminating an employee) based on a credit report you have obtained.	This form is required when you know you are taking adverse action based on information in the credit report (see "Background Checks and Testing" on page 31).	The employer.	Give it to the employee. Keep a copy in a private file away from personnel file. Restrict access to the form to a "need to know" basis.
Certification to Consumer Credit Reporting Agency	To obtain a credit report of any type.	This form is required before you obtain the report (see "Background Checks and Testing" on page 31).	The employer.	Send the form to the agency creating the report. Keep it in the personnel file. Restrict access to the form to a "need to know" basis.
Confidentiality Agreement	To obtain an employee's acknowledgment that there is information necessary for his/her job that he/she may not disclose.	At the time of hire or change in duties of an employee.	The employer prepares the agreement and it's reviewed by an attorney. The employee signs the agreement.	The original agreement goes in the employee's personnel record. Give the employee a copy.

Table 12. Forms and Checklists *(continued)*

Notice or Form	What Do I Use It For?	When Do I Use It?	Who Fills It Out?	Where Does It Go?
DE4 - California Employee's Withholding Certificate	All employees. This is the California tax withholding form if employees want different federal and state tax withholding.	Before employee's first pay date.	The employee.	Keep the form in the employee's personnel record. If you send the original to payroll, keep a copy of the form.
Direct Deposit Authorization	To get employees' permission to deposit paychecks directly into their bank account instead of receiving a paper check.	As part of the hiring process or whenever an employee requests direct deposit.	The employee.	Keep in personnel and/or payroll file (if separate).
Direct Deposit Authorization - Spanish	To get permission from employees whose primary language is Spanish to deposit paychecks directly into their bank account instead of receiving a paper check.	As part of the hiring process or whenever an employee requests direct deposit.	The employee.	Keep in personnel and/or payroll file (if separate).
Disclosure and Authorization to Obtain Consumer Credit Report - California	To obtain a credit report of any type.	This form is required before you obtain the report (see "Background Checks and Testing" in Chapter 2, page 31. It must be given separately from the federal report (listed below).	The employer.	Keep it in the personnel file. Restrict access to the form to a "need to know" basis.

Table 12. Forms and Checklists *(continued)*

Notice or Form	What Do I Use It For?	When Do I Use It?	Who Fills It Out?	Where Does It Go?
Disclosure and Authorization to Obtain Consumer Credit Report - Federal	To obtain a credit report of any type.	This form is required before you obtain the report (see "Background Checks and Testing" in Chapter 2, page 31. It must be given separately from the California report (listed above).	The employer.	Keep it in the personnel file. Restrict access to the form to a "need to know" basis.
Disclosure and Authorization to Obtain Investigative Consumer Report	To investigate and obtain an investigative consumer report.	This form is required before you obtain the report (see "Background Checks and Testing" in Chapter 2, page 31.	The employer.	Keep it in the personnel file. Restrict access to the form to a "need to know" basis.
Emergency Information	Recording important medical information and contacts in case of an emergency.	At the time of hire. Keep the form updated throughout employment.	The employee.	Keep emergency information readily accessible. You may keep the forms in your personnel records, but you might want to use a separate binder for quicker access.

Table 12. Forms and Checklists *(continued)*

Notice or Form	What Do I Use It For?	When Do I Use It?	Who Fills It Out?	Where Does It Go?
Emergency Information - Spanish	Recording important medical information and contacts in case of an emergency for employees whose primary language is Spanish.	At the time of hire. Keep the form updated throughout employment.	The employee.	Keep emergency information readily accessible. You may keep the form in your personnel records, but you might want to use a separate binder for quicker access.
Employee Orientation Checklist	Tracking completed orientation tasks.	In the first weeks of employment.	The managers.	Keep in the employee's personnel file.
Employing Minors Checklist	Tracking legal issues to consider when hiring a minor.	During the recruiting and hiring processes.	The employer.	Keep the checklist in the minor's personnel file.
Employment Application - Long Form	To gather more detailed information and employment history, and all other necessary sections.	During the recruiting process.	The applicant.	Keep in the employee's personnel file, if the applicant is hired. If you don't hire the applicant, keep the paperwork for two years.
Employment Application – Short Form	Gathering key work history information from an applicant, obtaining authorization to check references and background, and certification that all information is truthful.	During the recruiting process.	The applicant.	Keep in the employee's personnel file, if the applicant is hired. If you don't hire the applicant, keep the paperwork for two years.

Table 12. Forms and Checklists *(continued)*

Notice or Form	What Do I Use It For?	When Do I Use It?	Who Fills It Out?	Where Does It Go?
Employment Interview Checklist	Listing which questions to ask applicants during an interview.	During the applicant's interview.	The interviewer.	Keep in the employee's personnel file, if hired. If you don't hire the applicant, keep the paperwork for two years.
Employment Letter	Informing an applicant that he or she has been selected for employment.	When the employment decision has been made.	The employer.	Mail to the applicant. Keep a copy in the employee's personnel file.
Exempt Analysis Worksheet – Administrative Exemption	Determining whether an employee's duties meet the requirements for exempt status.	During the hiring process.	The employer.	Keep in the employee's personnel file.
Exempt Analysis Worksheet – Computer Professional Exemption	Determining whether an employee's duties meet the requirements for exempt status.	During the hiring process.	The employer.	Keep in the employee's personnel file.
Exempt Analysis Worksheet – Executive Managerial Exemption	Determining whether an employee's duties meet the requirements for exempt status.	During the hiring process.	The employer.	Keep in the employee's personnel file.
Exempt Analysis Worksheet – Professional Exemption	Determining whether an employee's duties meet the requirements for exempt status.	During the hiring process.	The employer.	Keep in the employee's personnel file.

Table 12. Forms and Checklists *(continued)*

Notice or Form	What Do I Use It For?	When Do I Use It?	Who Fills It Out?	Where Does It Go?
Exempt Analysis Worksheet – Salesperson Exemption	Determining whether an employee's duties meet the requirements for exempt status.	During the hiring process.	The employer.	Keep in the employee's personnel file.
Fair Credit Reporting Act - Summary of Your Rights	To obtain a credit report of any type.	This form is required when you give the employee a copy of the credit report.	N/A	Give it to applicant.
General Notice of COBRA Continuation Coverage Rights - California Employees	To inform California employees of their rights to continuation of health care coverage. Applies only to employers with 20 or more employees, and only to employees in California.	This form is required on the day the employee enrolls for the benefit.	N/A	Include this notice in the group health plan's Summary Plan Description. Send a copy of the notice to the spouse of a married employee, preferably by registered mail. Keep a record of the mailing and/or distribution at hire of this notice to both employee and spouse on the *Hiring Checklist*.

Table 12. Forms and Checklists *(continued)*

Notice or Form	What Do I Use It For?	When Do I Use It?	Who Fills It Out?	Where Does It Go?
General Notice of COBRA Continuation Coverage Rights - Outside California	To inform employees outside California of their rights to continuation of health care coverage. Applies only to employers with 20 or more employees, and only to employees outside California.	This form is required on the day the employee enrolls for the benefit.	N/A	Include this notice in the group health plan's Summary Plan Description. Send a copy of the notice to the spouse of a married employee, preferably by registered mail. Keep a record of the mailing and/or distribution at hire of this notice to both employee and spouse on the *Hiring Checklist*.
Guide for Pre-Employment Inquiries	Outlining what you can and can't ask during the recruiting process.	During the recruiting process.	N/A	Use as a reference.
Hiring Checklist	Tracking completion of recommended and required hiring procedures and forms.	During the recruiting and hiring process.	The manager or other person in charge of hiring employees.	Keep in the employee's personnel file.

Table 12. Forms and Checklists *(continued)*

Notice or Form	What Do I Use It For?	When Do I Use It?	Who Fills It Out?	Where Does It Go?
Form I-9 - Employment Eligibility Verification	To verify the employment eligibility of **all** employees.	Section 1: At the time of hire. Section 2: Within three business days after the employee's first day of work. Section 3: On or before the expiration date in Section 1.	Section 1: The employee fills out. Section 2: The employer fills out. Section 3: The employer fills out if necessary for updating or reverifying.	Keep the forms for all employees in a common file rather than separate personnel records.
Form I-9 - Employment Eligibility Verification - Instructions	Use these USCIS instructions to assist you in properly completing the *Form I-9*.	When the *Form I-9* is being completed.	N/A.	Keep the instructions with your file for *Forms I-9*.
Form I-9 - Employment Eligibility Verification - Supplement - Section 1	Use if extra space is needed to document that more than one preparer and/or translator assisted an employee in completing Section 1.	When the *Form I-9* is being completed.	The employee.	Keep the forms for all employees in a common file rather than separate personnel records.
Independent Contractors Report - DE542	All new independent contractors. The District Attorney uses the information in this form to locate parents who owe child support funds.	This form must be completed and submitted as soon as possible after signing the contract.	The employer.	Mail or fax the form to: Employment Development Department P.O. Box 997350 MIC 96 Sacramento, CA 95899-7350 Fax: 916-319-4410

Table 12. Forms and Checklists (continued)

Notice or Form	What Do I Use It For?	When Do I Use It?	Who Fills It Out?	Where Does It Go?
Letter to Applicants Not Hired	Informing an applicant that he or she wasn't selected for employment.	When the employment decision has been made.	The employer.	Mail to the applicant. You should keep a list of the applicants to whom the letter is mailed.
New Employees Report - Form DE34	All new employees. Permits registered domestic partners to file joint state income tax and have their earnings treated as community property on par with married couples. The District Attorney uses the information in this form to locate parents who owe child support funds.	This form must be completed and submitted within 20 days of hire.	The employer.	Mail or fax the form to: Employment Development Department Document Management Group P.O. Box 997016, MIC 96 West Sacramento, CA 95799-7016 Fax: 916-319-4400
New Health Insurance Marketplace Coverage Options and Your Health Coverage - for Employers That Do Not Offer a Health Plan	Under the Affordable Care Act, employers must provide a notice of coverage options to employees.	The U.S. Department of Labor provided this model notice for use by employers who do not offer a health plan.	The employer.	Keep a record of the distribution at hire of this notice to the employee on the *Hiring Checklist*.

Table 12. Forms and Checklists *(continued)*

Notice or Form	What Do I Use It For?	When Do I Use It?	Who Fills It Out?	Where Does It Go?
New Health Insurance Market-place Coverage Options and Your Health Coverage - for Employers That Offer a Health Plan	Under the Affordable Care Act, employers must provide a notice of coverage options to employees.	The U.S. Department of Labor provided this model notice for use by employers who offer a health plan to some or all employees.	The employer.	Keep a record of the distribution at hire of this notice to the employee on the *Hiring Checklist*.
Paid Family Leave pamphlet (available in the **2020 Required Notices Kit**)	To provide notice to employees of their rights to paid family leave benefits.	This pamphlet must be given it to all new employees and any employees taking leave for a covered reason.	N/A	Give the pamphlet to employees and make sure they understand its contents.
Permit to Employ and Work - Form B1-4	To obtain permission to employ a minor.	This is required before the minor begins working [and after the *Statement of Intent to Employ a Minor and Request for Work Permit - Form B1-1* has been approved]. See the form's description following in this table.	The minor's school district fills out and issues the permit.	Keep form (permit) on file as long as the minor is employed. Keep it in your personnel records or in a common binder for all minor employees.

Table 12. Forms and Checklists *(continued)*

Notice or Form	What Do I Use It For?	When Do I Use It?	Who Fills It Out?	Where Does It Go?
Pre-Adverse Action Disclosure	To notify an employee or potential employee of the possibility of adverse action.	This form is required when you know you're taking adverse action based on information in the credit report (see "Background Checks and Testing" on page 31).	The employer.	Give to the employee. Keep a copy in a private file away from personnel file. Restrict access to the form to a "need to know" basis.
Pre-Hire Checklist	Organizing the process of finding and preparing to hire an employee.	During the recruiting process.	The employer.	Keep the check-list in the employee's personnel file, if the applicant is hired.
Property Return Agreement	Obtaining employees' acknowledg-ment that they received property from you (tools, uniforms, etc.) and agree to return the property.	When your property is issued to the employee.	The employee signs the form.	Keep the original agreement in your personnel records.
Recruiting Checklist	Use this checklist to guide you through the recruiting process for new and existing positions.	When you need to advertise and recruit for a new position.	The employer.	In your files.

Table 12. Forms and Checklists *(continued)*

Notice or Form	What Do I Use It For?	When Do I Use It?	Who Fills It Out?	Where Does It Go?
Sexual Harassment Hurts Everyone pamphlet (available in the **2020 Required Notices Kit**)	This form describes the problem and the penalties of sexual harassment.	You must provide this pamphlet whenever you hire a new employee. It's recommended that this form is given to independent contractors.	N/A	Give a copy to your workers and make sure they understand its contents.
State Disability Insurance Provisions (SDI) pamphlet (available in the **2020 Required Notices Kit**)	The SDI pamphlet notifies employees of their right to disability insurance benefits should they sustain a non-work related injury.	Give to an employee upon hire and when an employee takes a leave of absence for a reason that is covered.	N/A	Give a copy to your workers and make sure they understand its contents.
Statement of Intent to Employ a Minor and Request for a Work Permit - Form B1-1	To obtain permission to employ a minor. Be sure to finish the permit process with the *Permit to Employ and Work (Form B1-4)*, supplied by the minor's school district.	Before the minor begins working.	Each completes the appropriate part: • Minor; • Employer; • Parent; and • School district.	File it with the minor's school district. Keep a copy in your personnel records.
W-4 – Employee's Withholding Allowance Certificate	All employees.	Before an employee's first pay date.	The employee.	Keep the form in the employee's personnel record. If you send the original to payroll, keep a copy of the form.

Table 12. Forms and Checklists *(continued)*

Notice or Form	What Do I Use It For?	When Do I Use It?	Who Fills It Out?	Where Does It Go?
Wage and Employment Notice to Employees (Labor Code section 2810.5)	To notify nonexempt employees of their hourly or piece rate of pay, pay dates, mandatory paid sick leave, and other information required by law.	At the time of hire, or on an employee's first day of employment.	The employer.	Give a copy to the new employee and keep a copy in the employee's personnel file.
Your Rights to Workers' Compensation Benefits and How to Obtain Them pamphlet (available in the **2020 Required Notices Kit**)	To provide notice to employees of their right to workers' compensation benefits should they sustain an on-the-job injury.	This must be given to all new employees at hire.	Employees fill out the *Personal Physician Designation Form* or the *Personal Chiropractor or Acupuncturist Designation Form*, then give it to their physician to sign, accepting the pre-designation; the rest is informational.	Put the designation form in the employee's regular personnel file and send a copy to your contact at your insurer or claims administrator. The employee keeps the rest of the brochure for reference.

Where Do I Go For More Information?

CalChamber and federal and state government agencies offer a variety of resources to help you hire employees in compliance with the law.

Table 13. Additional Resources

For information on	Check out these resources
General	From CalChamber: • The **2020 California Labor Law Digest**, the most comprehensive, California-specific resource to help employers comply with complex federal and state labor laws and regulations • **store.calchamber.com; www.hrcalifornia.com**
Equal opportunity	U.S. Equal Employment Opportunity Commission 1-800-669-4000 **www.eeoc.gov** California's Department of Fair Employment and Housing Toll-free: (800) 884-1684 **www.dfeh.ca.gov**
Consumer reporting agencies	Federal Trade Commission (202) 326-2222 **www.ftc.gov**
Immigration	U.S. Customs and Immigration Service 1-800-375-5283 **www.uscis.gov/I-9-central** Handbook for Employers at **www.uscis.gov/files/form/m-274.pdf**
Workers' compensation	California Division of Workers' Compensation **www.dir.ca.gov/dwc/dwc_home_page.htm**
Fingerprinting information	California Department of Justice **https://oag.ca.gov/fingerprints**

 TIP CalChamber also provides many ongoing and comprehensive educational opportunities for small business owners, HR beginners and experienced HR professionals alike. These include online training and special HR seminars and webinars. For more information, please visit our website at **store.calchamber.com**.

CalChamber®

Chapter 3

Leaves of Absence

A complicated mix of California and federal laws governs how employers administer leaves of absences.

In general, leaves of absence fall into two categories: mandatory and optional. This chapter describes mandatory and optional leaves of absence, and guides you through the processes of administering and providing them.

You'll get answers to questions about:

- Family and medical leaves (FMLA/CFRA).

- California New Parent Leave Act (NPLA).

- Pregnancy disability leave.

- Mandatory paid sick leave in California.

- Vacation.

- Other mandatory and optional leaves of absence.

When an employee goes on leave, make sure you know (and the employee knows) which type of leave it is. For example, if you fail to establish that the employee is taking leave under California's mandatory paid sick leave law, the NPLA, the FMLA or the CFRA, then the leave taken doesn't count toward the employee's limit.

California employers must provide paid sick leave benefits. For more information, see "Paid Sick Leave" on page 99. For more information on the interaction between mandatory paid sick leave and family and medical leaves, see "Pay and Benefits During Family and Medical Leave" on page 88. Please continue to look for guidance from the state Labor Commissioner at ***www.dir.ca.gov***.

Required and Optional Leaves of Absence

California and federal laws mandate employers to provide some leaves of absence, such as family and medical leaves, parental leave and pregnancy disability leave. Certain leaves of absence are required only for companies over a certain size.

Employers have the option to offer other leaves of absence, such as bereavement leave or unpaid personal leave. Because different types of leaves, both required and optional, can interact with each other, it is important to understand the different types of leaves and any legal requirements that apply to them. See "Does This Employment Law Apply to Me?" in Chapter 1, page 1. Family and medical leave laws apply only to private-sector employers with 50 or more employees on the payroll during each of any 20 or more calendar weeks in the current calendar or preceding calendar year (and to all public-sector employers).

Under the federal Family and Medical Leave Act and the California Family Rights Act, covered employers must provide up to 12 weeks of leave in a 12-month period for the employee's own serious health condition or the serious health condition of a covered family member. Family and medical leave laws impose several obligations on employers and require specific coordination with other leave laws.

If you are approaching 50 employees, you will want to consider the effect of both federal and state family and medical leave laws on your business. Consider consulting an employment law attorney to discuss the implications of reaching the 50-person threshold.

A new law requires employers with 20 or more employees to provide parental leave to eligible employees. For more information, see "New Parent Leave Act" in Chapter 3, page 90.

Required Leaves of Absence

Under California and federal law, you must provide certain leaves of absence to your employees:

- Family and medical leave (FMLA/CFRA), page 81
- New Parent Leave Act (NPLA), page 90.
- Pregnancy Disability Leave (PDL), page 93.
- Mandatory paid sick leave, page 99.
- Disability leave, page 109.
- Organ and bone marrow donor leave, page 113.

- Crime victims' leave, page 114.

- Domestic violence, sexual assault and stalking victims' leave, page 117.

- Jury/witness duty leave, page 119.

- Military service leave, page 120.

- Military spouse leave, page 122.

- School activities leave, page 122.

- School appearance leave, page 124.

- Volunteer emergency duty leave, page 125.

- Volunteer Civil Air Patrol leave, page 126.

- Voting lcave, page 126.

Optional Leaves of Absence

You have the option to offer a range of other leaves of absence to your employees, at your discretion:

- Vacation, page 106.

- Floating holidays and personal days, page 107.

- Paid holidays, page 108.

- Paid time off (PTO), page 108.

- Bereavement leave, page 127.

- Personal leaves of absence, page 127.

Family and Medical Leaves (FMLA/CFRA)

The federal Family and Medical Leave Act (FMLA) and the California Family Rights Act (CFRA) provide for overlapping as well as separate leaves.

 FMLA and CFRA require employers with 50 or more employees to provide family and medical leave to eligible employees. Employers with less than 50 employees may have to provide parental leave under a different California law. For more information, see "New Parent Leave Act" in Chapter 3, page 90.

Eligibility Requirements

Certain eligibility requirements must be met to qualify for FMLA/CFRA.

Table 14. Family and Medical Leave Eligibility Requirements

Question	Answer
Are we required to provide our employees with FMLA/CFRA leave?	Generally, you are a covered employer under the FMLA/CFRA if you: • Employ 50 or more employees; or • You are a public agency.
Which employees are eligible?	Eligible employees are those who worked: • For a covered employer for at least 12 months (not necessarily consecutively); • At least 1,250 hours in the past 12 months; and • At a worksite with at least 50 or more employees within a 75-mile radius.
Under which circumstances can eligible employees use FMLA/CFRA leave?	An employee can use FMLA and/or CFRA in the following circumstances: • The employee's own serious health condition (FMLA/CFRA). • A qualifying exigency relating to a close family member's military service (FMLA only). • To care for an ill or injured servicemember (FMLA only). For more information, see "Family and Medical Leaves (FMLA/CFRA)" on page 81. • Pregnancy-related disability (FMLA only). • Bonding with a newborn, an adopted child or a child placed in foster care with an employee (FMLA/CFRA or CFRA only). • Caring for a family member (parent, child, spouse) with a serious health condition (FMLA/CFRA). • Caring for a registered domestic partner with a serious health condition (CFRA only).

Private-sector employers with 50 or more employees on the payroll during any 20 or more nonconsecutive weeks within the current year, or any 20 or more nonconsecutive weeks within the preceding year, are covered under FMLA/CFRA.

This includes employees on the payroll who received no compensation, part-time employees, commissioned employees and employees on leave who are expected to return to active employment. Employees on layoff do not count.

Family and medical leave laws cover all public-sector employers, regardless of the number of employees.

 The 12 months of service don't have to include any employment prior to a break in service of seven years or more, unless the break was due to military service.

Eligible employees are also eligible for FMLA if they provide care to a member of the Armed Forces (including a member of the National Guard or Reserves). The servicemember only needs to have been a member of the armed forces at any time during the five years preceding the date the medical treatment began. Employees are also eligible for FMLA if they provide care to a member of the Armed Forces (including a member of the National Guard or Reserves) undergoing medical treatment, recuperation or therapy, and a veteran undergoing medical treatment, recuperation or therapy for a serious illness or injury and who was a member of the Armed Forces.

Pilots and flight attendants are also eligible for FMLA benefits to the same extent as other U.S. workers.

 Effective January 1, 2020, airline employees will be eligible for CFRA leave if they've worked for 12 or more months for the employer, worked at least 504 hours and have been paid at least 60 percent of the monthly guarantee, which means they worked at least 60 percent of the minimum number of hours scheduled in a given month.

Employees who are part of a same-sex marriage are also eligible for FMLA. Employers must allow employees to take FMLA leave to care for their same-sex spouse with a serious health condition, for a qualifying exigency and for other qualifying reasons.

Employees who assume the responsibilities of a parent for a child (stand *in loco parentis*) are eligible for FMLA.

Visit the Department of Labor's FMLA page at ***http://www.dol.gov/whd/fmla/*** for updated information.

 If an employee wants to take time off for baby bonding but the employee isn't eligible for FMLA/CFRA leave because the employee works at a worksite with less than 50 employees within a 75-mile radius, the employee may be eligible for leave under the NPLA if the employee's worksite has at least 20 employees within a 75- mile radius. For more information, see "New Parent Leave Act" in Chapter 3, page 90.

 Regulations defining "qualifying exigency" are described in the *FMLA - Family Member Leave for a Qualifying Exigency* form, available in your forms download.

 If you are in doubt about the standing of an employee who wishes to take leave under FMLA, consult with legal counsel before denying the leave.

Employer and Employee Notice Requirements

State and federal laws create specific posting and notice obligations for employers to explain employees' family and medical leave rights.

Employers may require employees to provide advance notice before FMLA/CFRA leaves begin.

Table 15. Employee Notice Requirements under FMLA/CFRA

Question	Answer
What notice must the employee give before I designate leave under FMLA/CFRA?	Generally, you can require that employees give you 30 days' notice when requesting family or medical leave (for example, the expected birth of a child or a planned medical treatment). The employee must consult with you and make a reasonable effort to schedule any planned medical treatment or supervision to minimize disruption of company operations (subject to the health care provider's approval).
	If the condition is not planned or foreseeable, employees must provide the notice as soon as practical. Employees must state the reason for the leave request. You cannot deny leave for an emergency or unforeseeable personal or family circumstances because the employee did not provide advance notice of the need for the leave.
	California regulations require an employee to provide at least verbal notice requesting a CFRA-qualifying leave and the anticipated timing and duration of the leave. An employee need not explicitly claim rights under, or even mention, CFRA or FMLA. However, the employee must communicate that the leave is needed for a protected reason to meet the notice requirement.
	The employer can inquire further to determine if the employee is seeking family and medical leave. The employee is required to respond to the employer's questions to determine if the leave qualifies for protection. Failure to respond may result in denial if the employer can't determine if the leave qualifies.

Table 15. Employee Notice Requirements under FMLA/CFRA *(continued)*

Question	Answer
What notices must I provide to the employee prior to designating leave under FMLA/CFRA?	Covered employers have both posting and notice obligations. You must post general family and medical leave notices in a conspicuous place where applicants and employees tend to congregate.
	There are two separate general notices: one for the federal FMLA and one for the state CFRA. Both describe employees' rights to leave under these laws. For more information, see "Required Posters" in Chapter 1, page 4.
	When an employee requests FMLA/CFRA leave or when you learn that an employee's leave may be for a FMLA/CFRA qualifying reason, you must notify the employee of the eligibility to take FMLA/CFRA leave and of that individual's rights and responsibilities within **five business days**, absent extenuating circumstances.
	Use the *FMLA/CFRA Designation Notice*, described in Table 40 on page 129, to respond to the leave request. If the employee is eligible for both PDL and FMLA concurrently, use the *FMLA/PDL Designation Notice*, described in Table 40 on page 129, to respond to the leave request.
	The *FMLA - Notice of Eligibility and Rights and Responsibilities* must state whether the employee is eligible for leave. If the employee is not eligible for FMLA/CFRA leave, the notice must state at least one reason why. For example, the notice may inform the employee that the employee is ineligible due to having worked less than 1,250 hours in the preceding 12 months.
	You must notify employees of the method you use to calculate the 12-month period in which the 12 weeks of entitlement occurs. The method that allows you the most control uses a "rolling" 12-month period measured backward from the date the employee first uses any leave.
	Under CFRA regulations, employers are required to notify employees of the consequences (such as denial of CFRA leave) if employees fail to provide a medical certification. The CFRA regulations provide a sample medical certification form that's updated consistent with new regulations.

You can require medical certification within 15 calendar days of your request. If you wish, you may require a second and third opinion of the employee's illness, but you must pay for them. See the *Certification of Health Care Provider - Employee's or Family Member's Serious Health Condition* form, described in Table 40 on page 129.

Designating Family and Medical Leave

Employers need to designate leave as family and medical leave, based on information provided by the employee or the employee's spokesperson, and to give the employee notice of the family and medical leave designation. If you do not believe you have sufficient information to evaluate the request, notify the employee and request additional information.

Table 16. Family and Medical Leave Eligibility Requirements

Question	Answer
How do I designate leave under FMLA/ CFRA?	When you have enough information to determine if the leave is being taken for a FMLA/CFRA qualifying reason, you must notify the employee in writing whether the leave will be designated and counted as FMLA/CFRA. FMLA and CFRA regulations require employers to notify an employee whether the leave will be designated and counted as FMLA/CFRA leave within **five business days** after you have enough information to determine whether the leave is for a qualifying reason (e.g., after receiving a medical certification). If you deny the request for leave, FMLA regulations require you to state at least one reason why.
Can I retro-actively designate leave under FMLA/ CFRA?	Employees may need leave for a FMLA/CFRA qualifying reason and be unable to provide advance notice. For example, a pregnant employee may deliver early or an employee and/or family member may experience a medical emergency. In these cases, you may not learn of the need for leave for a day or more. You may be able to retroactively designate the time as FMLA and/or CFRA, depending on the type of leave and the circumstances. For FMLA leave, employers can retroactively designate leave, or the employer and employee can mutually agree to do so, provided the failure to timely designate the leave as FMLA does not cause harm or injury to the employee. Under the CFRA regulations, employers may not retroactively designate leave after the employee returns to work unless: • The employer provides notice to the employee that the leave will be designated as CFRA; and • The failure to designate the leave in a timely manner does not cause harm or injury to the employee.

In 2019, the federal Department of Labor (DOL) issued an opinion letter that states employers are prohibited from:

- Delaying designation of FMLA-qualifying leave, even if the employee would prefer that the designation be delayed; and

- Designating more than 12 weeks of leave (or 26 weeks of military caregiver leave) as FMLA leave.

According to the DOL, a practice that allows employees to exhaust paid time off before starting FMLA leave would not be permissible because an employer can neither delay designation of leave as FMLA-qualifying nor provide the employee with more than 12 weeks of protected FMLA leave.

Exercise caution. This is a complicated compliance area and could lead to FMLA interference claims. Consult with legal counsel if you have an employee who does not want to use FMLA leave for a qualifying reason.

Duration and Timing of Family and Medical Leave

If an employee is eligible for FMLA/CFRA leave, that individual can take up to 12 workweeks of family and medical leave in a 12-month period, and can take all 12 weeks at once, or take leave in shorter increments of hours, days or weeks. FMLA and CFRA each provide up to 12 weeks of leave. They run concurrently for all purposes except:

- Leave to care for a registered domestic partner (CFRA only). Registered domestic partners enjoy the same rights under California law as spouses. An eligible employee who needs time off to care for a registered domestic partner would be entitled to a maximum of 12 weeks of leave under CFRA. FMLA does not cover registered domestic partners. For more information about registered domestic partner rights, see "Registered Domestic Partner Rights" in Chapter 4, page 149.

- Disabilities due to pregnancy or pregnancy-related condition (FMLA only).

- Leave for a qualifying exigency related to a family member's military service (FMLA only). If the leave is for a "qualifying exigency" relating to an employee's spouse, parent, son or daughter serving in the military, the employee will be eligible for 12 weeks of leave in a 12-month period. These 12 weeks may be in addition to 12 weeks the same employee is eligible for under CFRA.

- Leave to care for an ill or injured servicemember (FMLA only). If the leave is to care for a close family member injured during military service, the leave is a maximum of 26 weeks in a 12-month period. The 12-month period begins on the first day of leave for this purpose, regardless of how the 12-month period is defined for other types of FMLA leave.

Pay and Benefits During Family and Medical Leave

Family and medical leaves are generally unpaid, though employees have certain rights to substitute accrued paid leave for the otherwise unpaid time. You must continue providing any group health benefits at the same level and under the same conditions as if the employee were actively employed. This includes medical, dental, vision, mental health and other coverages, and coverage for dependents.

Table 17. Pay and Benefits During FMLA/CFRA

Question	Answer
Do employees get paid during FMLA/CFRA?	If an employee takes FMLA/CFRA leave for the employee's own serious injury or illness, the employee can receive State Disability Insurance (SDI) payments. SDI is an employee-funded insurance program administered by the California Employment Development Department (EDD). For more information, see "State Disability Insurance (SDI)" in Chapter 4, page 138.
	Employees who take FMLA/CFRA leave to care for a family member or for baby bonding may be eligible for Paid Family Leave (PFL) benefits. Like SDI, PFL is also an employee-funded insurance program administered by the EDD. For more information, see "Paid Family Leave Benefits" in Chapter 4, page 136.
Can I require employees to use paid sick leave, vacation, or PTO during FMLA/CFRA?	You can, as a matter of policy, require employees to use accrued sick pay, vacation or PTO during the unpaid portions of FMLA and CFRA leaves. One exception to this is when the leave is also pregnancy disability leave (PDL): You can't require use of vacation or PTO while the employee is on PDL or PDL/FMLA.
	If the employee is on FMLA/CFRA and receives any benefits (SDI, PFL, workers' compensation insurance or other disability benefit payments), you may not require use of paid sick leave, vacation or other accrued paid time off benefits. Employees may supplement disability benefits with any available sick pay, vacation or PTO.
How do I administer employee benefits while the employee is on FMLA/CFRA?	If you provide health benefits under any group health plan, you must continue providing those benefits during an employee's family and medical leave. The following rules apply: • You must maintain and pay for the employee's health coverage at the same level and under the same conditions as coverage would have been provided if the employee was continuously employed during the entire leave period (up to 12 weeks or up to 26 weeks during a leave to care for an ill or injured servicemember). • If your group health plan includes dental, vision, mental health counseling, etc., or coverage for both the employee's dependents and the employee, you also must continue this coverage to the same extent. • Your obligation to continue benefits may extend beyond12 weeks if you provide more than 12 weeks of benefits to employees on other leave types.

California employers must provide mandatory paid sick leave benefits, and can have a policy requiring an employee to use the mandatory paid sick leave days during unpaid FMLA/CFRA leave. However, the Healthy Workplaces, Healthy Families Act does not address the use of paid sick leave in conjunction with family and medical leaves. The interaction of the paid sick leave mandate with other leave laws is uncharted territory.

If the employee pays a portion of the premium, the employee is responsible for payment of that portion during the leave. Under the CFRA regulations, an employer must provide an employee with advance written notice regarding the terms and conditions under which the employee's portion of the premium must be paid.

The employer may not add additional charges to the employee's premium payments for administrative expenses while the employee is out on unpaid leave.

If the CFRA leave is paid, the premiums should be paid through the method normally used during paid leave, such as payroll deductions, unless the employee voluntarily agrees to pay the premium in another manner.

 The CFRA regulations provide extensive guidance and detail regarding providing health benefits to employees and how they are to be maintained and paid for and the consequences for untimely or missed payments.

The interaction of FMLA/CFRA leaves with other types of leaves can be confusing. For more information, see "Leave Interactions" on page 110. If you fail to comply with these laws, you face civil lawsuits that could result in compensatory and punitive damages, reinstatement and back pay, court costs and attorneys' fees.

Return to Work After Family and Medical Leave

You can require a medical release to allow the employee to return to work, but only if you also require medical releases for other employees returning to work after illness, injury or disability leaves.

The release should be completed by the employee's health care provider before the employee is back at work. The *Certification of Health Care Provider for Employee Return to Work*, described in Table 40 on page 129, can be used for this purpose.

You must reinstate the employee to that individual's position either by an agreed-upon date, or within two days of the employee's notification of readiness to return. You may reinstate an employee and then require the employee to take a fitness-for-duty exam if that exam is at your own expense and is job related and consistent with business necessity.

California law defines "job-related" as "tailored to assess the employee's ability to carry out the essential functions of the job or to determine whether the employee poses a danger to the employee or others due to disability." "Business necessity" is defined by California law as "vital" to the business.

Although employers are obligated under the Fair Employment and Housing Act (FEHA) to engage in the interactive process, employers have a separate obligation under the CFRA to engage in the interactive process with employees and to determine whether additional leave is an appropriate reasonable accommodation even if the employee's CFRA leave has ended.

 If you need to fire an employee on family and medical leave, seek legal counsel.

New Parent Leave Act

Employers with 20 or more employees must provide eligible employees with 12 weeks of parental leave under California's New Parent Leave Act (NPLA).

An eligible employee can use the NPLA to bond with a newborn, or a child placed with the employee for adoption or foster care.

You are liable if you fail to provide an eligible employee with parental leave under the NPLA, fail to guarantee that the employee may return to the same or comparable position at the end of NPLA leave, or take any adverse action against an employee for taking such leave or for exercising their rights under the law.

 The NPLA directs the California Fair Employment and Housing Council (FEHC) to incorporate, by reference, the state regulations interpreting the California Family Rights Act (CFRA) to govern NPLA leave, provided the CFRA regulations are within the scope of and are not inconsistent with the NPLA. The FEHC held a public hearing on proposed NPLA regulations on October 23, 2019. Employers can find updated information about the status of these proposed regulations at *www.dfeh.ca.gov*.

 Employers with questions about how to comply with the New Parent Leave Act should consult legal counsel.

Eligibility Requirements

NPLA leave defines covered employers and the employees eligible for the leave.

Table 18. New Parent Leave Act Eligibility Requirements

Question	Answer
Are we required to provide our employees with NPLA leave?	Generally, you are a covered employer under the NPLA if you: • Employ 20 or more employees and are not already covered under FMLA/CFRA; or • You are a public agency.
Which employees are eligible?	Eligible employees are those who worked: • For a covered employer for at least 12 months (not necessarily consecutively); • At least 1,250 hours in the past 12 months; and • At a worksite with at least 50 or more employees within a 75-mile radius.
Which circum-stances allow eligible employees to use NPLA leave?	An eligible employee may only use the NPLA to bond with a newborn, or a child placed with the employee for adoption or foster care.
How much leave must we provide to employees under the NPLA?	Eligible employees can take up to 12 weeks of NPLA leave to bond with a new child within one year of the child's birth, adoption or foster care placement. If both parents work for you and both are eligible for NPLA leave, you must allow both to take NPLA leave. However, you are not required to provide more than 12 weeks total for both employees. You may allow the employees to take the leave simultaneously, but are not required to do so.
What notices are required?	Before an employee takes leave under the NPLA, you must provide the employee with a guarantee that the employee will be reinstated to the same or comparable position at the conclusion of the employee's NPLA leave. The guarantee should be in writing. Use the *New Parent Leave Act (NPLA) Acknowledgment* contained in "Forms and Checklists" on page 129. If you fail to provide an employee with this guarantee of reinstatement before leave begins, you will be treated as having refused to allow the employee to take NPLA leave and can be held liable for a violation of the law.

Table 18. New Parent Leave Act Eligibility Requirements *(continued)*

Question	Answer
Do employees get paid during NPLA leave?	Leave under the NPLA is unpaid. However, during the parental leave, employees must be allowed (but cannot be required) to use accrued vacation pay, paid sick time, other accrued paid time off, or other paid or unpaid time off negotiated with the employer. Employees who take NPLA leave may also be eligible for PFL benefits. For more information, see "Paid Family Leave Benefits" on page 136.
How do I administer an employee's benefits while the employee is on NPLA leave?	If you provide health benefits under any group health plan, you must continue providing those benefits during an employee's NPLA leave. You must maintain and pay for the employee's health coverage at the same level and under the same conditions as coverage would have been provided if the employee was continuously employed during the entire leave period (up to 12 weeks). You can recover the premium you paid for maintaining the employee's coverage during NPLA leave if the employee fails to return to work after the leave, and the employee's failure to return to work was for a reason other than the continuation, recurrence, or onset of a serious health condition or other circumstances beyond the employee's control.

There may be times when an employer covered under FMLA/CFRA (50 or more employees) has an employee who isn't eligible for FMLA/CFRA but is eligible for NPLA leave. For instance, the employee might not be eligible for FMLA/CFRA because the employee works at a worksite with less than 50 employees within a 75-mile radius. This employee, however, will be eligible for NPLA leave if the employee has worked for you for at least 12 months, worked at least 1,250 hours in the last 12 months, and works at a worksite with at least 20 employees within a 75-mile radius.

The New Parent Leave Act is silent on whether employees can take such leave on an intermittent basis, and does not include any other posting or notice requirements. These may change once regulations are promulgated.

When an employee returns from leave under the NPLA, you must reinstate the employee to the same or comparable position.

If you are in doubt about the eligibility of an employee who wishes to take NPLA leave, consult with legal counsel before denying the leave.

If you need to terminate an employee on NPLA leave or have concerns about reinstatement, seek legal counsel.

The 12 weeks of NPLA leave is in addition to the up to four months of pregnancy disability leave available to eligible employees. For more information, see "Pregnancy Disability Leave" on page 93.

Pregnancy Disability Leave

 If you employ five or more full-time or part-time employees, you must make pregnancy disability leave (PDL) available to your employees. California state government, counties, cities and any other political or civil subdivision of the state must make PDL available, regardless of the number of employees.

PDL provides pregnant employees with time off from work when disabled by pregnancy, childbirth and related medical conditions. PDL also protects pregnant employees from being discriminated against.

 PDL also protects employees who need a transfer or reasonable accommodation because of pregnancy, childbirth or related medical condition.

If you refuse to provide PDL to an eligible employee or discriminate against an employee exercising the right to PDL, you can be penalized. See "Penalties Related to Discrimination" in Chapter 7, page 281.

However, employees may not take time off from work for baby bonding under PDL. After the employee is no longer disabled, that individual is not entitled to PDL to stay home with the new baby. For information about baby bonding leave, see "Family and Medical Leaves (FMLA/CFRA)" on page 81 and "New Parent Leave Act" on page 90.

PDL Eligibility and Use

There are eligibility requirements for both employers and employees under PDL.

Table 19. Pregnancy Disability Leave Eligibility and Use

Question	Answer
Are we required to provide our employees with PDL leave?	Generally, you are a covered employer under PDL if you: • Employ 5 or more employees; or • You are a public agency.
Which employees are eligible?	An employee is eligible for PDL leave after the employee's first day on the job. An employee does not need to meet a length of service requirement before becoming entitled to PDL.

Table 19. Pregnancy Disability Leave Eligibility and Use *(continued)*

Question	Answer
Under which circumstances can eligible employees use PDL leave?	PDL can be used for any time an eligible employee is disabled by pregnancy, childbirth or a related medical condition. An employee is "disabled by pregnancy" if that employee's health care provider deems that the individual is unable, because of pregnancy, to perform any one or more of the job's essential functions, or to perform any of these functions without undue risk to the individual, the successful completion of pregnancy or to other people.
How much leave must we provide to employees under PDL?	PDL starts when the employee's health care provider determines that the individual is disabled by pregnancy, childbirth or related medical conditions. PDL covers the actual period of disability, up to four months, even if your policy for other temporary disability leaves allows less. The four months' leave is the number of days or hours the employee would normally work in four calendar months (17 and 1/3 weeks): • If the employee works 40 hours per week, the individual is entitled to up to 693 hours of leave (40 hours per week x 17 1/3 weeks = 693 hours) • If the employee works 20 hours per week, the individual is entitled to 346.5 hours of leave (20 hours per week x 17 1/3 weeks = 346.5 hours) • If the employee works 48 hours per week, the individual is entitled to 832 hours of leave (48 hours per week x 17 1/3 weeks = 832 hours) If your policy provides for a longer leave period, you must allow the employee the extra time off. Also, an employee can use PDL intermittently, in increments as small as one hour. PDL time off also covers severe morning sickness and prenatal care, including doctors' visits.

An employee may continue to be disabled beyond four months of PDL. If so, you may be required to provide an extension of leave as a reasonable accommodation for a disability. For more information, see "Disability Leave" on page 109.

 Employers should not rule out the possibility of additional leave time for an employee who has exhausted PDL but is still unable to work.

 Some employers offer "maternity leave" to pregnant employees. Employers should know that no legal definition of "maternity leave" exists. Review your pregnancy and leave policies to make sure those policies conform with the law. If you do provide "maternity leave," make sure that your policy clearly defines what is meant by "maternity leave" and that this leave is offered in addition to any legally required leave, such as PDL.

 You can require or permit the employee to use accrued sick leave during the otherwise unpaid portion of PDL. You can also require or permit the use of sick leave benefits to supplement SDI benefits. The employee may choose to use accrued vacation (see page 106) or PTO (see page 108) during PDL, but you can't require that the employee use vacation or PTO during PDL.

PDL Notice and Response Requirements

Employers and employees both must follow notice requirements relating to PDL.

Table 20. PDL Notice and Response Requirements

Question	Answer
What notices must I provide?	Employers of five or more employees must post the Pregnancy Disability Leave Notice (*Your Rights and Obligations As A Pregnant Employee*) from the California Department of Fair Employment and Housing (DFEH). The poster is available in English or Spanish. CalChamber's *2020 California and Federal Labor Law Poster* includes the Pregnancy Disability Leave Notice. You must also give a copy of the PDL Notice to any employee who requests a pregnancy disability leave, a transfer or reasonable accommodation. Use the *Pregnancy Disability Leave Notice*, described in Table 40 on page 129.
What notice must the employee provide?	An employee must provide at least verbal notice to make you aware of the need for PDL, a reasonable accommodation or a transfer, and the expected timing and duration of the leave, reasonable accommodation or transfer. If possible, the employee must provide 30 days' advance notice whenever the need for PDL is foreseeable. The employee must consult with you and make a reasonable effort to schedule any planned medical treatment or supervision so as to minimize disruption to your operations. Any scheduling must be approved by the employee's health care provider. If 30 days' advance notice is not possible, the employee must notify you as soon as possible.

Table 20. PDL Notice and Response Requirements *(continued)*

Question	Answer
How do I respond to a request for PDL?	Respond to the request as soon as possible, but no later than 10 calendar days after the request. You should attempt to respond to the leave request before the date the leave is due to begin. Once the request for leave has been approved, it is retroactive to the first day of the leave. Use the *Employee Letter - PDL Only*, described in Table 40 on page 129, to respond to an employee's notice of absence due to PDL. If you are an employer covered by the FMLA (see page 81), and the employee is eligible for FMLA running concurrently with PDL, give the employee a copy of the *FMLA/PDL Designation Notice*, described in Table 40 on page 129.
Can I require medical certification in response to a request for PDL?	You can require a medical certification for the leave if you advise the employee of this requirement. See the *Certification of Health Care Provider for Pregnancy Disability Leave, Transfer Or Reasonable Accommodation*, described in Table 40 on page 129.

The PDL poster must be posted in conspicuous places on the employer's premises and must contain fully legible text that is large enough to be easily read. An electronic posting may be used to meet the posting requirement, as long as it is posted electronically in a conspicuous place or places where employees would tend to view it in the workplace.

 If 10 percent or more of your workforce at any location speaks a language other than English, you must translate the PDL notice into every language that is spoken by at least 10 percent of the workforce.

 If the pregnancy leave would also qualify as a leave under the FMLA, you must respond no later than five (5) business days, unless "extenuating

Pay and Benefits During PDL

Answers to pay and benefits questions for employees taking PDL include how to administer benefits; whether seniority is affected; and whether employees continue to accrue sick leave, vacation or PTO while on PDL.

Table 21. Pay and Benefits During PDL

Question	Answer
Are employees paid during PDL?	PDL is unpaid. You are not required to pay an employee on PDL unless you pay for other temporary disability leaves for similarly situated employees. However, an employee on PDL may be eligible for State Disability Insurance (SDI) benefits during the time the employee is disabled by pregnancy. For more information, see "State Disability Insurance (SDI)" on page 138.
How do I administer an employee's benefits while the employee is on PDL?	Employers must continue health benefits for employees taking PDL. When an employee takes PDL, an employer who provides health insurance under a group health plan (medical, dental, vision) must continue to maintain a pregnant employee's coverage under the plan as if that employee had not taken pregnancy disability leave. An employer must maintain health benefits for the duration of the pregnancy disability leave, up to a maximum of four months in a 12-month period per pregnancy. The 12-month period begins on the date the leave is taken. The benefits are at the same level and under the same conditions as if the employee had continued working during the leave period.
Does PDL affect an employee's seniority?	During PDL, an employee continues to accrue seniority to the same extent and under the same conditions as would apply to any other unpaid leave not related to pregnancy, and is also entitled to participate in the following: • Employee benefit plans, including life, short-term and long-term disability or accident insurance; • Pension and retirement plans; • Stock options; and • Supplemental unemployment benefit plans.
Do employees continue to accrue sick leave, vacation or PTO while on PDL?	Whether an employee on PDL will accrue sick leave, vacation and PTO will depend on your policy.

If an employer provides greater health benefits or health benefits for a longer period of time for other types of disability, the same level of benefits must be provided to the employee on PDL.

If the employee works for a state agency, the collective bargaining agreement governs the continuation of health care under the employer's group health plan.

An employer cannot use the time that it maintains and pays for group health coverage during PDL to meet the obligation to pay for 12 weeks of group health coverage during leave under CFRA. The continuation of group health care coverage during PDL and during CFRA are two separate and distinct entitlements.

COBRA/Cal-COBRA coverage may be triggered if the employee is disabled by pregnancy for more than the four months.

Return to Work After PDL

When you grant an employee's request for PDL, you must guarantee to reinstate the employee to the same position or to a virtually identical position. This guarantee must be put in writing if the employee requests a written guarantee. You can refuse to honor the guarantee of reinstatement only under very limited circumstances.

Under most circumstances, you must reinstate an employee returning from PDL to the same job that individual held before the leave, with no less seniority than when the employee's PDL began. This includes seniority for the purposes of layoff, recall, promotion, job assignment and seniority related benefits, such as vacation.

You must resume benefits upon the employee's reinstatement in the same manner and at the same levels as provided when the leave began without any new qualification period, physical exam, etc.

You can require a medical release to allow the employee to return to work if you require releases for other disability leaves. See the *Certification of Health Care Provider for Employee Return to Work*, described in Table 40 on page 129.

Paid Sick Leave

With the enactment of the Healthy Workplaces, Healthy Families Act of 2014, California requires employers to provide mandatory paid sick leave (PSL).

PSL Eligibility, Accrual, Usage

Paid Sick Leave has its own set of eligibility, accrual and usage requirements.

Table 22. PSL Eligibility

Question	Answer
Are we required to provide our employees with PSL?	The paid sick leave law applies to private and public employers regardless of size. Out-of-state employees can be covered if they spend enough time working in California. If a business is headquartered in Oregon but an employee routinely works in California for one week out of every month, the employee will be covered under the paid sick leave law because he/she will be working in California for 30 or more days in one year. You can impose a waiting period before employees can start using PSL, but it cannot be more than 90 days.
When are employees eligible for PSL?	All employees who have worked in California for the same employer for 30 or more days within a year from the commencement of employment will be entitled to paid sick leave. Part-time and full-time employees are covered, as well as exempt and nonexempt employees.

 There are a few narrow exemptions from the PSL law. Employers with questions regarding whether they are covered should consult legal counsel.

Table 23. PSL Accrual

Question	Answer
How do employees accrue PSL?	Employers have several different methods for providing PSL to employees — four different accrual methods and one lump-sum approach. • Statutory accrual method. • Optional accrual method that provides employees with no less than 24 hours by the 120th day. • Alternative accrual for new hires. • Pre-Existing Employer Policy (policy in effect prior to January 1, 2015). • "Lump-sum" method.
What is the statutory accrual method?	Under the statutory accrual method, employees earn one hour of PSL for every 30 hours worked. Both regular and overtime hours are counted toward the accrual rate of one hour for every 30 hours worked. Employees exempt under the administrative, executive or professional exemption are deemed to work 40 hours a week, but if they don't, then accrual will be based on their normal workweek.
Are there any other accrual options?	An employer may use a different accrual method, other than one hour for each 30 hours worked, if the accrual is on a regular basis so that the employee will have no less than 24 hours of accrued sick leave by the 120th calendar day of employment, or each calendar year or in each 12-month period. An employer may use an accrual method other than the statutory accrual method of one hour for every 30 hours worked if the employer provides no less than 24 hours or three days of paid sick leave that is available to use by the completion of the 120th calendar day of employment. This option applies only to paid sick leave — not paid time off (PTO) — and the time must be provided by the 120th calendar day of employment.

Table 23. PSL Accrual

Question	Answer
What if I already had a paid sick leave plan in place before the PSL law?	If your organization already had a policy that provided paid sick leave or PTO to a class of employees before January 1, 2015, you can continue using your pre-existing accrual method instead of the statutory accrual method of one hour per 30 hours worked, as long as the accrual method meets certain requirements. Accrual under the pre-existing policy must be on a regular basis and meet both of the following requirements: • An employee has no less than one day or eight (8) hours of accrued sick leave or PTO within three months of employment, each calendar year or each 12-month period. The employee was eligible to earn at least three days or 24 hours of sick leave or PTO within nine months of employment.
What happens if I change my paid sick leave plan I had in place before the PSL law?	If an employer makes modifications to the accrual method in the pre-existing policy, the employer will be required to select from one of the other accrual options or the lump-sum method. Employers can, however, increase the accrual rate.
Are there any other options besides accrual while the employee works?	Yes, an employer may provide paid sick leave in a lump sum. Under the lump-sum method, employees do not accrue paid sick leave. Instead, the employer places the full amount of leave (three days/24 hours) in the employee's leave bank at the beginning of each year of employment, calendar year or 12-month period.
Can I limit or cap the amount of paid sick leave an employee accrues?	If you use an accrual method, you can cap the employee's total accrual amount at six days/48 hours. If you use the lump-sum method you may limit the amount to three days/24 hours.

Table 23. PSL Accrual

Question	Answer
Does an employee's PSL balance carryover from year to year?	If you use an accrual method, all unused hours will carryover year-to-year. Under the lump-sum method, there is no carryover from year-to-year. Any time left in the employee's leave bank at the end of the 12-month period goes away and the employee gets three new sick days/24 hours placed into the employee's leave bank at the beginning of the following 12-month period.
Can I limit the amount of PSL an employee takes?	You can limit the amount of paid sick days an employee can use in each year of employment to 24 hours/three days.

Some employers have questions relating to how to provide "24 hours or three days" of PSL when employees don't work a traditional eight-hour day schedule. For example, what about workers with an alternative workweek schedule of four, 10-hour days? Or part-time employees who work six-hour shifts?

The Labor Commissioner issued an opinion letter to address such questions. The Opinion Letter clarifies that the accrual and usage method most beneficial to the employee is advised.

For example, if an employee works 10-hour days, that employee will get three days or 30 hours of paid sick time. Or, if an employee works six-hour days, he/she will get four days or 24 hours of paid sick time.

You can choose to have a more generous plan, allowing the employee to use and accrue more than the minimum amounts required under the Act.

If you choose to impose any of these limits on PSL, they must be in your PSL policy. Make sure your policy clearly explains what limits and/or caps you put in place and communicate that policy to employees.

PSL Usage, Employer Obligations

Paid Sick Leave comes with various usage requirements and employer obligations.

Table 24. PSL Usage

Question	Answer
For what reasons can an employee use PSL?	An employee can use paid sick time for an existing health condition or preventive care for themselves or a "family member." Under the PSL law, a family member is a: child. parent (or parent-in-law), spouse or registered domestic partner, grandparent, grandchild, or sibling. An employee who is a victim of domestic violence, sexual assault or stalking may also use PSL.
Does an employee have to provide advanced notice of PSL?	PSL must be provided upon an employee's verbal or written request. If the need for paid sick leave is foreseeable, an employee must provide reasonable advance notice. If not, the employee must provide notice as soon as practicable. You can't require an employee to search for or find a replacement worker for the days off.
In what increments can an employee use PSL?	An employee may determine how much paid sick leave he/she needs to use. An employer, however, can set a "reasonable minimum increment," not to exceed two hours, for the use of paid sick leave.

 Unless certification is required pursuant to another leave law, no provision in the PSL law allows an employer to require medical certification for paid sick time. According to the Department of Industrial Relations, an employer can't condition taking paid sick leave on a doctor's note. Moreover, an employer who denies leave because an employee failed to provide details about the leave can end up facing a claim for violating the PSL law.

Table 25. Employer Obligations Under PSL Law

Question	Answer
When must I pay an employee for PSL usage?	Paid sick leave must be paid no later than the next payday for the next regular payroll period after the sick leave was taken.
At what rate do I pay nonexempt employees?	Employers can use one of the following two methods to calculate how to pay nonexempt employees who take paid sick time: • Calculate paid sick time for a nonexempt employee in the same manner as the "regular rate of pay" for the workweek in which sick leave is taken, regardless of whether the employee actually works overtime in that workweek; or

Table 25. Employer Obligations Under PSL Law

Question	Answer
	• Calculate paid sick time for a nonexempt employee by "dividing the employee's total wages, not including overtime premium pay, by the employee's total hours worked in the full pay periods of the prior 90 days of employment."
At what rate do I pay exempt employees?	Employees exempt under the executive, administrative or professional exemptions are paid in the same manner as wages are calculated for other forms of paid leave time.
Are there any employer posting or notice requirements?	The paid sick leave law contains several notice and posting requirements: 1. Pay Stub Notice: You must provide an employee with a written notice setting forth the amount of paid sick leave available to the employee each pay period. You can either provide this notice to the employee on the already required itemized wage statement or in a separate written document provided to the employee with the payment of wages. 2. Employers with unlimited leave policies are in compliance if they note "unlimited" on employee pay stubs or in the separate written document. 3. The *Wage and Employment Notice (Labor Code section 2810.5)* contains information about an employee's right to accrue and use paid sick leave and about employee protections under the paid sick leave law. Employers are required to provide information about paid sick leave to all new hires and existing employees. 1. Poster: The Labor Commissioner produced a required poster advising employees of their sick leave rights. This poster must be placed in a conspicuous location. The poster is included in CalChamber's ***2020 California and Federal Labor Law Poster***, which can be purchased at ***store.calchamber.com***.
What records do I have to keep relating to PSL?	You will need to keep records that document the number of hours that employees worked and paid sick days accrued and used by the employees. You need to keep these records for at least three years. If you do not keep adequate records, there is a presumption that the employee is entitled to the maximum number of hours accruable.
Do I have to pay out any unused PSL balance at the end of employment?	Paid sick leave does not need to be paid out at the end of employment. However, if you combine the sick leave and vacation into a paid time off (PTO) policy, you will have to follow the rules relating to vacation and PTO, including paying out accrued but unused PTO upon termination.

Previously accrued and unused paid sick days must be reinstated if an employee leaves employment and then is rehired within one year, and the rehired employee must be allowed to use those previously accrued sick days and begin accruing additional paid sick days upon rehire.

Employers are **not** required to reinstate any PTO that is paid out to an employee at the time of separation.

In addition to the California PSL law, many cities have passed ordinances that also require paid sick leave benefits. Many of the local PSL ordinances provide more generous benefits and protections in some areas, while the state law is more generous in others. You will have to give whichever provision or benefit is more generous to the employee.

For a comparison of state and local paid sick leave laws, see the *Comparison of California State and Local Paid Sick Leave Laws* chart in your forms download, described in detail in "Online Forms" on page 9.

Cities that have PSL laws include, but are not limited to: Berkeley, Emeryville, Los Angeles, Oakland, San Diego, San Francisco and Santa Monica.

 Local PSL ordinances also contain posting and notice requirements that employers must comply with.

CalChamber members can visit HRCalifornia's Local Ordinances section, at ***https:// hrcalifornia.calchamber.com/hr-library/local-ordinances***, for detailed information on local employment-related ordinances in California, including paid sick leave ordinances.

 Any sick leave payment you provide to your employees can reduce the amount of SDI benefits they receive. For more information, see "State Disability Insurance (SDI)" on page 138. Pregnant employees must be allowed to use accrued sick leave during PDL. For more information, see "Pregnancy Disability Leave" on page 93.

Vacation

If you choose to offer paid vacation time to employees, you must follow California law concerning vacation benefits.

Table 26. Vacation Guidelines

Question	Answer
Do I have to offer my employees vacation?	You aren't required to offer vacation. You decide which employees are eligible to accrue vacation. Be consistent. Similarly situated employees should accrue vacation at the same rate.
How do employees accrue vacation?	Paid vacation time accrues, or "vests," as the employee renders services, so employees earn a portion of the annual vacation each day. **Example:** If your employees earn three weeks of vacation a year (120 hours), then vacation accrues at a rate of approximately 0.45 hours daily. If your employees receive one week of vacation per year (40 hours), vacation accrues at a rate of approximately 0.15 hours daily. You can allow employees to start accruing vacation from the day they start work. Or you can set a reasonable waiting period (30 days or 90 days, for example) before vacation begins to accrue.
Can I limit how much vacation an employee accrues?	You may institute a cap on vacation accrual, but the cap must be "reasonable" and must be greater than the amount the employee accrues in one year. Under a reasonable cap plan, after an employee accrues a certain level of vacation, but does not take the time, vacation no longer accrues until the employee takes some of the previously accrued time. After the employee takes some vacation, he/she begins to accrue time at the usual rate.
Can I limit when an employee uses vacation?	You have the right to determine when employees may or may not take vacations and the length of the vacations.

Table 26. Vacation Guidelines

Question	Answer
Can I require an employee to forfeit vacation if they don't use it?	After an employee earns vacation, you can't take it away. California courts and the Labor Code prohibit a "use it or lose it" policy, in which employees lose earned vacation if it is not taken by a specific time. You can't require employees to forfeit accrued vacation for any reason. You can require that your employees cash out their unused vacation once a year or that they stop accruing vacation after reaching a certain cap. When an employee leaves, you must pay out any accrued but unused vacation to the employee at the same time as the final paycheck. See "Calculating a Final Paycheck" in Chapter 9, page 322.
Do I need a written vacation policy?	Because paid vacation leave is a form of wages, paid vacation is also part of the "employment contract" between you and the employee. Due to a contract being created, it is critical that you clearly state your vacation policy. The policy should include how much vacation you offer and the rate at which vacation days are earned. The policy should also state whether an employee earns vacation days beginning on the first day of employment or after some period of time has passed.

Floating Holidays/Personal Holidays/Personal Days

Though not required to by law, employers can choose to offer employees floating holidays (sometimes called personal days) as a benefit.

The way your vacation policy defines floating holidays/personal holidays/personal days determines how you need to treat the time off. You can treat time off associated with an event, such as an employee's anniversary of his/her hire date, as a holiday (see "Holidays" on page 108). You must treat time off that an employee may take any time and for any reason as vacation (see "Vacation" on page 106).

You may place a cap on the accrual of these days off. But you must give employees reasonable opportunity to take the days off so that they can stay below the cap.

Paid Time Off

Some employers choose to lump various combinations of vacation, sick leave, holidays and personal days and/or floating holidays together into a benefit called "paid time off" (PTO). This allows employees a certain number of days off per year to use for planned and unplanned days off for illness, vacation, holidays and personal needs.

Though PTO is an acceptable benefit, be aware that California law treats the entire sum of accrued PTO like accrued vacation time because PTO is not tied to a specific event and may be taken at whatever time the employee chooses. For more information, see "Vacation" on page 106.

You must pay out the entire amount of accrued but unused PTO at the termination of the employment relationship. If you offer PTO, you must allow employees to use half of their annual PTO accrual for kin care.

Holidays

You are not required to offer employees paid time off for holidays, but many employers do so as an employment benefit. If you do offer paid holidays, you may choose the holidays that you observe.

Common holidays include New Year's Day, Presidents' Day, Memorial Day, the Fourth of July, Labor Day, Thanksgiving and the Friday after, and Christmas.

At the beginning of each year, announce which holidays you will grant, if any, and if you will pay for the time. You may need to accommodate religious holidays in certain circumstances (see "Religion" in Chapter 7, page 274).

Table 27. Holiday Guidelines

Question	Answer
Can I set rules for eligibility for holidays?	You may determine eligibility requirements for paid holidays, such as requiring that nonexempt employees be employed for some specified period of time before becoming eligible. All similarly situated employees should receive the same holiday benefits.
If I offer holidays, do I have to pay employees for the time off?	The law doesn't require you to pay nonexempt employees for holiday time, although many employers do. Exempt employees must be paid if they are ready, willing and able to work and no work is available, such as on a holiday when the company is shut down. Exempt employees who perform any work during the workweek in which a holiday occurs must be paid their full weekly salary, whether or not they work on the holiday.

Table 27. Holiday Guidelines

Question	Answer
What if a non-exempt employee works on a paid holiday?	The courts interpret the policy of giving a paid day off as a contract to do so. Therefore, you must make up the lost benefit to the employee in some manner, such as providing a separate holiday or providing holiday pay in addition to pay for actual hours worked.
Do I have to pay holiday pay on an employee's final paycheck?	Employees don't accrue or vest holiday pay. You don't need to pay a departing employee for any future holidays. However, floating holiday time must accrue, vest and must be paid out at termination. For more information, see "Floating Holidays/Personal Holidays/Personal Days" on page 107.

Certain leaves may affect holidays; please review:

- "Family and Medical Leave" on page 81.
- "Pregnancy Disability Leave" on page 93.
- "Disability Leave" on page 109.

Disability Leave

State and federal disability laws require covered employers to reasonably accommodate the disability of any individual if the employer knows of the disability. A leave of absence could be one form of a reasonable accommodation.

Employers must engage in the interactive process to determine what type of reasonable accommodation would enable an employee to perform the essential functions of a job.

Table 28. Disability Leave Guidelines

Question	Answer
Which employees are eligible for disability leave?	Certain leaves for disability are mandated by law. See "Pregnancy Disability Leave" on page 93and "Family and Medical Leaves (FMLA/CFRA)" on page 81.
	A leave of absence for an employee with a disability also may be a reasonable accommodation if the leave is likely to be effective in allowing an employee to return to work at the end of the leave and if the leave does not create an undue hardship for the employer.
	Disability leave will most likely start if one of your employees becomes disabled. The employee will notify you of the need for leave either verbally or in writing.

Table 28. Disability Leave Guidelines

Question	Answer
Do I have to pay the employee while on disability leave?	This leave is unpaid and your policy dictates whether an employee is allowed to use any accrued but unused vacation, sick leave or paid time off (PTO). The employee may be eligible for SDI benefits. For more details, see "Required and Optional Benefits" in Chapter 4, page 135.
How much time must I provide for disability leave?	Although you are not required to provide an indefinite leave of absence, a disability-related leave of absence could last weeks or months, depending on the circumstances.

 An employee who files a workers' compensation claim is not automatically eligible for disability leave. For information on workers' compensation, see "Workers' Compensation" in Chapter 4, page 142.

 If the need for leave may be related to a reasonable accommodation for a disability or if you have any questions on whether an employee's impairment requires accommodation, or if you need to fire an employee on disability leave, consult with legal counsel.

Leave Interactions

California and federal laws mandate employers to provide several different types of leave, some of which overlap. This section provides an overview of the ways FMLA/CFRA, PDL and disability leaves interact.

If you need help understanding the exact impact on your company, consult legal counsel.

 You must provide notice to the employee taking the leave as soon as possible before he/she takes the leave, or once you learn the employee is on a protected type of leave that runs concurrently with FMLA and/or CFRA. **Concurrently** means that as a week of leave type "A" is used up, so is a week of leave type "B."

You may be required to provide employees a leave of absence as a reasonable accommodation. For more information, see "Disability Discrimination" in Chapter 7, page 277.

Table 29. Types Of Leaves and Benefits and How They Interact

This Leave	Runs Concurrently With	Under These Conditions
PDL(see page 93)	FMLA	Always, if you notify the employee
	CFRA	Never
	Workers' Compensation	Never
	NPLA	Never
FMLA (see page 81)	CFRA	For all leaves except: Leave due to pregnancy disability Leave to care for a registered domestic partner; see "Duration and Timing of Family and Medical Leave" on page 87 Leave due to a qualifying exigency related to a family member's service in the military or to care for a servicemember, see "Family and Medical Leaves (FMLA/CFRA)" on page 81
	Workers' Compensation	If there is a work-related injury or illness, the employee can't work, and you notify the employee
	PDL	If the employee takes leave due to pregnancy disability and you notify the employee
	NPLA	Never; if the employee is eligible for FMLA, the employee will not be eligible for NPLA leave

Table 29. Types Of Leaves and Benefits and How They Interact *(continued)*

This Leave	Runs Concurrently With	Under These Conditions
CFRA (see page 81)	FMLA	For all leaves, except leave due to pregnancy disability, to care for a registered domestic partner or military related; see "Duration and Timing of Family and Medical Leave" on page 87
	Workers' Compensation	If there is a work-related injury or illness, the employee can't work, and you notify the employee
	PDL	Never
	NPLA	Never; if the employee is eligible for CFRA, the employee will not be eligible for NPLA leave
Workers' Compensation (see "Workers' Compensation" in Chapter 4, page 142)	FMLA/CFRA	Always, if there is a work-related injury or illness, the employee can't work, and you notify the employee
	PDL	Never
	NPLA	Never
New Parent Leave Act (see page 90)	FMLA/CFRA	Never; if the employee is eligible for FMLA/CFRA, the employee will not be eligible for NPLA leave
	Workers' Compensation	Never
	PDL	Never

Organ and Bone Marrow Donor Leave

 All employers with 15 or more employees must provide leave for employees who choose to donate organs and bone marrow.

Table 30. Organ and Bone Marrow Leave Guidelines

Question	Answer
Who is eligible for organ and marrow donor leave?	The employee must take the leave to donate an organ or bone marrow to another person. The employee must have worked for you for at least 90 days prior to taking leave.
Can I request certification before providing this leave?	Yes, the employee must provide you with written verification of the need for donation leave. The verification must state that the employee is a bone marrow or organ donor and that the donation is medically necessary.
How much leave must I provide?	Bone marrow donors may take up to five business days of leave in a one-year period. **New** Effective January 1, 2020, organ donors may take up to 60 business days of leave in a one-year period. The "one-year period" starts the day the leave begins and consists of 12 consecutive months.
Do I have to pay employees while they are on this leave?	Employees who take leave to donate bone marrow are entitled to be paid for the full leave, unless the employer's policy requires the use of vacation or sick leave. **New** Employees who take leave to donate an organ are entitled to be paid for 30 business days, unless the employer's policy requires the use of vacation or sick leave. The subsequent 30 business days, if taken, may be unpaid. You may require that bone marrow donors use up to five days of paid sick leave, vacation time or paid time off. You may require organ donors to use two weeks of paid sick leave, vacation time or paid time off. After that, or if the employee does not have any accrued time, the employer must provide paid leave up to the time limits provided. If you will require the use of paid sick leave/ vacation/paid time off, be sure to state the requirement in your employee handbook policy.
How do I administer an employee's benefits during this leave?	You must continue the employee's health benefits coverage and pay for the coverage during the leave of absence. The time off for donor leave is not a break in service for the purpose of salary adjustments, sick leave, vacation, paid time off, annual leave or seniority.

 Donor leave does not run concurrently with leave under the CFRA or the FMLA.

Employees returning from donor leave must be reinstated to the position held when the leave began, or to a position with equivalent seniority status, employee benefits, pay, and other terms and conditions of employment.

You cannot terminate, discriminate or retaliate against an employee for exercising his/her right to use this type of protected leave.

Crime Victims' Leave

State law creates protected time off for employees who are victims of crime and who meet the eligibility requirements to take crime victims' leave to attend judicial proceedings related to the crime.

State law also creates protected leave for crime victims to attend any proceeding in which the rights of the victim are at issue (for more information on this leave, see "Leave for a Proceeding Involving Victims' Rights" on page 115).

Leave to Attend Judicial Proceedings Related to the Crime

This is a required leave for eligible employees.

Table 31. Criminal Judicial Proceedings Leave Guidelines

Question	Answer
Do I have to provide this leave?	All employers must grant leave for eligible employees to attend judicial proceedings related to a: • Violent felony; • Serious felony; and • Felony theft or felony embezzlement.
Who is eligible for leave to attend judicial proceedings related to a crime?	You must allow an employee to take time off from work to attend judicial proceedings related to one of the above crimes if the employee is: • A victim of a crime; • A crime victim's immediate family member; • A crime victim's registered domestic partner; or • of a registered domestic partner who is a crime victim. Immediate family members include the employee's: spouse, child or stepchild, brother or stepbrother, sister or stepsister, mother or stepmother, and father or stepfather.

Table 31. Criminal Judicial Proceedings Leave Guidelines

Question	Answer
Do employees have notice requirements?	Before taking leave to attend the judicial proceeding, the employee must give you a copy of the notice of each scheduled proceeding. These notices are provided to the victim by the pertinent government agency. Documentation can come from any of the following sources: • The court or government agency setting the hearing; • The district attorney or prosecuting attorney's office; or • The victim or witness assistance office advocating on the victim's behalf. When advance notice is not feasible or if an unscheduled absence occurs, you can't take action against the employee if, within a reasonable time after the absence, he/she provides documentation from one of the above sources confirming the judicial proceeding.
How much leave must I provide?	There are no restrictions on the length of time. However, the time off from work must be used to attend judicial proceedings related to the violent crime.
Do I have to pay employees taking this leave?	This leave is unpaid. Employees may choose to use accrued paid vacation, PTO or sick leave.

 You cannot terminate, discriminate or retaliate against an employee for exercising his/her right to use this type of protected leave.

Leave for a Proceeding Involving Victims' Rights

California law provides protections for crime victims to take time off from work, at the victim's request, to appear in court to be heard at any proceeding in which a right of the victim is at issue.

Table 32. Victims' Rights Leave Guidelines

Question	Answer
Do I have to provide this leave?	All employers are required to provide time off from work to a "victim," which is defined as "any person who suffers direct or threatened physical, psychological, or financial harm as a result of the commission or attempted commission of a crime or a delinquent act." "Victim" also includes an employee's family members, including: spouse, parent, child, sibling and guardian.

Table 32. Victims' Rights Leave Guidelines

Question	Answer
Are there limitations on the crimes that qualify under this leave?	Yes, the employee, or the employee's family member, must be a victim of one of the following covered offenses: • Vehicular manslaughter while intoxicated; • Felony child abuse likely to produce great bodily harm or a death; • Assault resulting in the death of a child under eight years of age; • Felony domestic violence; • Felony physical abuse of an elder or dependent adult; • Felony stalking; • Solicitation for murder; • A serious felony, such as kidnapping, rape or assault; • Hit-and-run causing death or injury; • Felony driving under the influence causing injury; or • Specified sexual assault.

Do employees have notice requirements?	Before taking this type of leave, the employee must give you reasonable advance notice of their intention to take the time off.
	
	When advance notice is not feasible, or if an unscheduled absence occurs, you cannot take action against the employee if he/she, within a reasonable time after the absence, provides you with certification.
	
	Any one of the following forms will be sufficient:
	
	• A police report indicating that the employee was a victim of one of the specified offenses.
	
	• A court order protecting or separating the employee from the perpetrator of one of the specified offenses.
	
	• Documentation verifying that the employee was undergoing treatment for physical or mental injuries or abuse as a result of being a victim of one of the specified offenses. Documentation must be accepted from a:
	
	  — Medical professional;
	
	  — Domestic violence advocate;
	
	  — Victims of sexual assault advocate;
	
	  — Health care provider; or
	
	  — Counselor.

Table 32. Victims' Rights Leave Guidelines

Question	Answer
How much leave must I provide?	The leave can be of any length. Unlike judicial proceedings for crime victims' leave, this leave can be initiated at the victim's request and does not need to be initiated by a notice from a government agency. The law protects time off to attend any "proceeding" involving victim's rights, including any delinquency proceeding, involving a post-arrest release decision, plea, sentencing, post-conviction release decision; or any proceeding in which a right of the victim is at issue.
Do I have to pay employees taking this leave?	Leave to attend proceedings involving victims' rights is unpaid. Employees can use available vacation or personal leave while on leave. Unlike crime victims' leave, sick leave is not specifically included.

Domestic Violence, Sexual Assault and Stalking Victims' Leave

An employee who is victimized by domestic violence, sexual assault or stalking may request time off from work to attend legal proceedings or medical treatment, and to ensure his/her health, safety or welfare, or that of his/her children.

Employers must maintain the confidentiality of any employee who requests leave as a result of domestic violence, sexual assault or stalking.

In addition, state law contains a reasonable accommodation requirement for employers with employees who are victims of domestic violence, sexual assault or stalking. Reasonable accommodations under the statute may include implementation of safety measures.

Table 33. Domestic Violence, Sexual Assault and Stalking Victims' Leave Guidelines

Question	Answer
Do I have to provide this leave?	Yes, all employers must provide leave to attend judicial proceedings to any employee who is victimized by domestic violence, sexual assault or stalking. **25+** In addition, if you have 25 or more employees, you must provide leave for medical treatment to an employee victimized by domestic violence, sexual assault or stalking.

Table 33. Domestic Violence, Sexual Assault and Stalking Victims' Leave Guidelines

Question	Answer
Under what circumstances do I have to provide leave for judicial proceedings?	All employers, regardless of size, must provide eligible employees with time off work to appear in court to comply with a subpoena or other court order or to serve as a witness in any judicial proceeding. All employers must also provide employees with time off to obtain or attempt to obtain any relief, such as a temporary restraining order, or other court-ordered relief to help ensure the health, safety or welfare of the employee or employee's child.
Under what circumstances do I have to provide leave for medical treatment?	If you are a covered employer, you must also provide eligible employees with unpaid time off for the following reasons: • To seek medical attention for injuries caused by domestic violence, sexual assault or stalking. • To obtain services from a domestic violence shelter, program or rape crisis center as a result of domestic violence sexual assault or stalking. • To obtain psychological counseling related to domestic violence sexual assault or stalking. To participate in safety planning and take other actions to increase safety from future domestic violence, sexual assault or stalking, including temporary or permanent relocation time off from work.
Do employees have notice requirements?	If feasible, your employee will provide you with reasonable advance notice of his/her intent to take time off. If your employee is unable to provide reasonable advance notice and an unscheduled absence occurs, you may not take any action against the employee. However, the employee must provide one of the following within a reasonable time after the absence: • A police report regarding the domestic violence, sexual assault or stalking. • A court order protecting or separating the employee from the abuser, or other evidence from the court or prosecuting attorney that the employee appeared in court. • Documentation from a medical professional, domestic violence advocate, health advocate, health care provider or counselor that the employee underwent treatment for injuries resulting from domestic violence.

Table 33. Domestic Violence, Sexual Assault and Stalking Victims' Leave Guidelines

Question	Answer
Do I have notice requirements?	All employers must provide employees with written notice about the rights of victims of domestic violence, sexual assault and stalking to take protected time off for medical treatment or legal proceedings. The required notice must be given to all new hires and to other employees upon request.
How much leave must I provide?	There is no limit on the amount of leave that can be taken to attend legal proceedings.
Do I have to pay employees taking this leave?	No, this leave is unpaid. Employees may use any available leave under California's Paid Sick Leave law or may use vacation, personal leave or PTO.

Leave for medical treatment does not give an employee the right to take leave that exceeds or is in addition to the leave available under FMLA/CFRA (12 weeks in a 12-month period).

Time Off for Jury/Witness Duty

According to state law, a person called to serve on a jury or participate as a witness in a trial must do so, unless the court releases the person from service.

Table 34. Jury/Witness Duty Leave Guidelines

Question	Answer
Do I have to provide this leave?	Yes, all employers must provide employees with time off to serve as a juror or as a witness.
Do employees have notice requirements?	Yes, your employee will receive a summons for jury duty or a subpoena to appear in court as a witness. Your employee then gives you notice of the summons or subpoena.

Table 34. Jury/Witness Duty Leave Guidelines

Question	Answer
How much leave must I provide?	The duration of leave depends on how long the court proceeding lasts, or how long the employee's responsibilities as a witness last.
Do I have to pay employees taking this leave?	Whether you must pay wages to an employee who takes time off for jury or witness duty depends on whether the employee is exempt or nonexempt.
	You don't need to pay a nonexempt employee who takes time off for jury/witness duty; the nonexempt employee can use available vacation or PTO.
	You can't make deductions from an exempt employee's salary for absences caused by jury/witness duty. But you can make deductions from an exempt employee's pay if the employee performs no work at all in the workweek.

Military Service Leave

All employers must provide this leave. When your employees serve in the military during their employment, you must either hold their jobs or re-employ them in similar positions when they return.

Table 35. Military Service Leave Guidelines

Question	Answer
Do I have to provide this leave?	Yes, all employers must provide leave to any employee in service in the military.
Which employees are eligible for service in the military leave?	An employee absent from work due to "service in the uniformed services" is eligible. "Service" includes active duty, active duty for training, initial active duty for training, inactive duty training, full-time National Guard duty and examinations to determine fitness for duty.
	"Uniformed services" include:
	• The Army, Navy, Air Force, Marine Corps and Coast Guard (and the Reserves for each of those branches);
	• The Army National Guard, Air National Guard and commissioned corps of the Public Health Service;
	• The National Disaster Medical System; and
	Any other category of persons designated by the president in time of war or emergency.

Table 35. Military Service Leave Guidelines

Question	Answer
Do I have any notice requirements?	The Veterans Benefits Improvement Act requires all employers to provide a notice of rights under the Uniformed Services Employment and Reemployment Rights Act (USERRA) to all persons entitled to rights and benefits under USERRA. The only official version of this poster is provided in English because the federal Department of Labor (DOl) stated that all military service personnel must be able to read and understand English. The most efficient way to comply is to post the notice in a prominent place where employees customarily check for such information. The notice is part of CalChamber's **California and Federal Labor Law Poster**. You can purchase this product, available in English or Spanish, at **store.calchamber.com**.
How much leave must I provide?	Military service leave may take almost any length, with a maximum of a cumulative five years. Ask your employee to notify you upon learning of the need for military leave. When the service is over, the employee will provide you with a notice of intent to return. Under most circumstances, you must reinstate the employee. For exceptions, see the USERRA websiteat **www.dol.gov/elaws/userra.htm**.
Do I have to pay employees taking this leave?	This leave is unpaid, however, employees taking this leave are entitled to all rights and benefits as if they had remained continuously employed. The employee can also choose COBRA-like health care coverage.

California law provides additional protections and return rights for members of the National Guard ordered into active state service for emergency purposes and for reservists called to active duty.

These protections are extended to California employees who are members of the National Guard in another state and are called into service by the other state or by the president, causing them to leave a private job in California.

Military Spouse Leave

State law provides for a leave of absence for military personnel spouses if employed by a covered employer. You must reinstate any employee to his/her position upon return from military spouse leave.

Table 36. Military Service Leave Guidelines

Question	Answer
Do I have to provide this leave?	**25+** All California employers with 25 or more employees must provide an unpaid leave of absence for employees whose spouses are in the military and on leave from deployment during a time of military conflict.
Which employees are eligible for military spouse leave?	To be eligible for the leave, an employee must work an average of 20 hours or more per week and have a spouse in the United States Armed Forces, National Guard or Army Reserve who was deployed during a period of military conflict.
How much leave must I provide?	The leave lasts for up to 10 days. The employee must provide the employer with notice within two business days of receiving official notice that their spouse will be on leave from deployment.
Do I have to pay employees taking this leave?	This leave is unpaid. You can allow an employee to use accrued sick time, vacation or PTO during this leave, but you can't require the employee to do so.

School and Child Care Activities Leave

Parents or guardians of a child in school may occasionally need to participate in school activities, such as parent/teacher conferences, field trips or meetings. For this reason, California law provides employees with School and Child Care Activities Leave.

Table 37. School and Child Care Activities Leave Guidelines

Question	Answer
Do I have to provide this leave?	**25+** All California employers with 25 or more employees **at the same location** must provide employees with time off to participate in certain school or child care activities.
Which employees are eligible for school and child care activities leave?	An eligible employee is any employee who is the parent, guardian, step-parent, foster parent, grandparent or a person who stands *in loco parentis* (in the place of a parent or acting as a parent) to a child who is in grades K–12 or who is with a licensed day-care provider.

CalChamber®

Table 37. School and Child Care Activities Leave Guidelines

Question	Answer
For what reasons can an eligible employee take this leave?	An employee can take time off to: • Find, enroll, or re-enroll his/her child in a school or with a licensed child care provider; • Participate in activities of the school or licensed child care provider; or • Address a "child care provider or school emergency."
What is a child care provider or school emergency?	A "child care provider or school emergency" means that the employee's child cannot remain in a school or with a child care provider due to one of the following: • The school or child care provider has requested that the child be picked up, or has an attendance policy (excluding planned holidays) that prohibits the child from attending or requires the child to be picked up from the school or child care provider; • Behavioral or discipline problems; • Closure or unexpected unavailability of the school or child care provider, excluding planned holidays; or • A natural disaster, including, but not limited to, fire, earthquake or flood.
How much leave must I provide?	You must provide up to 40 hours off per calendar year for school activities. You can limit the use of this time off to no more than eight hours in any one calendar month. However, you can't limit the use of this time off to eight hours per month when the time off is necessary to address a childcare provider or school emergency.
Do employees have to provide notice of the need for this leave?	If an absence for school or child care activities is planned, the employee must give reasonable prior notice. If there is a child care provider or school emergency, the employee need only give notice. You can require employees to provide documentation from the school or child care provider that the employee was participating in school or child care activities. Acceptable documentation is any written verification of participation that the school or licensed child care provider deems appropriate and reasonable.

Table 37. School and Child Care Activities Leave Guidelines

Question	Answer
Do I have to pay employees on this leave?	This leave is unpaid. You can require the employee to use available vacation, PTO or other personal leave. The employee may use paid sick leave if the need for leave would qualify as a permissible use of sick leave; for example, if the employee was asked to pick up the child from school because the child was sick. If the employee is on company paid leave, then sick pay, vacation and PTO continue to accrue. If on unpaid leave, they only accrue if your other policies require it.

School Appearances Leave

Parents or guardians of a child in school may need time off work to appear at school when a child has been suspended from school. All employers must provide employees with unpaid leave for this purpose.

You cannot terminate, discriminate or retaliate against an employee for exercising their right to use this type of protected leave.

The parent or guardian should receive a written notice from the school stating that they must attend a class. You can require a copy of the notice or some other certification from the school stating that the employee's presence is required.

Volunteer Civil Service and Training Leave

You may employ people who also volunteer to provide emergency services in times of crisis. They may be called away during work hours to help in an emergency or go through training.

Table 38. Volunteer Civil Service Leave Guidelines

Question	Answer
Do I have to provide this leave?	All employers must provide time off for employees who are required to perform emergency duty.
Which employees are eligible for volunteer civil service leave?	The leave extends to volunteer firefighters, reserve police officers and emergency rescue personnel. "Emergency rescue personnel" is defined as any person who is: <ul><li>An officer, employee or member of a fire department, fire protection or firefighting agency of the federal government, California state government, local government, special district or other public or municipal corporation or political subdivision of California.</li><li>An officer of a sheriff's department, police department or private fire department.</li><li>An officer, employee or member of a disaster medical response team sponsored or requested by the state.</li></ul>
How much leave must I provide?	The leave lasts for the duration of the emergency duty.
Do I have to pay employees taking this leave?	This leave is unpaid.

An employee who is a health care provider, as defined, is required to notify their employer when they're designated as emergency rescue personnel and also to notify the employer at the time that the employee learns that they'll be deployed for emergency duty.

Time Off for Civil Service Training

If you employ 50 or more people, you must allow an employee who is a volunteer firefighter, reserve peace officer or emergency rescue personnel to take temporary leaves of absence, up to a total of 14 days per calendar year, to engage in fire, law enforcement or emergency rescue training. The leave is unpaid.

Civil Air Patrol Leave.

 California law requires all employers with more than 15 employees to provide leave to participate in Civil Air Patrol duty.

Table 39. Volunteer Civil Air Patrol Guidelines

Question	Answer
Do I have to provide this leave?	All employers with more than 15 employees must provide time off for employees who are required to perform emergency duty.
Which employees are eligible for volunteer civil service leave?	An eligible employee is any employee who is a volunteer member of the California Wing of the civilian auxiliary of the U.S. Air Force (Civil Air Patrol), responding to an emergency operation mission. The employee must have been employed for at least 90 days before the start of the leave.
How much leave must I provide?	An employee is entitled up to 10 days of leave per year. The leave for a single emergency mission can't exceed three days, unless the emergency is extended by the entity in charge of the operation and the extension of leave is approved by the employer.
Do I have to pay employees taking this leave?	This leave is unpaid. Employees who take leave under this law can't be required to exhaust all accrued vacation, personal, sick, disability or other leave available to the employee.
	The employer and employee can negotiate for the employer to maintain the benefits of the employee at the expense of the employer during the leave. The leave can't result in a loss of benefits accrued before the date on which the leave began.

Employees must be reinstated to the position held when the leave began, or to an equivalent position.

Voting Leave

All employers must allow an employee up to two hours of paid time off to vote in a statewide election if the employee does not have sufficient time outside of work to do so.

Employees must notify you at least two working days in advance to arrange time off for voting. You can grant time off at the beginning or end of the employee's regular working shift, whichever allows the most free time for voting and the least time off from work.

You must grant up to two hours of leave on election days. The time off is paid. You also must post the voting leave requirements in a conspicuous place at least 10 days before every statewide election.

 The notice is part of CalChamber's *California and Federal Labor Law Poster*. You can purchase this product, available in English or Spanish, at *store.calchamber.com*.

Bereavement Leave

When an employee experiences the death of a family member or friend, he/she may request time off for a funeral or for mourning. Bereavement leave is not required by law.

Whether you provide this leave is entirely a matter of company policy. If you do provide this leave, your policy should communicate how much time is allowed, which family members are covered by your policy, whether the time off is paid, and what notice or documentation employees must provide.

You can determine eligibility requirements for this leave. You might designate bereavement leave as applicable only to family deaths, or you might extend it for other circumstances.

Personal Leaves of Absence

Employers are not legally required to provide time off for employees who want to take a leave of absence for personal reasons. Whether you grant a personal leave of absence is entirely a matter of company policy. If you do allow personal leaves, be consistent in how you apply your personal leave policy.

 If you provide this benefit for one employee, you set a precedent for other employees and could create the potential for a discrimination claim if you deny another employee's request for the same type of leave.

Minimum Compliance Elements

1. Hang your ***2020 California and Federal Labor Law Poster*** (available from ***store.calchamber.com***), which includes mandatory postings that all employees and applicants must be able to see, in a prominent place (such as a break room). It includes the Healthy Workplaces, Healthy Families Act of 2014 Paid Sick Leave poster.

    If you have employees working in a city or county with a local minimum wage and/or paid sick leave ordinance, you may also need to post required local ordinances and provide additional notices to employees at the time of hire.

2. Provide employees with a written notice setting forth the amount of paid sick leave available to them each pay period. Also, the *Wage and Employment Notice (Labor Code section 2810.5)* needs to contain information about an employee's right to accrue and use paid sick leave and about employee protections. See "Paid Sick Leave" on page 99.

3. Give employees information on their workers' compensation, paid family leave and disability insurance benefits (all located in the ***Required Notices Kit***, available at ***store.calchamber.com***).

4. Pay particular attention to the overlapping requirements of pregnancy disability leave, family and medical leave and workers' compensation. For more information, see:

    - "Pregnancy Disability Leave" on page 93;

    - "Family and Medical Leaves (FMLA/CFRA)" on page 81;

    - "Leave Interactions" on page 110; and

    - "Workers' Compensation" on page 142.

Forms and Checklists

The following table describes forms associated with leaves of absence.

TIP You can find these forms in your forms download, described in detail in "Online Forms" on page 9.

Table 40. Forms and Checklists

Notice or Form	What Do I Use It For?	When Do I Use It?	Who Fills It Out?	Where Does It Go?
Certification of Health Care Provider for Employee Return to Work	To obtain physician or medical practitioner approval for the employee to return to work.	Just before the employee returns to work.	The employee's physician or medical practitioner.	Keep a copy in employees' confidential medical files, separate from their personnel files.
Certification of Health Care Provider - Employee's or Family Member's Serious Health Condition	To obtain physician or medical practitioner certification that the employee or family member is disabled due to "a serious health condition."	At the time of the medical leave.	The patient's health care provider. (The patient could be either the employee or a family member.)	Keep a copy in employees' confidential medical files, separate from their personnel files.
Certification of Health Care Provider for Pregnancy Disability Leave, Transfer Or Reasonable Accommodation	To obtain physician or medical practitioner certification that the employee requires a leave.	At the time of a disability leave related to pregnancy, childbirth or a related medical condition.	The employee's physician or medical practitioner.	Keep a copy in employees' confidential medical files, separate from their personnel files.

Table 40. Forms and Checklists *(continued)*

Notice or Form	What Do I Use It For?	When Do I Use It?	Who Fills It Out?	Where Does It Go?
COBRA Administration Guide	To ensure you use the proper, required forms relating to COBRA (20 or more employees) and Cal-COBRA (2 to 19 employees), as applicable.	Use when an employee is hired and refer back to it when a qualifying event occurs.	N/A	N/A
Employee Letter - PDL Only	To respond to notice of an employee's absence due to Pregnancy Disability Leave (PDL).	Respond within 10 calendar days of the request or no later than the following payday, whichever is sooner.	The employer.	Send a copy to the employee and keep a copy in the employee's confidential medical file, separate from his/her personnel file.
Family Care and Medical Leave and Pregnancy Disability Leave notice — 20 or More Employees	To inform employees of their leave rights under the NPLA, CFRA and FMLA.	When an employee is seeking PDL or reasonable accommodation/ transfer for pregnancy, childbirth or related medical condition and/or who is seeking family care or medical leave.	N/A	Post in a place commonly used by employees. Employers are also encouraged to give this notice at time of hire to each new employee.
FMLA/CFRA Designation Notice	To notify the employee of the type of leave granted.	At the beginning of the leave.	The employer.	Send a copy to the employee and keep a copy in the employee's confidential medical file, separate from his/her personnel file.

Table 40. Forms and Checklists *(continued)*

Notice or Form	What Do I Use It For?	When Do I Use It?	Who Fills It Out?	Where Does It Go?
FMLA/PDL - Designation Notice	To notify the employee of the type of leave granted.	At the beginning of the leave.	The employer.	Send a copy to the employee and keep a copy in the employee's confidential medical file, separate from her personnel file.
Leave Interaction	Use this form to determine the relationships among the various state-mandated leaves of absence and benefits during the time off.	When an employee considers a leave.	N/A	Your employee would also benefit from this information.
Military Spouse Request for Leave - 25 or More Employees	For employees to request military spouse leave in writing.	At the time an employee requests military spouse leave.	The employee.	In the employee's personnel file.
New Parent Leave Act (NPLA) Acknowledgment	Use this notice to respond to a request for NPLA leave and to comply with your obligation to guarantee the employee's right to reinstatement	Give to an employee who is seeking leave under the NPLA to bond with a newborn, adopted child or foster child. Provide before the leave is taken.	The employer.	Give a copy to the employee and keep a copy in the employee's personnel file.

Table 40. Forms and Checklists *(continued)*

Notice or Form	What Do I Use It For?	When Do I Use It?	Who Fills It Out?	Where Does It Go?
Pregnancy Disability Leave Notice	Use this notice to inform employees about pregnancy disability leave.	Give to an employee who is seeking PDL or reasonable accommodation/ transfer for pregnancy, childbirth or related medical condition.	N/A	Give a copy to the employee and keep a copy in the employee's confidential medical file, separate from his/ her personnel file.
Request for Leave of Absence - FMLA/CFRA/ PDL	Give to employees who request or may need a leave of absence under FMLA, CFRA or PDL.	Provide this form when an employee requests a leave of absence or you recognize the need.	The employee.	The employee's personnel file - medical file if the request for leave is for the employee's own medical condition.
Request for Leave of Absence - FMLA/CFRA/ PDL - Spanish	Give to employees who request or may need a leave of absence under FMLA, CFRA or PDL.	Provide this form when an employee requests a leave of absence or you recognize the need.	The employee.	The employee's personnel file - medical file if the request for leave is for the employee's own medical condition.
Temporary Modified Duty Agree- ment	To document a temporary modified duty assignment.	When an employee can't perform the essential functions of a job without accommodation.	The employee.	Keep a copy in the employee's confidential medical file, separate from his/ her personnel file.

Table 40. Forms and Checklists *(continued)*

Notice or Form	What Do I Use It For?	When Do I Use It?	Who Fills It Out?	Where Does It Go?
Wage and Employment Notice to Employees (Labor Code section 2810.5)	To notify employees about mandatory paid sick leave.	Provide this form to all nonexempt employees at the time of hire. If any change is made to the information on this form, notify employees of the change in writing within seven calendar days after the time a change was made unless notice is provided in another writing required by law within seven days of the change.	You do.	In your files.
Workers' Compensation Insurance Shopper's Checklist	Use this form to ask potential brokers and carriers important questions as you shop for a workers' compensation policy.	When shopping for a workers' compensation insurance policy.	N/A	In your files.

Where Do I Go for More Information?

CalChamber and federal and state government agencies offer a variety of resources to help you develop written employee policies.

Table 41. Additional Resources

For Information On	Check Out These Resources
General	From CalChamber: • **2020 California Labor Law Digest** • **Employee Handbook Creator** • **Required Notices Kit with Poster** • **www.hrcalifornia.com** • **store.calchamber.com**
Paid sick leave	• **www.dir.ca.gov**
Military leave	• Veterans' Employment and Training Service "eLaws Advisor" **www.dol.gov/elaws/userra.htm** • Employer Support of the Guard and Reserve (ESGR) at **www.esgr.mil** (800) 336-4590 • Non-technical Resource Guide to the USERRA at **www.dol.gov/vets/whatsnew/uguide.pdf** • **www.dol.gov/vets/programs/userra/**

TIP CalChamber also provides many ongoing and comprehensive educational opportunities for small business owners, HR beginners and experienced HR professionals alike. These include online training, webinars and special HR seminars. For more information, please visit our website at *store.calchamber.com*.

Chapter 4

Providing Benefits

This chapter guides you through the processes of providing and administering to your employees. Make sure that you offer benefits evenly. Don't discriminate amongst your employees.

You'll get answers to questions about:

- Required and optional benefits.

- Paid family leave.

- State disability insurance.

- Unemployment insurance.

- Workers' compensation.

Required and Optional Benefits

Employers must offer certain benefits, such as Unemployment Insurance or State Disability Insurance. Certain benefits are required only for companies over a certain size. See "Does This Employment Law Apply to Me?" in Chapter 1, page 1.

California recognizes same-sex marriages as lawful and same-sex marriage is also lawful in all 50 states. In addition, it is unlawful to exclude same-sex spouses from the definition of "spouse" under federal law.

California employers should be aware that this impacts federal benefits, such as coverage under the Consolidated Omnibus Budget Reconciliation Act (COBRA) and eligibility for Employee Retirement Income Security Act (ERISA) benefit plans, for partners in same-sex marriages.

Employers have the option to offer extra benefits, such as health care and retirement plans. You must comply with certain legal guidelines that expand your employees' rights to use the optional benefits you offer. California and federal law regulate how you provide benefits.

Benefits	
Required	**Optional**
• State Disability Insurance (SDI), page 138 • Paid Family Leave (PFL), page 136 • Workers' Compensation, page 142 • Unemployment Insurance (UI), page 140 • Health care, if you are covered by the employer mandate of the Affordable Care Act, page 152.	• Health care, if you are not covered by the employer mandate of the Affordable Care Act, page 149 • Voluntary disability insurance, page 153 • Bonuses, page 153 • Retirement and pension plans, page 154

Paid Family Leave Benefits

Employees may apply for wage replacement benefits under California's PFL program when they take a leave of absence to care for certain seriously ill family members or bond with a new baby.

Employers with one or more employees are covered by PFL. PFL is not a leave of absence. It does not give employees the right to take time off work.

California's Employment Development Department (EDD) administers the PFL program. Employers do not fund PFL; employee payroll deductions fund the program.

 Beginning July 1, 2020, the maximum duration of PFL benefits individuals may receive from California's SDI program will be extended from six to eight weeks.

Table 42. Paid Family Leave

Question	Answer
Does the law require me to provide this benefit?	Yes. If you pay into the SDI program, you also pay into the PFL program. You must withhold part of an employee's pay and send it to the PFL program, which is administered by the EDD. You face steep penalties for failing to comply. When you register with the EDD, you will receive a registration number and information concerning your tax and reporting requirements.

Table 42. Paid Family Leave *(continued)*

Question	Answer
Is this time off paid?	Benefit payments represent approximately 55 percent of the employee's regular wages and may be used for a maximum of eight weeks in a 12-month period.
Who's eligible?	Almost everyone is covered by PFL. The EDD determines eligibility and administers the benefit uniformly.
How does the leave start?	Your employee will be absent for a reason that qualifies for PFL benefits. He/she will notify you.
How long does it last?	Employees are eligible for benefit payments for a maximum of eight weeks in a 12-month period.
What's the process like?	1. Provide all new employees and employees absent for a qualifying reason with a copy of the *Paid Family Leave* pamphlet (located in the **Required Notices Kit** available from **store.calchamber.com**). 2. Keep records of employee pay as required by state and federal law. 3. When an employee files a PFL claim, the EDD will contact you and provide you with any paperwork required from you. The EDD does the rest.
What if the employment relationship ends?	The law doesn't require you to hold the employee's job merely because he/she collects PFL benefits. However, other laws may protect the employee's job (such as FMLA and CFRA).
What other benefits are related/can be affected?	PFL covers loss of earnings not covered by workers' compensation and SDI benefits. If a person receives Unemployment Insurance benefits, he/she can't receive PFL benefits for the same period. If the employee receives full replacement wages, such as sick leave and PTO, then he/she is ineligible for PFL benefits during that time. Employers can coordinate sick leave and PTO benefits with the EDD to maximize PFL payments. An employee receiving vacation pay doesn't affect PFL benefits. However, employers may require that employees take up to two weeks of accrued, unused vacation before PFL payments begin. The first week of vacation would be the seven-day waiting period for PFL payments. For information about specific leave benefits, see "Required and Optional Benefits" on page 135.

Beginning January 1, 2021, the PFL wage replacement program will be expanded so that employees can collect PFL benefits if they take time off for activities related to the covered active duty status of their spouse, registered domestic partner, child or parent who is a member of the U.S. Armed Forces.

Called "qualifying exigencies," these activities might include such things as official military ceremonies; briefings; changes to child care or financial or legal arrangements as a result of military service; counseling; or spending time with the covered servicemember during rest and recuperation leave, among others.

PFL does not give employees the right to take a leave. If you have 20 or more employees, you must provide parental leave to eligible employees. For more information, see "New Parent Leave Act" on page 90. If you have fewer than 20 employees, applicable state and federal laws, such as the FMLA/CFRA, or your own policy will determine whether the employee is eligible for a leave of absence. For instance, you may choose to provide new parents with a certain amount of parental leave after the birth or adoption of a new child. If your policy allows such time off, the employee could also seek PFL benefits during the time in order to receive partial wage replacement. Or you may have a PTO policy that allows the employee to take time off for any reason, including care of a family member.

State law may also dictate whether the employee is eligible for leave. For example, your employee may have accrued enough paid sick leave under your mandatory California paid sick leave policy to take protected time off to care for a sick family member. For more information, see "Paid Sick Leave" in Chapter 3, page 99.

If your small business grows to 50 or more employees, you will then need to be concerned about other applicable state and federal family and medical leave laws that may grant an employee time off to care for a family member or bond with a new child. For more information, see "Required and Optional Leaves of Absence" in Chapter 3, page 80.

The EDD determines eligibility and administers the benefit.

State Disability Insurance (SDI)

California's SDI program provides wage-replacement benefits for California employees who are unable to work due to a non-work-related illness, injury or disability, including pregnancy and pregnancy-related conditions.

SDI provides short-term benefits to eligible workers who suffer a loss of wages when unable to work due to a non-work-related illness or injury, or when medically disabled due to pregnancy or childbirth.

California's EDD administers the SDI program. Employers do not fund SDI; employee payroll deductions fund the program. For more information, visit the EDD's website at ***www.edd.ca.gov/***.

Table 43. State Disability Insurance

Question	Answer
Does the law require me to provide this benefit?	Yes, almost every employer must comply. You must withhold part of an employee's pay and send it to the SDI program, which is administered by the EDD. You face steep penalties for failing to comply. When you register with the EDD, you will receive a registration number and information concerning your tax and reporting requirements. Its website is ***www.edd.ca.gov/***.
Is this time off paid?	The time off is governed by applicable leave of absence laws or your company policy, not the SDI program. Any benefits get paid through SDI in an amount equaling approximately 60-70 percent of the employee's weekly wages. The employee may choose to take accrued vacation or PTO, or you may require that the employee do so. Payment of vacation or PTO does not affect the employee's SDI benefits. If you pay out accrued sick leave, the employee's SDI benefits get reduced by the amount of sick pay. To avoid reduction of SDI benefits, you may coordinate the payment of sick leave with SDI benefits.
Who's eligible?	Almost everyone is covered by SDI. The EDD determines eligibility and administers the benefit uniformly.
How does the leave start?	Your employee becomes disabled. He/she will notify you in some way.
How long does it last?	SDI benefit payments can't exceed 52 times the employee's weekly benefit amount or the total wages subject to SDI tax paid in the base period, whichever is less.
What's the process like?	1. Provide the employee with a copy of the *State Disability Insurance Provisions* pamphlet (located in the ***Required Notices Kit*** available at ***store.calchamber.com***). 2. Keep records of employee pay, as required by state and federal law. 3. When an employee files an SDI claim, the EDD will contact you and provide you with the appropriate paperwork. You fill out the employer portion of the form. The EDD does the rest.

Table 43. State Disability Insurance *(continued)*

Question	Answer
What if the employment relationship ends?	The law doesn't require you to hold the employee's job merely because he/she collects SDI benefits. However, other laws may protect the employee's job (such as family leave, PDL or the ADA).
What other benefits are related/can be affected?	SDI covers loss of earnings not covered by workers' compensation. If someone receives workers' compensation, then he/she is only eligible for SDI benefits in the amount of the difference between normal wages and workers' compensation. If a person receives Unemployment Insurance (UI) benefits, he/she can't receive SDI benefits for the same period. When employees receive full pay, they are ineligible for SDI benefits during that time. Employers can coordinate sick leave, PTO benefits or other pay (excluding vacation) with the EDD to maximize SDI payments. An employee's receipt of vacation pay doesn't affect SDI benefits.

For information about coordinating SDI with specific leaves of absence or other benefits, see:

- "Leave Interactions" in Chapter 3, page 110.

- "Pregnancy Disability Leave" in Chapter 3, page 93.

- "Family and Medical Leaves (FMLA/CFRA)" in Chapter 3, page 81.

- "Disability Leave" in Chapter 3, page 109.

- "Workers' Compensation" on page 142.

Unemployment Insurance

The unemployment insurance (UI) system is a state program required by federal law. Typically funded by taxes paid by employers, UI benefits are sometimes extended by federal law, particularly during times of high unemployment.

Almost all California employers must pay the tax, and employers face steep penalties for failing to pay their share. Employers with employees that work in multiple states should contact legal counsel or the EDD to determine how to file. For more information, visit the EDD's website at ***www.edd.ca.gov***.

Table 44. Unemployment Insurance

Question	Answer
Does the law require me to provide this benefit?	Yes. Almost all California employers must pay the tax. You face steep penalties for failing to pay your share. If your employees work in multiple states, contact legal counsel or the EDD to determine how to file. For more information, visit the EDD's website at ***www.edd.ca.gov***.
Is this time off paid?	This is not time off from work. Employees must be unemployed or going through a reduction in hours to receive UI benefits.
Who's eligible?	To be eligible for UI, a claimant must: • Make a claim for benefits in accordance with the regulations. • Be unemployed through no fault of his/her own, including circumstances where an employee leaves employment to protect his/her family, or himself/herself from domestic violence. • Have earned $1,300 in one quarter, or have high quarter wages of $900 and total base period earnings of 1.25 times that amount. • Be able to work and available for work (including part-time work, if appropriate). • Be actively looking for work. • Register for work and conduct a search for suitable work, as directed. A claimant is ineligible if he/she is out of work for one of the following reasons: • Voluntarily quitting without just cause. • Termination for willful misconduct. • Refusing to perform suitable work. See Chapter 9, "Terminating Employment" for further information.
How does this start?	An employee files an unemployment insurance claim with the EDD. The EDD will then send you a "Notice of Unemployment Insurance Claim Filed."
How long does it last?	UI benefits may be paid for a maximum of 26 weeks. However, this time is often extended, depending on the unemployment situation.

Table 44. Unemployment Insurance *(continued)*

Question	Answer
What's the process like?	1. An employee may file for UI benefits when he/she is out of work or when his/her hours get significantly reduced. 2. Respond to the EDD's request for information. 3. You face penalties for providing false information as to the reason for an employee's termination in connection with a UI claim. See "Ending the Employment Relationship" in Chapter 9, page 321 for the steps to follow when the employment relationship ends. 4. UI benefits get paid every two weeks (after a one-week waiting period) for up to 26 weeks. 5. Keep records of employee pay as required by state and federal law. See "Records Retention" in Chapter 5, page 198 for more information. 6. If you disagree with EDD's determination, you can protest the claim. You must appeal in a timely manner. You can use *Unemployment Insurance - Responding to a Claim Checklist*, *Unemployment Insurance Claim - Appealing to an Administrative Law Judge Checklist* and *Unemployment Insurance Claim - Appealing to the Appeals Board Checklist*, described in Table 94 on page 330.
What other benefits are related/can be affected?	An unemployed person can't draw both UI and SDI or PFL benefits. For information about specific leave benefits, see "Required and Optional Benefits" on page 135 and "Paid Family Leave Benefits" on page 136" for details.

Workers' Compensation

Every employer, including nonprofit organizations, government entities and every person employing another person, must carry workers' compensation insurance.

Workers' compensation insurance provides payments without regard to fault for any injury or death "arising out of and in the course of employment."

An employer must maintain coverage at all times while its business is in operation. If an employer fails to provide coverage and an injury occurs, the employer still has to pay the employee's medical costs, in addition to penalties and possible financial damages from lawsuits.

Injured workers receive the necessary medical care, at no cost to them, to cure or relieve the effects of the injury. Employees generally give up their rights to sue you for civil damages in exchange for certain, though limited, benefits, which may include pay for time away from work. However, workers' compensation does not create a separate job-protected leave of absence. Employees who suffer a workplace injury may be entitled to leave under the rules of FMLA/CFRA, or as a reasonable accommodation under FEHA. For more information, see "Reasonable Accommodation Defined" in Chapter 7, page 278.

 An employer doesn't pay any benefits directly to an employee. The employee may receive temporary disability benefits, medical expenses and possibly a permanent disability award from the workers' compensation insurance carrier.

For information on preventing injuries at work, see Chapter 6, "Ensuring Workplace Safety."

Table 45. Workers' Compensation

Question	Answer
Does the law require me to provide this benefit?	Every employer must comply, including nonprofit organizations, government entities and every person employing another person. You must maintain coverage at all times while your business is in operation. If you fail to provide coverage and an injury occurs, you still have to pay the employee's medical costs, in addition to penalties and possible financial damages from lawsuits.
Is this time off paid?	The employer doesn't pay for the time off directly. The workers' compensation insurance carrier pays the injured employee.
Who's eligible?	Just about everybody, including non-U.S. citizens, casual workers (if they work at least 52 hours in a 90-day period) and minors. Independent contractors are excluded (see Table 5, "Types of Workers," on page 15 for more information). An employee may be ineligible if they were: • Under the influence of alcohol or drugs at the time of the injury. • Intentionally inflicting the injury or committing suicide. • Engaging in an "altercation" in which he/she was the initial physical aggressor. • Committing a felony for which he/she was later convicted. • Engaging in horseplay. • Voluntarily participating in off-duty recreational, social or athletic activity not constituting his/her work-related activities (unless those activities are expected of employees). • Going to or coming from work, unless you control the route or mode of transportation.

Table 45. Workers' Compensation *(continued)*

Question	Answer
How does the leave start?	Employees are protected as soon as they start performing work on your behalf. You must provide all new employees with the current *Workers' Compensation Rights and Benefits* pamphlet, described in Table 12 in Chapter 2, page 65, and part of the **Required Notices Kit** available from **store.calchamber.com**. Workers' compensation law covers four types of injuries: • Specific physical injury • Cumulative physical injury • Specific mental/psychiatric injury • Cumulative mental/psychiatric injury Workers' compensation law covers any one of these injuries, regardless of whether first aid or surgery is required or if the injury is work-disabling, even if no medical treatment is required. An injury is deemed job-related when: • It arises out of and in the course of employment • The job played an "active" role and was a "positive" factor in the injury • The injury was caused only by something to which the employee was exposed in his/her employment period • The employment brought the employee to the place where the accident occurred • The injury happened at home, if the employee's work duties require tasks at home Typically, courts will resolve any reasonable doubt about whether an injury occurred in the course of employment in favor of the injured claimant. If an employee suffers from a specific injury and a cumulative injury, regardless of when the injury occurred, the employee is entitled to two separate awards — one for each injury — but not a combined award with a longer payout period.

Table 45. Workers' Compensation *(continued)*

Question	Answer
How does the leave start? (continued)	Psychiatric injuries fall under slightly different standards. Work-related stress must be "predominant as to all causes of the psychiatric injury combined." Unless a "sudden and extraordinary" employment condition is involved, the employee must have worked for you for at least six months. Work-related stress (not stress from the employee's family, health or other issues) must account for more than half of the employee's injury. Psychiatric injuries must meet *all* of the following criteria: • Diagnosis as a mental disorder, based on the published criteria of the American Psychiatric Association • Determination that the mental disorder results in disability or requires medical treatment • Proof that the "actual events of employment were predominant as to all causes combined," except in situations involving a significant violent act As soon as you get workers' compensation insurance, you should identify health care providers and hospital facilities designated by the insurance company and/or are familiar with occupational injuries and the workers' compensation system. In most circumstances, you may designate the treating physician for at least the first 30 days following an injury. For more on designating physicians, see "Predesignating a Personal Physician, Chiropractor or Acupuncturist" on page 146.
How long does the leave last?	This is determined by the workers' compensation carrier and the treating physician.
What if the employment relationship ends?	Don't take adverse action against an employee involved in a workers' compensation claim, unless you first consult legal counsel. The law explicitly prohibits you from discharging, threatening or discriminating in any way against an employee because he/she received an award from, filed or intends to file a workers' compensation claim. If the employee decides to leave the company (voluntary quit), workers' compensation leave ends. The workers' compensation carrier handles medical treatment and disability benefits, which may continue even if the employee no longer works for you. If you need to fire an employee on workers' compensation leave, consult legal counsel. If you need to lay off an employee on workers' compensation leave, remember that the employee enjoys the same rights and seniority that he/she would have earned if he/she was at work. See "Separation Types" in Chapter 9, page 318, for more information.

Table 45. Workers' Compensation *(continued)*

Question	Answer
What other benefits are related/can be affected?	An employee who suffers a workplace injury may be eligible for family and medical leave. During this time, the employee may receive the following health benefits: • Up to 12 weeks of continued health benefits as if the employee was still at work • COBRA coverage, if triggered by absences related to the workers' compensation injury. Contact your insurance provider for information Workers' compensation covers the following employee benefits: • Seniority — employees continue to accrue seniority as defined by your paid and unpaid leave policies • Holidays — you determine whether an employee on workers' compensation leave receives holiday pay. Treat the employee on workers' compensation the same as you treat employees on other types of disability leave • Sick leave, vacation and PTO — if the employee takes company-paid leave, these benefits continue to accrue. If unpaid leave, they only accrue if your other disability policies allow. • You may allow the use of sick pay ("Paid Sick Leave" in Chapter 3, page 99), vacation time ("Vacation" in Chapter 3, page 106) or PTO ("Paid Time Off" in Chapter 3, page 108) to supplement workers' compensation benefits.

Predesignating a Personal Physician, Chiropractor or Acupuncturist

Before an injury occurs, each employee has the right to designate a personal physician as well as a personal chiropractor and a personal acupuncturist. Unless the employee works for an employer who has a medical provider network (MPN), the employee may choose to be treated by a physician of his/her own choice. The employee must predesignate, in writing, before an injury occurs, his/her personal physician.

After an injury occurs, the predesignated physician becomes the medical provider for injury-related treatment. Within the first 30 days following an injury, the employee may make a one-time request for a change of physician. After the first 30 days, employees may choose their own treatment provider, subject only to any applicable MPN.

Employees that properly predesignate a personal physician are entitled to be treated by that physician. Employees may make a valid physician predesignation if:

- The employee has health care coverage for injuries or illnesses that are not work related.

- The physician is the employee's regular physician, who limits his/her practice of medicine to general practice or is a board-certified or board-eligible internist, pediatrician, obstetrician/gynecologist or family practitioner. In addition, the physician must have previously directed the employee's medical treatment and must maintain the employee's medical records.

- Prior to the injury, the employee's physician agrees to treat him/her for work injuries or illnesses.

- Prior to the injury, the employee provided you the following information in writing:

  - Notice that the employee wants his/her personal physician to treat him/her for a work-related injury or illness; and

  - The employee's personal physician's name and business address.

Employers must notify employees of the right to predesignate a personal physician and must provide new employees with a physician predesignation form upon hire or by the end of the first pay period.

Employers must notify employees in writing of the right for employees to request a change to a treating physician of their choice 30 days after reporting an injury if the original treating physician was selected by the employer or its insurer.

Some employees may want to predesignate a personal chiropractor or acupuncturist, instead of a medical doctor. Unless covered by an MPN, the rules also require employers to provide their employees with a form for predesignating a personal chiropractor or acupuncturist, upon hire or by the end of the first pay period.

The chiropractor or acupuncturist must:

- Have previously directed treatment of the employee;

- Be licensed under the Business and Professions Code; and

- Retain the employee's treatment records and history.

There is no requirement for acceptance by the health care provider as there is with the personal physician. For injuries after January 1, 2004, the personal chiropractor may be designated as the treating physician for a maximum of 24 visits per injury, unless additional visits are authorized in writing. After that, the employee must choose a non-chiropractic treating physician.

What to do if an Injury Occurs

1. Should a work-related injury or illness occur, your company's first duty is to provide the employee with first aid or emergency medical care, if needed.

   To meet the obligation to furnish medical care, you or your insurance carrier can designate the physician who provides medical treatment for the first 30 days after an injury.

   An employee can predesignate a personal physician. If the employee has made a valid predesignation, then the personal physician may immediately assume treatment for a work-related injury.

    Need help finding a medical provider? Visit the State Compensation Insurance Fund's website at *http://statefundca.com/claims/mpnforers.asp.*

2. If the injury requires more than first aid, give the employee the *Workers' Compensation Claim Form - DWC 1* as soon as possible after the incident.

   Although you can postpone acceptance of a workers' compensation claim for up to 90 days, pending an investigation to determine if the injury is work-related, you must provide all appropriate medical care immediately upon learning of the injury. Your potential liability for medical care costs is limited to $10,000 for treatment prior to the decision to accept or reject the claim.

3. File the *Employer's Report of Occupational Injury or Illness - Form 5020* with your insurance company.

4. Conduct an investigation into the circumstances surrounding the injury. Document any findings and use this information to prevent future injuries.

5. If the law requires you to record and report injuries on the Cal/OSHA *Log 300* forms, fill out the forms appropriately. To find out if these requirements apply to you, see "Reporting and Recording Work-Related Injuries and Illnesses" in Chapter 6, page 240.

6. Communicate with your injured employee and focus on his/her recovery and return to work. Make sure the employee knows about available benefits and when the benefit services will be furnished. Make sure that employees receive the benefit checks they're entitled to. Stay informed.

7. Take corrective action to eliminate any workplace hazards discovered during the injury investigation.

8. Respect employee confidentiality. Like most types of medical information, workers' compensation claim information must be kept private.

✕ *CalChamber*®

Registered Domestic Partner Rights

California law requires equal civil rights, legal status and benefits for registered domestic partners as for spouses. Effective January 1, 2020, registered domestic partners are any couples who have registered their relationship with the California Secretary of State.

California law:

- Gives registered domestic partners the same rights, protections and benefits as those granted to, and imposed on, spouses.

- Subjects registered domestic partners to the same responsibilities, obligations and duties under law — whether they derive from statutes, administrative regulations, court rules, government policies, common law or any other provisions or sources of law — as those granted to and imposed on spouses.

- Provides registered domestic partners with the same rights, with respect to a child of either of them, as spouses would have with respect to a child of either of the spouses.

- Gives registered domestic partners the same rights for leave under the California Family Rights Act (CFRA) as that given to spouses and their children (see "Duration and Timing of Family and Medical Leave" in Chapter 3, page 87).

Employers with state contracts for $100,000 or more must certify that they comply with legislation regarding benefits for registered domestic partners. If you want to contract with the state, you must provide the same benefits to registered domestic partners of employees as those provided to spouses of employees.

 If you do business with the state, consult with your legal counsel and benefits expert.

Health Insurance

Some employers offer voluntary health insurance plans covering medical, dental, vision, prescription drugs and mental health care. These types of benefit are complicated; consult a benefits expert when setting up your plan.

This section does not address requirements under the Patient Protection and Affordable Care Act (ACA). For more information, see "Federal Health Care Reform" on page 152.

Providing Health Insurance

Unless you are covered by the ACA's employer mandate, the law does not require you to provide health insurance to your employees. The law does not require small businesses to provide health insurance to employees. If you do offer it, you must offer it in accordance with the applicable laws.

Your insurance carrier can offer advice and suggestions. You also decide who is eligible. Make sure that similarly situated employees are similarly eligible.

If you offer a health insurance plan, you may fall under ERISA regulations relating to notifying your employees about changes to benefits and to other employer duties. Check with your legal counsel. ERISA is very complicated. This section does not address the health care mandate of the Affordable Care Act, because the employer mandate does not apply to small businesses with 50 or less full-time employees (including full-time-equivalent (FTE) employees who work an average of 30 or more hours per week). If you are approaching this employee threshold, consult a benefits expert for information on how the ACA may affect your business.

See "Glossary of Terms, Laws and Agencies" on page 339 for details about COBRA and ERISA.

Continuing Health Insurance After the Employment Relationship Ends

If you offer health insurance, you must give ex-employees the opportunity to continue coverage by paying their own premiums.

2+ Employers with between two and 19 employees are covered by Cal-COBRA.

20+ Employers with more than 20 employees are covered by COBRA.

For details, see Chapter 9, "Terminating Employment."

Health Insurance and Other Benefits

During certain leaves, health insurance benefits must be extended to cover the leave. For details, see "Family and Medical Leaves (FMLA/CFRA)" in Chapter 3, page 81, "New Parent Leave Act" in Chapter 3, page 90 and "Pregnancy Disability Leave" in Chapter 3, page 93.

Effective January 1, 2020, employers are required to notify employees who participate in flexible spending accounts of any deadline to withdraw funds before the plan year's end in two different ways, which may include email, telephone, text message, postal mail and in-person notification.

Registered Domestic Partners and Health Insurance Plans

California law requires group health care service plans and health insurance policies to provide group coverage to the registered domestic partner of the employee or insured equal to the coverage provided to the spouse of those persons. This rule applies to every group health care service plan contract and every group health insurance policy that is marketed, issued or delivered to a California resident. The employer still has the option to offer only employee coverage, and no spouse or registered domestic partner coverage.

Even if the employer's principal place of business and majority of employees are located outside of California, no policy or certificate of health insurance marketed, issued or delivered to a California resident may discriminate between spouses or registered domestic partners of a different sex and spouses or registered domestic partners of a same sex.

A willful violation of this provision by a health care service plan is a crime.

Registered Domestic Partners and COBRA

A registered domestic partner is not a qualified beneficiary under COBRA because federal law does not treat a registered domestic partner the same as a spouse. COBRA covers employers with 20 or more employees. A former employee's registered domestic partner may be enrolled as a dependent at open enrollment time, but the duration of that coverage is determined by that of the former employee.

Example: If an employee in your health plan terminates employment, the employee is eligible for COBRA, followed by Cal-COBRA, for a total of 36 months. The employee's registered domestic partner is not eligible for COBRA. If the employee was married, his/her spouse would have an independent right to COBRA.

At open enrollment, the employee on COBRA may choose to add his/her registered domestic partner as a dependent. This does not give the registered domestic partner any COBRA rights. The registered domestic partner is entitled to dependent coverage only for the remaining length of time that your former employee is entitled to COBRA coverage. If the former employee and his/her registered domestic partner end their relationship, the dependent coverage for the registered domestic partner also ends.

However, the child of a registered domestic partner has COBRA rights independent of the former employee if the child was covered as a dependent under the former employee's plan on the day before the COBRA-qualifying event.

Registered Domestic Partners and Cal-COBRA

Registered domestic partners are qualified beneficiaries under Cal-COBRA, which covers employers with between two and 19 employees. If a registered domestic partner was a health plan participant on the day before a qualifying event, he or she would be entitled to continuation benefits.

The Cal-COBRA extension of federal COBRA continuation benefits does not apply to a registered domestic partner. A person must have been a COBRA-qualified beneficiary to be entitled to this extension, and COBRA doesn't cover registered domestic partners. Once COBRA benefits are exhausted, a registered domestic partner may be eligible to continue benefits by converting to an individual policy.

Federal Health Care Reform

The Patient Protection and Affordable Care Act, as amended by the Health Care and Education Affordability Reconciliation Act (together the Act or ACA), was signed into law by President Obama in March 2010.

The ACA's employer mandate requires all employers with more than 50 full-time employees (including full-time equivalent (FTE) employees) to provide health insurance for their full-time employees, or pay a per-month "employer shared responsibility payment" on their federal tax return. A "full-time" employee is someone who works an average of 30 or more hours per week.

The ACA also imposes plan design mandates applicable to insurance plans, including requirements related to restrictions on annual and lifetime limits, dependent coverage of children to age 26, rescissions, and pre-existing condition exclusions.

In addition, under the ACA, the maximum eligibility waiting period for group health plan participation is no more than 90 days.

Employers with questions about how the ACA applies to their employees should consult legal counsel.

Other Benefits

Employers can also choose to add other benefits to the total benefits package offered to employees. These optional benefits — such as life insurance, voluntary disability insurance plans, bonuses and retirement plans — can help employers attract and retain employees.

Life Insurance Plans

Many employers include life insurance among the benefits they offer to their employees. This type of benefit is complicated. Consult a benefits expert when setting up your plan.

Voluntary Disability Insurance Plans

Most employers must contribute to the SDI program. Employers can establish their own voluntary disability insurance program with the EDD and employee approval. A voluntary disability insurance plan must offer coverage, benefits and rights equal to the state program in all aspects, and better in at least one.

Your employees can still opt into the state program. See "Required and Optional Benefits" on page 135. Check with your legal counsel if you want to set up a voluntary program.

Bonuses

A bonus is money promised to an employee in addition to the salary or hourly rate usually due as compensation. Bonuses can be based on various factors, such as a company's overall production numbers or annual revenue.

Employers can choose to pay "objective" or "discretionary" bonuses:

- An objective bonus is tied to certain goals (such as working a certain number of hours or making a certain dollar amount of sales)

- A discretionary bonus is awarded at the employer's discretion (such as a holiday bonus)

This type of benefit is complicated. Consult a benefits expert when setting up your plan. For additional information, see "Bonuses" in Chapter 5, page 175.

Retirement or Pension Plans

Although not required by law, a company-sponsored qualified retirement plan (one that meets IRS specifications) is an excellent benefit that can attract and reward employees and provide you with tax advantages.

You can choose from a wide range of options, from complex plans requiring advice from experts to simple plans that you can establish without any outside consultants. Some examples:

- Individual Retirement Accounts (IRAs);

- Simplified Employee Pensions (SEPs);

- Profit-sharing plans (including 401(k) plans); and

- Employee Stock Ownership Plans (ESOPs).

Retirement plans fall into two general categories:

- Defined benefit plans — a predetermined formula determines the benefits received, tied to the employee's salary, length of service or both. You bear the responsibility for funding and investment risks.

- Defined contribution plans — a specified amount is placed in a participant's account. The amount of funds accumulated and the investment gains or losses determine the benefit received at retirement. You bear no responsibility for investment returns, but you must provide a good selection of sound investment options.

ERISA regulates retirement plans. See "Glossary of Terms, Laws and Agencies" on page 339 for more details about ERISA. Consult legal counsel to make sure you establish and maintain your plans according to this complex and technical area of the law.

California enacted the Secure Choice Retirement Savings Program, also known as the CalSavers Retirement Program (CalSavers), which is a state-run retirement plan for private-sector workers whose employers do not offer a retirement plan.

The CalSavers program requires employers with five or more employees that do not offer specified retirement plans to put a payroll arrangement into place that allows employees to contribute a portion of their salary or wages to a retirement saving plan in the CalSavers program.

Employers that already offer a qualified retirement savings program do not have to allow employees to participate in the CalSavers program. Employers retain the right at all times to set up and offer their own qualified retirement plan.

Employers won't have to comply with the CalSavers program mandate until the program is open for enrollment, and compliance will be phased in over a three-year period based on the size of the employer.

Deadlines for participating in the CalSavers program are as follows:

- By June 30, 2020, eligible employers with more than 100 eligible employees, and do not offer a retirement savings program must allow employees to participate.

- By June 30, 2021, eligible employers with more than 50 eligible employees, and do not offer a retirement savings program must allow employees to participate.

- By June 30, 2022, all other eligible employers that do not offer a retirement savings program must allow employees to participate.

Employers will have some administrative duties, including:

- Register for the CalSavers program in compliance with the above schedule.

- Within 30 days of registering, provide the CalSavers program administrator with a collection of personal information about each individual employee. This information includes: the name, Social Security number, date of birth, and contact information for each eligible employee.

- Ensure that each employee receives a packet of information from the program administrator.

- Calculate the appropriate rate of deduction for each employee based on a schedule contained in the regulation.

- Deduct each employee's contributions to the CalSavers program from their salary.

- Remit the employee's contributions to the program administrator within seven days of deduction.

Minimum Compliance Elements

1. Hang your ***2020 California and Federal Labor Law Poster*** (available from ***store.calchamber.com***), which includes mandatory postings that all employees and applicants must be able to see, in a prominent place (such as a break room). It includes the required workers' compensation notice.

    If you have employees working in a city or county with a local minimum wage and/or paid sick leave ordinance, you may also need to post required local notices and provide additional notices to employees at the time of hire.

2. Give employees information on their workers' compensation, paid family leave, unemployment insurance and disability insurance benefits (all located in the ***Required Notices Kit***, available at ***store.calchamber.com***). Pay particular attention to the overlapping requirements of pregnancy disability leave, family and medical leave and workers' compensation. For more information, see:

    - "Pregnancy Disability Leave" on page 93;

    - "Family and Medical Leaves (FMLA/CFRA)" on page 81;

    - "New Parent Leave Act" on page 90;

    - "Types Of Leaves and Benefits and How They Interact" on page 111;

    - "Paid Family Leave Benefits" on page 136; and

3. "Workers' Compensation" on page 142.

Forms and Checklists

The following table describes forms associated with leaves of absence and other benefits.

 TIP You can find these forms in your forms download, described in detail in "Online Forms" on page 9.

Table 46. Forms and Checklists

Notice or Form	What Do I Use It For?	When Do I Use It?	Who Fills It Out?	Where Does It Go?
COBRA Administration Guide	To ensure you use the proper, required forms relating to COBRA (20 or more employees) and Cal-COBRA (2 to 19 employees), as applicable.	Use when an employee is hired and refer back to it when a qualifying event occurs.	N/A	N/A
Leave Interaction	Use this form to determine the relationships among the various state-mandated leaves of absence and benefits during the time off.	When an employee considers a leave.	N/A	Your employee would also benefit from this information.
Personal Physician Designation Form This form is also a tear-out in the ***Workers' Compensation Rights and Benefits*** pamphlet (in the ***Required Notices Kit***).	To notify employees of their right to choose medical treatment by their personal physician.	Give it to the employee at the time of hire.	The employee.	Keep a copy in the employee's personnel file, and send a copy to your contact at your insurer or claims administrator.

Table 46. Forms and Checklists *(continued)*

Notice or Form	What Do I Use It For?	When Do I Use It?	Who Fills It Out?	Where Does It Go?
Personal Chiropractor or Acupuncturist Designation Form This form is also a tear-out in the **Workers' Compensation Rights and Benefits** pamphlet (in the **Required Notices Kit**).	To notify employees of their right to choose medical treatment by their personal chiropractor or acupuncturist.	Give it to the employee at the time of hire.	The employee.	Keep a copy in the employee's personnel file, and send a copy to your contact at your insurer or claims administrator.
Workers' Compensation Insurance Shopper's Checklist	Use this form to ask potential brokers and carriers important questions as you shop for a workers' compensation policy.	When shopping for a workers' compensation insurance policy.	N/A	In your files.

Where Do I Go for More Information?

CalChamber and federal and state government agencies offer a variety of resources to help you develop written employee policies.

Table 47. Additional Resources

For Information On	Check Out These Resources
General	From CalChamber: • *2020 California Labor Law Digest* • *Employee Handbook Creator* • *Required Notices Kit with Poster* • *HRCalifornia.com* • *store.calchamber.com*
Self-insured employers	Department of Industrial Relations (DIR) (916) 464-7000 *www.dir.ca.gov/osip/*
State Disability Insurance	Employment Development Department (EDD) 1-800-480-3287 *www.edd.ca.gov/Disability/*
Unemployment Insurance	Employment Development Department (EDD) 1-866-333-4606 *www.edd.ca.gov/Unemployment/*

Table 47. Additional Resources *(continued)*

For Information On	Check Out These Resources
Workers' Compensation	CalChamber's ***2019 Labor Law Digest*** The Division of Workers' Compensation within the Department of Industrial Relations will provide assistance and advice; ***www.dir.ca.gov/dwc/contactdwc.htm*** The Equal Employment Opportunity Commission (EEOC) at ***www.eeoc.gov/policy/docs/workcomp.html*** State Compensation Insurance Fund at ***www.statefundca.com*** Workers' Compensation Offices 455 Golden Gate Avenue, 2nd Floor San Francisco, CA 94102-7014 (415) 703-5020 (800) 736-7401
Work Sharing	EDD Special Claims Office (916) 464-3343 ***www.edd.ca.gov/unemployment/Work_Sharing_Program.htm***

TIP CalChamber also provides many ongoing and comprehensive educational opportunities for small business owners, HR beginners and experienced HR professionals alike. These include online training, webinars and special HR seminars. For more information, please visit our website at ***store.calchamber.com***.

Chapter 5

Paying Employees

In California, an exhaustive set of rules govern employee pay. In this chapter you can find answers to questions about:

- California Wage Orders.
- Work schedules.
- Wages and salaries.
- Other compensation.
- *De minimis* time.
- Paid non-work time.
- Overtime.
- Pay rules.
- Deductions.

California Wage Orders

California's Department of Industrial Relations (DIR) regulates wages and hours of nonexempt employees. California's Wage Orders define the minimum wages, hours and working conditions for nonexempt employees in a specific industry.

Currently, California law contains 17 Wage Orders, plus a Wage Order Summary and a Minimum Wage Order. Each of the Wage Orders is specific to the industry or occupations it covers, and each Wage Order contains different requirements for different occupations. Wage Orders are numbered 1 through 17, with each number followed by the year in which the Wage Order was last amended and reprinted.

The DIR recently updated Wage Orders 1 through 13, 15 and 16 to reflect the 2019 increase to the minimum wage and meal and lodging rates. The correct revision date for these Wage Orders is Rev. 11/2018. There was no change to Wage Order 17, and Wage Order 14 was not updated at the time of publication.

California employers must comply with one or more of 17 Wage Orders, plus a Minimum Wage Order, as well as any applicable statute. Be sure you understand which Wage Order applies to your business. In some cases, more than one Wage Order will apply — depending on the type of work performed.

Each Wage Order contains regulations on the following topics:

Table 48. Wage Order Regulation Topics

Alternative workweeks	Meals and lodging	Rest breaks
Cash shortage and breakage	Minimum wages	Seats
Changing rooms and resting facilities	Overtime	Special licenses for disabled employees
Hours and days of work	Record retention	Temperature
Meal breaks	Reporting time pay	Uniforms and equipment

Wage Order Provisions

Although each Wage Order includes comparable information, pay special attention to some of the more obscure provisions of the Wage Orders. For example, a provision in many Wage Orders requires "suitable seats when the nature of the work reasonably permits the use of seats."

The California Supreme Court issued a decision affirming these requirements. If work allows the employee to sit, you must provide suitable seats. If the work does not allow for sitting, you must provide seats close to the work area and permit employees to use them. If an employer fails to provide suitable seating, employees can sue under the Private Attorneys General Act of 2004.

 As a result of the guidelines issued by the California Supreme Court, as well as continuing litigation in this area, employers with any questions on their obligations should seek advice of legal counsel.

The purpose of your business determines which Wage Order applies to you. For help determining the correct wage order for your business, use CalChamber's free Wage Order wizard at ***https://hrcalifornia.calchamber.com/forms-tools/wizards/wage-order-wizard***.

Setting Work Schedules

You can set a work schedule that suits your company or a particular job in your company. Base your work schedule(s) on workdays and workweeks. You can start the workday and workweek at a specific date and time of your choosing, but from then on you must follow this schedule as a uniform rule.

The schedule you choose and how you set up that schedule will have an effect on pay-related issues, such as overtime pay for nonexempt employees. Your schedule must comply with the day and hour limits and overtime regulations for your industry.

Defining Workdays and Workweeks

Employers must keep certain facts in mind when defining workdays and workweeks:

Table 49. Definition Of Workday And Workweek

Workday	A workday is not simply the hours an employee normally works; for example, 8 a.m. to 5 p.m. A "workday" is any consecutive 24-hour period starting at the same time each calendar day. If you don't define the workday, California's Labor Commissioner will presume a workday of 12:01 a.m. to midnight.
Workweek	Similarly, a workweek is not just the days that an employee normally works; for example, Monday through Friday. A "workweek" is any seven consecutive 24-hour periods starting on the same calendar day each week. If you don't define the workweek, California's Labor Commissioner will presume a workweek of Sunday through Saturday.

Whatever schedule you set, it must follow regulations that govern day and hour limits, overtime, paydays and meal and rest breaks for nonexempt employees. California's Wage Orders explain these regulations for various industries.

Mandatory Days Off

Generally, every employee is entitled to at least one day off in a seven-day workweek or, under some circumstances, the equivalent to one day's rest in seven during each calendar month. You cannot cause an employee to go without a day of rest in the workweek.

The day of rest requirement does not apply if the employee does not work more than six hours on any day of the workweek.

Overtime

The definition of workweek becomes extremely important when calculating overtime under the "seventh-day" rule. This rule applies only on the last day of your defined workweek, not any time an employee works seven days in a row.

In a Sunday through Saturday workweek, the seventh day rule applies only if an employee works each day, Sunday through Saturday. Even if the employee works each day beginning on Monday of the first workweek and ending on Sunday of the next workweek (seven consecutive days), Sunday does not count as the seventh consecutive day in that "workweek"— Sunday starts the new workweek. In the first workweek, the employee worked only six days — Monday through Saturday.

For more information, see "Overtime Pay" on page 184.

Scheduling Options

You can choose from a variety of scheduling options for your employees. You may define different workdays or workweeks for different groups of employees if all the employees in the group follow the same schedule. Make sure to observe meal and rest break requirements, whatever schedule you choose. For more information, see "Meal and Rest Breaks" on page 176.

Table 50. Scheduling Options

Type Of Schedule	Definition
Regular Workweek	A seven-day workweek where any work performed in excess of eight hours in one workday or 40 hours in one workweek is considered overtime. See "Defining Workdays and Workweeks" on page 163.
Flexible Schedule	A workweek schedule of eight hours per day where some employees begin the shift early in the day and others begin their work later in the day. Ordinary overtime rules apply. See "Defining Workdays and Workweeks" on page 163.
Split Shift	Any two distinct work periods established by the employer that are separated by more than a one-hour unpaid break. You must pay the employee at least one hour's pay, at no less than minimum wage, for the time between shifts. Any hourly amount the employee earns above minimum wage can be used to partially or fully offset the split shift requirement.

Table 50. Scheduling Options *(continued)*

Type Of Schedule	Definition
Alternative Work-week ⚠ **Use extreme caution when setting up an alternative work-week.** Consult your industry's Wage Order to learn the specific steps you must follow to create, implement, follow and repeal an alternative work-week.	An alternative workweek is any regularly scheduled workweek requiring an employee to work more than eight hours in a 24-hour period. Common schedules include: • 4/10 — a four-day workweek of 10 hours per day • 9/80 — a two-week schedule of nine-hour days with every other Friday off Employees on an alternative workweek earn overtime differently than those employees eligible for overtime after eight hours per day. Employers wanting to adopt an alternative workweek schedule must follow certain requirements, including holding an election and submitting the results of the election to the Labor Commissioner. Failure to comply with even one requirement may invalidate the schedule.

Wages and Salaries

What you pay your workers depends on what type of workers they are classified as (see "Properly Classify Workers" in Chapter 2, page 18 for more information) and what type of earnings you designate for the job, such as an hourly rate or a salary.

California and federal law create minimum wage and overtime requirements for nonexempt employees and minimum salary requirements for exempt employees. You must adhere to these requirements.

California law prohibits employers from paying its employees wage rates that are less than the rates paid to employees of another gender, race or ethnicity if they are performing "substantially similar work." Employees may file complaints alleging pay gaps between people doing substantially similar jobs at different work-sites.

Nonexempt Employees

Nonexempt workers are typically paid an hourly rate and receive at least the minimum wage for each hour they work. California regulates nonexempt employees' wages and hours through Wage Orders. Get to know the Wage Order for your industry. Local ordinances can also affect nonexempt employees' wages. For more information, see "Local Minimum Wage Ordinances" on page 167.

California Minimum Wage

Legislation passed in 2016 will increase the minimum wage in California every year until it reaches $15 per hour by 2022.

Increases began for employers with 26 or more employees in 2017, but there was a one-year implementation delay for companies employing 25 or fewer people.

 Effective January 1, 2020, employers with 26 or more employees must pay a minimum wage of $13 per hour, and employers with 25 or fewer employees must pay a minimum wage of $12 per hour.

Table 51. Increases to California's Minimum Wage

Dates	Employers with 25 or Fewer Employees	Employers with 26 or More Employees
01/01/2020	$12 per hour	$13 per hour
01/01/2021	$13 per hour	$14 per hour
01/01/2022	$14 per hour	$15 per hour
01/01/2023	$15 per hour*	$15 per hour*

*Once the minimum wage reaches $15 per hour for all businesses, wages could then be increased each year up to 3.5 percent (rounded to the nearest 10 cents) for inflation as measured by the national Consumer Price Index.

The federal minimum wage is $7.25 per hour. When state and federal law differ, you must comply with the more restrictive requirement. The California minimum wage is higher so you must pay employees that rate in California.

If your company policies create special pay rates based upon the applicable minimum wage rate, those policies will need to be updated annually. For example, a policy that stipulates that travel pay is paid at minimum wage will need to be updated.

Not paying the minimum wage can get you in trouble (see "Failing to Pay the Minimum Wage" on page 205).

Local Minimum Wage Ordinances

Many cities and counties in California have adopted their own local minimum wage rates that are higher than the state's rate. This is part of a growing trend. Keep in mind that the minimum salary requirement for exempt employees is based on the current state minimum wage, not any applicable local minimum wage.

 Cities in California continue to pass local ordinances relating to the minimum wage. Eligibility rules may vary from city to city. The minimum wages rates in these cities may change at any time; employers should closely monitor them. Check with your local city government as to whether any local minimum wage ordinance might apply to your workforce.

At the date of this book's publication, the following localities have passed minimum wage ordinances:

Table 52. Localities With Minimum Wage Ordinances

Alameda	Los Angeles County (ordinance applies only to unincorporated parts of Los Angeles County)	Richmond
Belmont	Menlo Park	San Francisco
Berkeley	Milpitas	San Jose
Cupertino	Mountain View	San Leandro
Daly City	Novato	San Mateo
El Cerrito	Oakland	Santa Clara
Emeryville	Palo Alto	Santa Monica
Fremont	Pasadena	Santa Rosa*
Los Altos	Petaluma	Sonoma
Los Angeles City	Redwood City	South San Francisco
Malibu	San Diego	Sunnyvale

*Santa Rosa's minimum wage ordinance is effective July 1, 2020.

For a list of local minimum wages, please see the *Local Minimum Wage and Paid Sick Leave Ordinances* chart in your forms download, described in detail in "Online Forms" on page 9.

CalChamber members can visit HRCalifornia's Local Ordinances section, *at https:// hrcalifornia.calchamber.com/hr-library/local-ordinances*, for detailed information on local employment-related ordinances in California, including minimum wage ordinances.

"Living Wage" Ordinances

Many California cities and counties adopted local "living wage" ordinances. These ordinances generally require employers who contract with a city or county to pay their employees at a higher rate than the state (or local) minimum wage for work that's performed related to the contract.

Exempt Employees

Exempt employees are typically paid on a salary and receive a fixed amount for each payroll period, whether weekly, bi-weekly, semi-monthly or monthly. Salary is limited to cash wages. It may not include payments "in kind," such as the value of meals and lodging.

 If you fail to pay an exempt employee the minimum salary or misclassify an exempt employee who should be nonexempt, the employee's exempt status can change, which would force you to pay for overtime worked and any missed meal and rest breaks.

Executive, Administrative and Professional Exemptions

Under California law, the most common exemptions (the executive, administrative and professional exemptions) require employees to earn a minimum monthly salary of no less than two times the state minimum wage for full-time employment, and the salary must be a pre-determined sum.

There are different rules for some employees, such as hourly physicians, computer professionals and outside salespersons.

 The exempt minimum salary requirement is based on the current state minimum wage, **not** any applicable local minimum wage.

The 2020 minimum salary threshold for the executive, administrative and professional exemptions is as follows:

- For employers with **26 or more employees**, the state minimum wage increases on January 1, 2020, to $13 per hour. Accordingly, the minimum monthly salary test for these exemptions will be $4,506.67 per month ($54,080 per year).

- For employers with **25 or fewer employees**, the minimum wage increases on January 1, 2020, to $12 per hour. Accordingly, the minimum monthly salary test will be $4,160 per month ($49,920 per year).

The minimum salary calculation for employers with 26 or more employees is:

- California minimum wage = $13/hour

- Number of hours a full-time employee works in a week = 40

- Number of weeks in a year = 52

- Number of hours a full-time employee works in a year = 40 x 52 = 2,080

- Minimum annual salary for a full-time exempt employee beginning January 1, 2020 = $13 x 2 = $26 x 2,080 = $54,080

- Minimum monthly salary for a full-time exempt employee beginning January 1, 2019 = $54,080 ÷ 12 = $4,506.67

The minimum salary calculation for employers with 25 or fewer employees is:

- California minimum wage = $12 per hour

- Number of hours a full-time employee works in a week = 40

- Number of weeks in a year = 52

- Number of hours a full-time employee works in a year = 40 x 52 = 2,080

- Minimum annual salary for a full-time exempt employee beginning January 1, 2020 = $12 x 2 = $24 x 2,080 = $49,920

- Minimum monthly salary for a full-time exempt employee beginning January 1, 2020 = $49,920 ÷ 12 = $4,160

Because the minimum wage and salary requirements will change annually, each year employers should evaluate their exempt employees' pay to ensure it complies with the upcoming year's minimum salary requirements.

Federal Salary Test

Effective January 1, 2020, the federal salary test now requires employers to pay white-collar exempt employees a salary of at least $684 per week ($35,568 per year.) Also, the "highly-compensated employee" exemption now requires a minimum salary of $107,432 per year.

However, employers with California employees must continue to follow the California salary test rules described above because the salary threshold is higher.

Computer Professional Exemption

Employees exempt under the computer professional exemption may be paid on a salaried basis, either monthly or annually. This exemption allows for salaried pay without having to break down the payment by hour. These rates usually change annually, based on the California Consumer Price Index for Urban Wage Earners and Clerical Workers.

The hourly rates for the computer professional exemption increased, effective **January 1, 2020**:

- The minimum hourly rate of pay exemption increased to $46.55 from its previous rate of $45.41.

- The minimum monthly salary increased to $8,080.71 from its previous rate of $7,883.62.

- The minimum annual salary exemption increased to $96,968.33 from its previous rate of $94,603.25.

Computer professionals must meet separate exemption requirements regarding their job duties (see the *Exempt Analysis Worksheet – Computer Professional Exemption* in Table 12 in Chapter 2, page 65).

Computer professionals who meet the job duties and minimum wage requirements of this exemption are exempt from overtime pursuant to Labor Code section 515.5; they must still take mandatory meal and rest breaks. For more information, see "Meal and Rest Breaks" on page 176.

Outside Salesperson Exemption

Outside salespeople are exempt from overtime pay, minimum wage, and meal and rest breaks if they meet both of the following criteria:

- Are 18 years of age or older; and

- Customarily and regularly work more than 50 percent of their working time away from your place of business selling tangible or intangible items or obtaining orders or contracts for products, services or use of facilities.

Outside salespeople do not need to meet the minimum salary requirement that covers the executive, administrative and professional exemptions.

Commissioned Inside Sales Employee Exemption

Wage Order 4, Professional, Technical, Clerical, Mechanical and Similar Occupations, and Wage Order 7, Mercantile Industry, contain exemptions for some commissioned sales employees. However, the exemption is from overtime, not from the other requirements of the wage orders — such as minimum wage, meal and rest breaks and tracking hours worked.

Generally, the exemption applies if:

- The employee earns more than 1.5 times the state minimum wage; and

- More than half of the employee's compensation represents commission earnings.

This is a narrow exemption. Consult legal counsel with any questions regarding whether your inside sales employees meet the commission exemption.

Licensed Physicians and Surgeons

The hourly rate for the licensed physician or surgeon exemption increased, effective **January 1, 2020**. The minimum hourly rate of pay exemption increased to $84.79 from $82.72.

The exemption applies to a licensed physician or surgeon primarily engaged in performing duties that require a license. This exemption does not apply to employees in medical internships or resident programs, physician employees covered by collective bargaining agreements or veterinarians.

Other Compensation

In some businesses, other forms of compensation make up part of employees' pay in addition to wages, such as:

Table 53. Other Forms of Compensation

Piece Rate	An amount paid based on completing a particular task or making a particular good. See "Piece Rate" on page 172 for detailed information.
Meals and Lodging	This applies to nonexempt employees only. See "Meals and Lodging (Nonexempt Employees)" on page 173 for details.
Tips and Gratuities	This includes tip pools, and automatic gratuities and mandatory service charges. See "Tips and Gratuities" on page 173 for more information.
Commissions	Compensation paid to any person for services rendered in the sale of the employer's property or services. See "Commissions" on page 175 for details.
Bonuses	Money given to an employee in addition to the salary or hourly rate usually due as compensation. See "Bonuses" on page 175 for detailed information.
De Minimis Time	Small amounts of time spent either before the employee clocks in or after the employee clocks out. See "De Minimis Time" on page 176 for more information.

Piece Rate

A piece rate includes only time spent producing a particular good or completing a particular task, and not time spent on non-piece-rate work. Non-piece-rate work must be compensated separately, and at least at the minimum wage.

Example: If employees have time where they are not performing the work to produce the particular good or completing the particular task but must wait at the worksite until more work is available, that time must be compensated at least at minimum wage.

Also, the piece-rate system does not include compensation for employees' rest breaks. Rest breaks must be compensated for separately, and at least at the minimum wage. At the end of the payroll period, the employee must receive at least minimum wage for each hour worked, despite slow production hours or slow production days.

Piece-rate employees are entitled to overtime wages. To determine the regular rate of pay, divide total earnings by total hours (even if more than 40 hours).

Employers paying employees on a piece-rate system must include the following information on the itemized pay statement provided to employees:

- The total hours of compensable rest and recovery periods, the rate of compensation and the gross wages paid for those periods during the pay period;

- The total hours of other nonproductive time (defined as time under the employer's control, exclusive of rest and recovery periods, that is not directly related to the activity being compensated on a piece-rate basis);

- The rate of compensation; and

- The gross wages paid for that time during the pay period.

Piece-rate employees must be compensated for rest and recovery periods and other nonproductive time at or above minimum wage, separately from any piece-rate compensation.

 If you're using a piece-rate compensation system, consult legal counsel to make sure your system complies with recent changes in the law.

Meals and Lodging (Nonexempt Employees)

Employer-provided food and lodging counts as wages and can help you meet minimum wage requirements. However, meals or lodging can't be credited against the minimum wage without a voluntary written agreement between the employer and the employee. Be sure to consult your Wage Order regarding the regulatory requirements as applied to your industry.

Meals must be varied and nutritious, and lodging must meet sanitary standards. Employees can't be required to share beds.

Tips and Gratuities

Tips and gratuities are any money left by patrons for employees only. Employers can't count tips against minimum wage requirements.

If tips get paid by credit card, payment can be delayed only until the next payday.

Tip Pools

The restaurant and hospitality industries commonly create tip pools for employees. In a tip pool, employees who receive tips share those tips with other employees. Tip pools spread the risk of low-tipping patrons among all tipped employees. Tip pools also create a way for tips to be shared with employees who aren't directly tipped by customers, such as table bussers.

California law does not specifically prohibit mandatory tip pooling, in which you require employees to pool all or a portion of their tips and then share those tips with other employees who contribute to the customers' service, including back-of-house staff. But the employer and any supervisors may not share in the tips.

 Employers who use tip pools should consult with legal counsel to ensure they comply with California and federal law.

Automatic Gratuities and Mandatory Service Charges

Restaurants commonly add an automatic gratuity or mandatory service charge to bills for large parties. An example would be a 15-percent charge added to the cost of a banquet.

In most instances, mandatory service charges are not considered tips, according to the California Division of Labor Standards Enforcement (DLSE). When a business establishes a non-voluntary, flat charge or a set percentage of a bill that must be paid by the customer, that amount belongs to the business and is not classified as a tip or gratuity left for the employee.

This practice also has wage and tax implications for employers. The Internal Revenue Service treats automatic gratuities as "wages" for payroll tax purposes. Besides the payroll tax implications, the distinction between whether the amount added is a "tip" or a "service charge" can affect employee wages. A "service charge" belongs to the business; it's not left for the employee.

According to the DLSE, if an employer pays out all or a portion of the service charges to employees, these payouts must be included in the employee's regular rate of pay and must be factored into any overtime calculation.

Commissions

Commission wages are defined as compensation paid to any person for services rendered in the sale of the employer's property or services, and based proportionately on the amount or value of the property or services. An employee's main task must be selling a product or service, not making the product or rendering the service.

Employers who pay commission wages to employees working in California must put commission agreements into writing. The agreement must contain the method by which the commissions are computed and paid. Also, the agreement must specify when commissions are earned, paid out and how the employee's termination impacts the commission payment.

Employers must give the employee a signed copy of their contract, as well as obtain a signed receipt from each employee acknowledging that the employee received a copy of the agreement. If the contract expires and the employee continues working for the employer, the terms of the expired contract are presumed to be in effect.

"Commissions" do not include short-term productivity bonuses. Bonus and profit-sharing plans are not included in this requirement unless the employer offers to pay a fixed percentage of sales or profits as compensation for work.

Excluded from the contract requirement are temporary, variable incentive payments that increase, but do not decrease, payment under the written contract.

Bonuses

A bonus is money paid to an employee in addition to the salary or hourly rate usually due as compensation. There are generally two types of bonuses:

Table 54. Types of Bonuses

Discretionary Bonus	Generally in the form of a gratuity where there's no promise for their payment, such as an end-of-year holiday bonus, discretionary bonuses need not be included in the employee's regular rate of pay.
Non-discretionary Bonus	May be a contractually required payment where a promise is made that a bonus will be paid in return for a specific result, such as exceeding a minimum sales figure or piece quota, or as an inducement to remain in the employ of the employer for a certain period of time. Non-discretionary bonuses must be included in the employee's regular rate of pay forpurposes of determining overtime rates. For more information, see "Calculating Overtime for Nonexempt Employees With Nondiscretionary Bonuses" on page 188.

De Minimis **Time**

In recent years, employers have faced lawsuits over small or *de minimis* amounts of unpaid time spent either before the employee clocks in or after the employee clocks out — like time spent booting up your computer or locking up the store.

The California Supreme Court has declined to adopt the federal *de minimis* rule that excuses payment for small amounts of time when the employer can show these amounts are administratively difficult to keep track of. California labor laws, according to the Court, don't allow employers to require that employees routinely work for minutes off the clock without being paid — because California labor laws require pay for "all hours worked."

The Court's ruling left open whether there are some circumstances where the time is so "minute or irregular" that keeping track of it is unreasonable — leaving employers with little definitive guidance.

Employers who routinely have employees engage in tasks before or after clocking in and out for their scheduled shift should ensure employees are compensated for all time — no matter how small the amount may seem.

Meal and Rest Breaks

Meal and rest break compliance has been the source of a great deal of litigation. California employers face costly consequences for violating meal and rest break rules. Court decisions have increased the potential for large financial fines.

It is imperative that you understand the complex meal and rest break requirements. You must do everything you can to communicate the legal requirements to employees and give them opportunities to take the requisite breaks.

Meal Break Requirements

Nonexempt employees are entitled to an uninterrupted, 30-minute meal break if they will work five hours or more. However, if six hours of work will complete the day's work, the employee and employer can mutually agree, in writing, to waive the meal break.

The California Supreme Court, in *Brinker Restaurant Corp. v. Superior Court*, set forth specific guidelines relating to meal breaks. The court clarified that an employer's obligation is to "provide" the meal break, and underscored the need for employers to maintain time records demonstrating that they have provided meal breaks to their employees. A court of appeals case recently reaffirmed the standard established in *Brinker*, and held that although employers must provide meal breaks, they're not required to police whether employees are taking them.

Table 55. Meal Break Requirements

Employer Obligations	An employer must: • Relieve its employees of all duty; • Relinquish control over their activities; • Permit them a reasonable opportunity to take an uninterrupted, 30-minute break; and • Not impede or discourage them from doing so.
Timing	Employers must provide a meal break by the end of the employee's fifth hour of work. For example, if an employee begins a shift at 8 a.m., the meal break must begin by 12:59 p.m. If necessary, employers must provide a second meal break by the end of an employee's 10th hour of work. Refer to the Wage Order for your industry for any exceptions, especially if your employees work shifts between 10 and 12 hours long. For example, Wage Order 5 authorizes allows health care workers to voluntarily waive one of their two meal breaks, even when an employee's shift exceeds 12 hours.
On-Duty Meal Breaks	In limited circumstances, employees can take an on-duty meal break if: • The nature of the work prevents an employee from being relieved of all duty; • The employer and employee agree in writing to the on-duty meal break; • The meal break is paid; and • The on-duty meal break agreement can be revoked at any time in writing by the employee (except under Wage Order 14) If the meal break does not clearly meet all of these conditions, it will not be a lawful on-duty meal break, and the employer will owe one hour of premium pay. Consult legal counsel before implementing on-duty meal breaks.

Rest Break Requirements

Nonexempt employees are entitled to a paid rest break of 10 consecutive minutes for each four hours (or major fraction thereof) worked. If the employee's total daily work time is less than 3.5 hours, a rest break need not be given.

The Labor Code states that an employer may not require an employee "to work" during a rest break.

Table 56. Meal Break Requirements

Employer Obligations	An employer must: • Relieve its employees of all duty; • Relinquish control over their activities; and • Permit them a reasonable opportunity to take an uninterrupted break ⓘ Even though rest breaks are paid time, employers may not require employees to remain on call during rest breaks (even if employees don't actually perform any work) and can't require employees to remain on the premises during rest breaks. Employers with rest break policies and practices that restrict or dictate what employees can and can't do during rest breaks should consult an attorney.
Timing	Generally, rest breaks should occur near the middle of a work period before and after a meal period, if applicable. If necessary, employers may deviate from this rule if: **1.** The departure will not unduly affect employee welfare; and **2.** The departure is tailored to alleviate a material burden that would be imposed on the employer. ⓘ Employers should be cautious about departing from the general rule to provide rest breaks in the middle of each work period and should consult with counsel if practical considerations unique to their industry seem to warrant a departure from the general rule.

A departure from the preferred schedule that is "merely advantageous" to the employer will not meet the above test. Instead, the employer must show that providing the rest break in the middle of each work period imposes a material burden and that a departure from the norm is necessary to alleviate that burden.

Missed Meal or Rest Break

You must pay an employee one additional hour of wages if you don't provide the employee with a timely, uninterrupted, 30-minute off-duty unpaid *meal* break. You must also pay one additional hour of wages if you don't provide an employee with an off-duty, 10-minute, paid *rest* break.

You must pay an employee an amount equal to the employee's regular rate of compensation, up to a maximum of two hours a day (one hour for any meal break violations and one hour for any rest break violations.)

 A 2019 California Court of Appeal decision determined that regular rate of compensation means an employee's base hourly rate. This decision may be subject to reversal so consult with legal counsel prior to changing any premium pay practices.

Employees may be entitled to up to two hours of premium pay per day: one hour for any meal break violations and one hour for any rest break violations. Failure to pay the premiums due may result in civil penalties. For more information, see "Failing to Pay Wages Due" on page 206.

This time is **not** included in overtime pay calculations.

Meal and Rest Break Policies

Employers should have a legally compliant meal and rest break policy as part of their employee handbook.

You should draft specific break policies for your operation. Vague policies that are subject to interpretation by the employee increase your risk of liability.

Meal and rest break policies should stress the timing of the breaks. Consider formally scheduling breaks for your employees as evidence that the rest breaks have been provided. Distribute the policies to all employees and periodically remind employees of your policy. Train all supervisors and managers to make sure breaks are taken and employees are not discouraged from taking all required breaks. Discipline employees who violate your meal and rest break policies.

Paid Non-Working Time

At times, you need to pay a nonexempt employee for time not spent performing their regular work duties. If you will pay a special rate for travel time or other special circumstances, you must establish and communicate the rate to employees in advance of the event. The amount and duration depend on what they do during that time. The special rate can't be less than the minimum wage.

Table 57. Meal Break Requirements

Time Spent Between Split Shifts	If there is more than one hour between shifts, the employee must receive one hour's pay at no less than the minimum wage rate for the time between shifts. See page 181 for details.
Reporting Time Pay	This is owed when you require employees to report to work at a specific time, and you don't put them to work or you give them less than half the hours they were scheduled to work. See page 181 for more information.
On-Call (Standby) Time	If you require employees to stay at home or at work on an on-call or standby status, that time may qualify as hours worked depending on the restrictions you put on their ability to actually have free time. See page 182 for additional details.
Travel Time	You must pay for the time your employee is traveling for work-related purposes in various circumstances. See page 183 for more information.
Uniform Changing/ Washing Up	Time spent changing uniforms, washing or cleaning up at work, or engaging in other preparatory activity that's required for the job must generally be counted as hours worked. See page 183 for details.
Employee Meetings	You must pay employees for attending meetings if you require them to attend. This time is included in overtime pay calculations. If you schedule a meeting or require employees to report to work for a specific amount of time on a day they're not normally scheduled to work, you must pay the employees only for the time they attended the meeting; this is to be distinguished from "reporting time" requirements.
Employer-Sponsored Activities	You must pay employees for attending training, lectures or work courses that you sponsor if you require employees' attendance or if the training relates to the employees' regular job. This time is included in overtime pay calculations.
Reimbursing Expenses	You must reimburse exempt and nonexempt employees for all the expenses they incur in performing their duties. See page 184 for additional details.

Time Spent Between Split Shifts

You must pay employees an amount equal to one hour of pay of at least the current minimum wage if the time between shifts is more than one hour in duration. You can use any hourly amount the employee earns above minimum wage to offset the split shift requirement.

This time is **not** included in overtime calculations because the time wasn't actually spent working.

 The California Labor Commissioner states that the split shift premium owed is one hour at the state minimum wage, or the local minimum wage if there is one, whichever is greater. Historically, the split shift premium has been based only on the statewide minimum wage. There has been no change to the IWC Wage Orders that require split shift pay, but the language from the Labor Commissioner means employers in areas with local minimum wages that are higher than the statewide rates may want to consult legal counsel to consider whether they should change their split shift pay practices.

Reporting Time

You must pay reporting time when you require employees to report at a specific time and you don't put them to work or give them less than half the hours they were scheduled to work.

 A 2019 California court of appeal decision significantly expanded the reporting time pay requirement. The court determined that under Wage Order 7, reporting time pay is due when an employee is required to call in two hours before a previously scheduled "on-call" shift. The court determined that employees were "reporting" for work when they called in and therefore entitled to reporting time pay if they were told not to come into work. While this case was decided under Wage Order 7, employers with similar policies should consult with legal counsel to determine whether this case impacts their particular workplace policies and practices.

Employees must be paid for at least half of their scheduled hours, but a minimum of two hours of reporting time pay (for shifts that are four hours or less) but not more than four hours of reporting time pay (for shifts greater than 8 hours). Employees must be paid at their regular rate of pay.

This time is **not** included in overtime calculations.

You must also pay reporting time if you require employees to report to work a second time in any one workday and give them less than two hours of work. Such employees must be paid for at least two hours at their regular rate of pay. Only the time the employee actually worked is included in overtime calculations.

You must also pay reporting time for on-call employees who are not being paid while they are on-call. These employees typically have the freedom to spend their on-call time as they wish and have a reasonable amount of time to report to work when called.

You do not have to pay reporting time for on-call employees who are being paid for their on-call time. You must only pay the time employees actually work.

You also do not have to pay reporting time when your business operations are disrupted by threats to your property, utility failure or acts of God.

On-Call (Standby) Time

If you require an employee to stay at home or at work on an on-call or standby status, that time may qualify as hours worked depending on the restrictions you put on his/her ability to actually have free time.

Courts typically consider the following factors in looking at whether on-call time should be paid:

- Are there excessive geographic restrictions on the employee's movements?

- Is the frequency of calls unduly restrictive?

- Is there a fixed time limit for the employee to respond to the call that is unduly restrictive?

- Can the on-call employee easily trade on-call responsibilities with another employee?

- Can the employee engage in personal activities during on-call periods? If so, to what extent?

- What is the nature of the employment relationship and the industry practice?

- Are there any other limitations on employees' ability to use the time for their own benefit?

The more restrictions on an employee's use of personal time while on call, the more likely the on-call time is compensable.

You must pay on-call time for any time spent on-call that can't be used for the employee's benefit. You must also pay for time spent on call-backs and time spent traveling from the point summoned to the worksite and the return trip.

You must pay the employee at the applicable rate (straight time or overtime). This time is included in overtime pay calculations. On-call time is *not* compensable if the employee can use the time spent on-call primarily for personal purposes.

Travel Time

You must pay for travel time if the employee reports to the regular site and then has to go to another site. You must pay the employee for the time spent traveling between sites.

You must also pay for travel time if the employee has to work at another site. In this circumstance, you must pay the employee for the time in excess of the employee's normal commute.

Finally, you must pay for travel time if the employee must travel to a distant place, such as another city. You must pay employees for time spent in transit from their home or office to the destination where they're no longer under the employer's control.

Employers may pay for travel time at a rate that is lower than an employee's usual hourly rate, as long as it is at least minimum wage. If you will pay a separate rate for travel time, notify employees of that rate in advance of the travel, preferably through a company policy.

All travel time is included in overtime pay calculations. For more information, see "Calculating Overtime for Nonexempt Employees" on page 185.

Mandatory Mode of Transportation

You must also pay for travel time if you require your employees to travel to the worksite on employer-provided transportation. You must pay employees at least minimum wage for duration of travel. This time is included in overtime pay calculations.

Uniform Changing/Washing Up

If employees must change uniforms, wash up or clean up at work, or engage in other preparatory activity that's required for the job, that time must generally be counted as hours worked in California. You must pay these employees at their applicable rate (straight time or overtime). This time is included in overtime pay calculations.

Federal law generally considers this time non-compensable. When in doubt as to whether you should count the time toward an employee's pay, consult legal counsel.

Reimbursing Employees for Their Expenses

You must reimburse all employees (exempt and nonexempt) for all the expenses they incur in performing their duties. Common examples include mileage, travel and dining expenses, and personal cell phone usage. The mileage reimbursement rate considered most reasonable in California is set by the Internal Revenue Service.

 The IRS did not announce the optional standard mileage rates for 2020 at the time of publication. For the most recent rate, please visit the IRS website at www.irs.gov.

Under California law, an employer must reimburse an employee only if it requires the employee to use a personal cell phone for work-related reasons. This is true even when employees don't incur an extra expense when using the phone for work-related reasons.. To comply with the Labor Code, the employer must pay "some reasonable percentage" of the employee's cell phone bill; however, the law does not clearly define what is a "reasonable percentage."

 If you have any questions about whether you should reimburse employees, and at what rate, for using their personal cell phone to make work-related calls, consult legal counsel.

 There is a broad array of reimbursable expenses. In extreme cases, employers must reimburse employees sued by third parties for conduct within the scope of employment. Consult legal counsel to audit your expense compensation practices to ensure you are complying with the law.

Overtime Pay

When your nonexempt employees work beyond a "normal" number of hours, you must compensate them at a higher rate. In most cases, this means you pay overtime to a nonexempt employee who works more than eight hours per day or 40 hours per week. Failing to pay overtime can get you into trouble. For more information, see "Failing to Pay Overtime" on page 206.

 Remember — exempt employees do not receive overtime pay.

Employees with an alternative workweek schedule earn overtime differently (see "Scheduling Options" on page 164). Be sure to consult the Wage Order that applies to your industry.

 Sometimes a collective bargaining agreement can affect overtime rules, so check yours if you have one.

Overtime Rates of Pay

Generally in California, nonexempt employees must be paid overtime at the following rates:

Table 58. Rates of Overtime Pay

Hours Worked	Employee's Regular Pay Rate Multiplied by ...
Beyond eight in one workday	1.5 (time-and-one-half)
Beyond 12 in one workday	2.0 (double-time)
Up to eight hours on the seventh consecutive day of the workweek	1.5 (time-and-one-half)
Beyond eight on the seventh consecutive day of the workweek	2.0 (double-time)
Beyond 40 straight-time hours in one workweek	1.5 (time-and-one-half)

 Some wage Orders contain special provisions regarding overtime. Always follow the Wage Order that applies to your industry.

Calculating Overtime for Nonexempt Employees

1. Determine the employee's regular rate of pay:

- For hourly workers, total the amount earned for each hour actually worked plus any nondiscretionary bonuses and commissions, and divide that by the total number of actual hours worked.

- For piece-rate workers, total the amount earned for units produced and divide that by the total number of actual hours worked, even if it's more than 40.

 The **regular rate of pay** equals an employee's actual earnings, which may include an hourly rate, commissions, nondiscretionary bonuses, piece work and the value of meals and lodging. For examples of other compensation, see "Other Compensation" on page 172.

Though you need to include nondiscretionary bonuses and commissions in the regular rate of pay, you do not need to include:

- Hours paid but not worked (vacation, reporting time, etc.). See "Paid Non-Working Time" on page 180.

- Reimbursement of expenses. See "Reimbursing Employees for Their Expenses" on page 184.

- Gifts or discretionary bonuses (in recognition of services performed during a given period).

- Benefits payments (profit sharing plan, health care plan, etc...).

- Overtime premium pay.

 For a sample calculation, see "Calculating Overtime for Nonexempt Employees With More Than One Rate of Pay" on page 187.

2. Determine how many hours the employee worked in excess of the maximum allowed in a workday. For most nonexempt employees, this is the first eight hours of that employee's workday. Any hours actually worked in excess of the maximum allowed in a workday are considered overtime hours. To determine any additional workweek overtime hours, determine how many straight-time hours the employee worked for that workweek. Straight-time hours are hours that the employee works in a workday that are not considered overtime hours (usually the first eight hours of that individual's workday). For information on defining your workday and workweek, "Setting Work Schedules" on page 163.

Only hours worked at straight time apply to the weekly 40-hour limit. This prevents "pyramiding" of overtime, where an employee earns overtime on top of overtime already paid. For example, once an employee is paid overtime for hours over eight in one workday, those overtime hours do not count toward the weekly 40-hour limit.

Example: Assume the workweek is Monday through Sunday. A nonexempt employee works 10 hours each day Monday through Thursday. Eight of those hours worked each day are straight time, while the remaining two hours each day are considered overtime. On Friday, the employee doesn't begin earning weekly overtime until after working eight more hours. Although that individual already worked 40 hours in the workweek, only 32 hours of that was straight time.

The employee works 10 hours on Friday — another eight straight time hours and two overtime hours. Because the employee now has worked 40 hours of straight time, any other straight time hours worked in this workweek will be considered overtime hours.

3. For any overtime hours, pay the appropriate rate listed in Table 59 on page 187.

Calculating Overtime for Nonexempt Employees With More Than One Rate of Pay

Different rates may be paid for different jobs so long as the work involved is objectively different. For example, travel time pay may be paid at a lower rate than the employee's regular rate of pay, but travel time must be paid at least the minimum wage. Accurate recordkeeping is imperative in such scenarios.

TIP When employees travel to a different time zone, ask them to track all hours based on California time — it will make the math much easier and your payroll department will sincerely appreciate it. Consistent communication by email or phone can also cut down on later disputes regarding hours actually worked.

Especially with travel time, employers should communicate with nonexempt employees regarding these obligations. In this case, there's a difference between the hourly rate and the regular rate of pay when employees work overtime and earn:

- Time and one-half: You must pay them the hourly rate for the job theydo, plus one-half of the regular rate of pay.

- Double-time: You must pay them two times the regular rate of pay.

If your employee works an alternative workweek, you must use different calculations. See "Scheduling Options" on page 164.

Table 59. Regular Rate of Pay for Multiple Hourly Rates

An employee normally earns $15 per hour working at trade shows for his/her employer and $12 per hour for travel time. In one week, the employee works 40 hours at the trade show and spends 10 hours traveling.	
Total rate 1	$15 per hour x 40 hours = $600
Total rate 2	$12 per hour x 10 hours = $120
Total weekly wages before overtime premiums	$600 + $120 = $720
Regular rate of pay	$720 ÷ 50 hours = $14.40
Overtime premium for time-and-one-half	$14.40 ÷ 2 = $7.20

For more than two rates, multiply the additional rates by the number of hours worked at those rates and include them in the total weekly compensation. If the employee earned commissions or bonuses in addition to the hourly rates, include those amounts in the total weekly compensation.

Calculating Overtime for Nonexempt Employees With Nondiscretionary Bonuses

A "non-discretionary bonus" is extra wages provided to an employee based on predetermined factors that can't be withheld unless the employee doesn't meet the stated goal.

The exact method for calculating overtime on a non-discretionary bonus depends on whether it's a production bonus or a flat-sum bonus.

 Correctly calculating overtime on bonuses under California law is complicated. Consult legal counsel regarding calculating overtime on bonuses.

Production Bonus

A production bonus is based on a percentage of production or some formula other than a flat amount.

- The regular rate for a production bonus is calculated by dividing the bonus by the total hours worked (including overtime) during the period to which the bonus applies. The overtime pay on the bonus is then calculated by multiplying one-half of this regular bonus rate by the number of overtime hours worked during the period in which the bonus was earned (or multiply by one for double time hours).

An employee earning $12 per hour worked 50 hours in a workweek (40 hours of straight time and 10 hours of overtime). The employee also received a $125 production bonus. The employee's wages for the week would be calculated as follows:	
Regular hourly rate of pay	$12 per hour x 40 hours = $480
Overtime rate (time and one-half)	$18 per hour x 10 hours = $180
Bonus attributable to the workweek	$125
Regular bonus rate	$125 ÷ 50 hours = $2.50 $2.50 x .5 = $1.25 $1.25x 10 overtime hours = $12.50
Total earnings due for the workweek	$797.50 ($480 +$180 + $125 + $12.50)

Flat-Sum Bonus

A flat-sum bonus is not designed as an incentive for increased production, but so the employee remains with the employer.

The Division of Labor Standards Enforcement's method for calculating overtime on nondiscretionary flat-sum bonuses is as follows:

- Divide the employee's bonus by the employee's *nonovertime hours worked* (not by the total hours worked). This provides the per-hour value of the bonus, which is multiplied using 1.5, not 0.5, as the multiplier for determining the employee's overtime rate. The multiplier is 1.5 for time and a half and 2.0 for double time.

An employee earning $12 per hour worked 50 hours in a workweek (40 hours of straight time and 10 hours of overtime). The employee also received a $20 flat-sum bonus for working a weekend shift. The employee's wages for the week would be calculated as follows:

Regular hourly rate of pay	$12 per hour x 40 hours = $480
Overtime rate (time and one-half)	$18 per hour x 10 hours = $180
Bonus	$20
Overtime on bonus	$20 bonus ÷ 40 regular hours = $0.50 $0.50 x 1.5 = $0.75 $0.75 x 10 overtime hours = $7.50
Total earnings due for the workweek	$687.50 ($480 + $180 + $20 + $7.50)

 Employers who want to give "extra pay" to hourly workers should consult legal counsel.

Requiring Employees to Work Overtime

With a couple of limited exceptions, there is no lawful basis for employees to refuse your request that they work overtime. You can often find employees who will voluntarily work overtime.

A good approach is to first request volunteers among qualified employees, and then require overtime only in the absence of such volunteers. You can enforce overtime requests with disciplinary action if the employee refuses.

Overtime and Agricultural Employees

Different overtime rules apply to agricultural employees. In the past, agricultural laborers earned overtime pay after working 10 hours per day or working the seventh consecutive day in a workweek. The overtime pay rate is 1.5 times the regular rate of pay after 10 hours per day and for the first 8 hours on the seventh consecutive workday in a workweek. The overtime pay rate is two times the regular rate of pay after eight hours on the seventh day.

 California is phasing in increased overtime requirements for agricultural employees over the course of four years from 2019 to 2022. Starting January 1, 2020, employers with 26 or more employees must pay agricultural employees overtime when they work more than 9.5 hours per day and 50.5 hours per week. This number will decrease yearly until it reaches 8 hours per day and 40 hours per week by January 1, 2022.

Employers with 25 or fewer employees will have an additional three years to comply with the phasing in of these requirements and won't start paying overtime until 2022.

In addition, agricultural employers are no longer exempt from the requirement of one day's rest in seven and employers cannot cause employees to work more than six days in seven.

Overtime and Non-Resident Employees

The California Supreme Court ruled that California overtime laws apply to non-resident employees when they perform work in California for California-based employers. Although the case involved full weeks of work by employees not based in California, it's possible that future decisions will find in favor of employees who work less than a full work week in California.

The court did not address meal and rest breaks, pay stubs and other California issues related to nonexempt employees. The court also did not make a decision about out-of-state employees working in California for an employer based outside of California.

 Employers who send out-of-state employees to California to work should consult legal counsel for advice on how to pay those employees.

Makeup Time and Compensatory Time Off

You can choose to offer makeup time to your nonexempt employees if they want to request time off for a personal obligation and make up the time without receiving overtime pay.

The law doesn't require you to offer this option, but if you offer it, you must abide by these rules:

- You can't ask or encourage employees to use makeup time.

- The time must be made up within the same workweek.

- The employee is limited to 11 hours per day and 40 hours per week when working makeup time.

- Before taking off or making up the time, the employee must provide you with a signed, written request for each occasion that makeup time is desired, unless the time off is for a recurring event, such as a college course.

Make sure your time-recording system shows which hours you will pay at an overtime rate and which hours you will pay at a normal rate as makeup time. The sample *Makeup Time Checklist* and *Makeup Time Request* forms are described in Table 63 on page 210.

Compensatory time off (CTO) is lawful only for public-sector employers. CTO is time off given to employees in exchange for extra hours worked. CTO is not "makeup time."

 It is illegal for all private-sector employers to provide CTO under any circumstances; not only in California, but nationwide.

Pay Rules

California has extensive rules that determine how employees are paid. It is important that you understand the laws pertaining to amount, timeliness and form of payment.

When Do I Pay My Workers?

If you fail to pay your workers in a timely manner, you face certain penalties (see "Failing to Pay Wages Due" on page 206). You must pay employees according to guidelines that apply to the type of payment.

Table 60. Payment Types

Payment Type	Must Be Paid
Regular Wages (nonexempt)	All employees must be paid at least twice each calendar month on days designated in advance (see "Notifying Employees About Paydays" on page 194). • Twice-monthly (semi-monthly): For hours worked between the 1st and the 15th day of the month (no later than the 26th day of the same month); and for hours worked between the 16th and the last day of the month (no later than the 10th day of next month). • Weekly or bi-weekly: Within seven days of the end of the pay period.
Regular Wages (exempt)	Employees exempt under the executive, administrative and professional exemptions may be paid once per month as long as payment is made by the 26th day of the month for all wages, including those yet unearned, for the month.
Overtime	Overtime wages must be paid no later than the next work period's payday. For a complete discussion, please see "Overtime Pay" on page 184.
Tips/Gratuities Paid by Credit Card	Credit card tips or gratuities must be paid no later than the next scheduled payday following the date the patron authorized the credit card payment.
Expense Reimbursements	Reimbursements may be paid on any reasonable schedule. Expense reimbursements to terminated employees are not subject to final paycheck deadlines and can be paid at the same time as reimbursements to active employees. Put a policy or procedure in place regarding reimbursements and follow it consistently.

Table 60. Payment Types *(continued)*

Payment Type	Must Be Paid
Vehicle Salespeople Commission Wages	These wages must be paid once per month.
Farm Labor Contractor Employees	These employees must be paid at least once every week on a day designated in advance. ⓘ Payment must include all wages earned up to and including the fourth day.
Temporary Service Employees	These employees must be paid at least weekly, and daily if an employee is assigned to a client on a day-to-day basis or to a client engaged in a trade dispute. This requirement also applies to security guards employed by private patrol operators who are temporary services employers. ⓘ There is an exception to these pay rules — employees assigned to a client for more than 90 consecutive calendar days are not subject to this requirement unless the employer pays the employee weekly. In California, employers are jointly liable for wage-and-hour and Workers' Compensation coverage violations against workers hired through temporary service employers. Exercise due diligence to make sure that the companies you hire workers through are complying with the law. Ask legal counsel to review all contracts between you and the temporary service company and include an indemnification clause to protect your company. For more information, see "Labor Contractor Violations" on page 207.

Exceptions to Payday Rules

Under certain circumstances, you can make exceptions to the payday requirements:

- Agriculture workers may be paid once per month if you lodge and board them.

- Domestic employees may be paid once per month if you lodge and board them.

- Striking employees may be paid on the next regularly scheduled payday when they come back to work.

Notifying Employees About Paydays

You must post the day, time and place of the regular payday in a way that your employees can understand. As a convenience, the state provides a small form for this purpose, which CalChamber includes as part of the **2020 California and Federal Labor Law Poster** (available from **store.calchamber.com**).

If you change the payday schedule, notify your employees of the change at least one full payroll cycle in advance.

Wage Information Notice to Employees

Nonexempt employees must be provided with specific written wage information, at the time of hire. Use the *Wage and Employment Notice to Employees (Labor Code section 2810.5)* form, described in Table 63 on page 210.

The Labor Commissioner designed a template that complies with the specific notice requirements, which include:

- The rate/rates of pay and basis — hourly, by a shift, day, week, salary, piece, commission or otherwise, including applicable overtime rates.

- Allowances, if any, claimed as part of minimum wage, including meal or lodging allowances.

- The regular payday designated by the employer.

- The name of the employer, including any "doing business as" names used.

- The physical address of the employer's main office or principal place of business, and a mailing address, if different.

- The employer's phone number.

- The name, address and telephone number of the employer's workers' compensation carrier.

- Information about mandatory paid sick leave.

- Any other information the Labor Commissioner deems material and necessary.

Temporary service employers must also include the name, physical address of the main office, mailing address if different from the physical address of the main office, and the telephone number of the legal entity for whom the employee will perform work, as well as any other information the Labor Commissioner deems material and necessary. Security service companies are exempt from this requirement.

Additionally, the employer is required to notify employees in writing of any changes to the information above, within seven calendar days after the time a change is made, unless:

- All changes are reflected on a timely wage statement (must meet all legal requirements).

- Notice is provided in another writing required by law within seven days of the changes.

Employees exempt from the payment of overtime wages by statute or Wage Order, employees of the state or any political subdivision (city, county, city and county or special district) and employees covered by a collective bargaining agreement are not covered by the written statement requirement.

Payday on a Sunday or Holiday

If your business is closed on a payday that falls on a Saturday, Sunday or a legal holiday, you must pay wages no later than the next business day. Make sure you state your policy in your employee handbook.

Failure to Turn in a Time Card

Even when a nonexempt employee fails to turn in a record of time worked, the law requires you to pay that individual on the established payday.

Since you have no time record to verify actual hours worked, pay all wages that would normally be due for the employee's work period and defer payment of overtime until the next pay period. If the payment results in an overpayment of wages, deducting the wages from the next payroll can be risky. Consult legal counsel before taking such action.

 Exempt employees should not turn in time cards for pay purposes.

Rounding Practices

When calculating the number of hours worked by employees, the California Labor Commissioner will accept the practice of computing working time by rounding to the nearest 5 minutes or one-tenth or one-quarter of an hour. However, the rounding must be used in such a manner that it will won't result in failure to compensate the employees properly for all the time they actually worked in a pay period.

Courts have also approved the ability of California employers to round a nonexempt employee's time to the nearest quarter of an hour as long as the practice is neutral on its face and in practice, meaning that over time, it favors neither the employer nor the employee.

Form of Payment

All paychecks must be payable in cash, on demand and without discount, at a bank that does business in California. The bank's name and address must appear on the paycheck. At the time the paycheck is issued, and for at least 30 days after, you must maintain sufficient funds in the payroll account, or credit, for payment. Paying any wage with a check that is backed by insufficient funds is unlawful. See "Paychecks Returned for Insufficient Funds" on page 208.

You can also use an electronic transfer system (direct deposit) to transfer wages to a bank, savings and loan or credit union if the employee chooses to do so. You may not force employees to use a direct deposit system. Even though the money is transferred electronically, you must still provide a written statement of wages and deductions to the employee.

You may deposit final wages by direct deposit if the payment complies with existing laws concerning final payment and the employee authorizes you to do so.

Itemized Wage Statement

California employers have a legal obligation to provide employees with specified information regarding their wages. You must provide each employee an itemized statement, in writing and at the time wages are paid, that contains the following information:

- Gross wages earned.
- Total hours worked (except employees who are exempt from the payment of minimum wage and overtime).
- All deductions, including taxes, disability insurance and health and welfare payments.
  - Deductions ordered by the employee can be aggregated and shown as one item.
- Net wages earned.
- The pay period's inclusive dates.

- Name of the employee and last four digits of the individual's Social Security number (SSN).

  – All employers can print no more than the last four digits of an employee's Social Security number on check stubs or similar documents (they can substitute some other identifying number).

- Name and address of employer or legal entity.

- All applicable hourly rates in effect during the pay period and the corresponding number of hours the employee worked at each hourly rate.

- Piece rate units and applicable piece rate, if the employee is paid on a piece rate basis.

- Temporary service employers must also include the rate of pay and the total hours worked for each temporary services assignment. Licensed security services companies are specifically excluded from this law.

California's mandatory PSL law requires employers to provide employees with a written notice that sets forth the amount of paid sick leave available for use, or paid time off leave an employer provides in lieu of sick leave. Employers can provide the information on either:

- The employee's itemized wage statement; or

- A separate writing provided on the designated pay date with the employee's payment of wages.

Failing to provide an itemized wage statement or to include the correct information on the wage statement may subject you to a Private Attorneys General Act (PAGA) claim which contains additional penalties (for more information, see "Private Attorneys General Act (PAGA) Claims" on page 208).

Employers can be liable under PAGA even if the employer didn't knowingly or intentionally violate the wage statement statute, and the employee was not harmed in the violation.

California law provides employers a limited time period to fix specific technical violations (failing to list the inclusive dates of the pay period or the employer's proper legal name and address) on itemized wage statements before civil litigation begins.

The period of time is very short, so employers should respond promptly and consult legal counsel when faced with litigation from employees seeking financial penalties related to technical violations on wage statements.

Reporting Payroll Information

You must provide information to assist district attorneys with the enforcement of garnishments for child support. In an effort to collect child support, federal law requires all employers to report certain information on their newly hired employees to the EDD within 20 days of hire. All businesses and government entities that use independent contractors must file similar reports. For more details, see "Independent Contractors" in Chapter 2, page 55.

Records Retention

You must maintain an accurate record of employees' hours of work and compensation. The basic recordkeeping obligation includes the employee's:

- Name.

- Home address.

- Date of birth (if under 18 years of age).

- Occupation/job title.

- Total wages and other compensation paid during each payroll period.

- And for nonexempt employees:

    - Clock time when each work period and off-duty meal break begins and ends (for more information, see "Meal and Rest Breaks" on page 176).

    - Total hours worked in each payroll period and applicable rates of pay.

    - Number of piece-rate units earned, if applicable, and any piece rate paid.

Access to Payroll Files

You must keep records of all payments and deductions for each employee for at least three years. The employee, upon reasonable request, can inspect and/or receive a copy of these records. Employers must make and provide the copies; they can't require employees to find ways to make the copies themselves. A copy can be either a duplicate of the itemized statement provided to an employee or a computer-generated record that accurately shows all of the information required by law to be included in the itemized statement.

If an employee or ex-employee requests to review or receive copies of the payments and deductions listed in "Wage Garnishments" on page 201, you must comply with the request within 21 calendar days. You may charge the individual for the actual cost of reproducing the requested information.

The penalty (for actual damages) for failure to comply may be up to $4,000 plus costs and attorneys' fees for the employee. The Labor Commissioner may also impose a penalty of up to $750. For more information, see "Failing to Provide a Statement of Wage Deductions" on page 207.

Execution of Release on Account of Wages Due

You can't ask or require an employee to forgo wages due or "execute a release" of wages due. The phrase "execute a release" includes requiring an employee, as a condition of being paid, to sign a false statement of the hours that individual worked during a pay period. Employers who violate this law are guilty of a misdemeanor.

Deductions from Employee Pay

You must make certain deductions from the total compensation of both exempt and nonexempt employees. You must take out taxes and wage garnishments, if any.

Federal and State Taxes

You must make certain tax deductions from employee paychecks.

Table 61. Tax Deductions

Tax	Deductions
Federal Income Tax	Use the W-4 – *Employee's Withholding Allowance* Certificate (described in Table 12 in Chapter 2, page 65) and the withholding methods described in the Employer's Tax Guide (Publication 15) from the IRS. You can download the Employer's Tax Guide from the IRS website at **www.irs.gov**.
State Income Tax	Use the DE4 - *California Employee's Withholding Certificate* (described in Table 12 in Chapter 2, page 65). For information about rates, forms, exemptions and withholdings, contact the EDD or visit its website at www.edd.ca.gov.

Table 61. Tax Deductions *(continued)*

Tax	Deductions
Social Security (FICA)	Both you and your employee must pay Social Security taxes. You must withhold and deposit the employee's withheld taxes and pay a matching amount. **New** The withholding rate for 2020 is 6.2 percent (unchanged from 2019). However, the wage base limit for 2020 increased to $137,700.
Medicare	Both you and your employee must pay Medicare taxes. You must withhold and deposit the employee's withheld taxes and pay a matching amount at the rate of 1.45 percent (no wage base limit). The Medicare tax rate is unchanged from 2019.
State Disability Insurance (SDI) Tax	SDI provides temporary disability benefits for employees disabled by a non-work- related illness or injury. You must withhold monies from each paycheck. The SDI withholding rate, taxable wage limit and annual maximum withholding for 2020 were not announced at the time of publication. For the most recent data, please visit the EDD website at ***www.edd.ca.gov***.
Paid Family Leave (PFL) Tax	PFL provides temporary disability benefits for employees who can't work because of the need to care for a family member or bond with a child. You must withhold monies from each paycheck. The SDI withholding includes the PFL tax.

Wage Garnishments

A public agency or court judgment may require you to withhold money from an employee's paycheck. This is known as a "wage garnishment." The money is distributed to a third party pursuant to the order from a public agency or a court judgment. These third parties could be government agencies, debt collection companies or divorced spouses, for example. Make these deductions after taking out taxes. If you have any questions about wage garnishments, please visit the Judicial Council's website at ***www.courts.ca.gov/documents/wg002.pdf*** to download the *Form WG-002*, which contains instructions for employers.

Table 62. Wage Garnishment and Back Taxes

Child Support	Court orders for child support take precedence over all other garnishments. If the employee has multiple child support garnishments, current support takes priority over past due support. Regardless of the number of garnishments, you can't deduct more of the employee's disposable income than: • 50 percent if the employee has current spouse/child dependents; or • 60 percent if the employee has no dependents. An additional 5 percent may be garnished for support payments that are more than 12 weeks behind. Different limits apply for child support (50 percent of amount remaining after deductions). Any person or business entity that knowingly helps someone escape, evade or avoid current payment of unpaid child support obligations can be subject to a penalty. The penalty can be up to the total amount of the entire child support obligation due. Prohibited actions, when an individual or entity knows or should have known of the child support obligation, include: • Hiring or employing a person who owes child support without making a timely report to the EDD's New Employee Registry. • Retaining an independent contractor who owes child support and failing to file a timely report of such engagement with the EDD. • Paying wages or other forms of compensation (including cash, barter or trade) not reported to the EDD. Visit the California Department of Child Support Services website at ***www.childsup.ca.gov/Portals/0/employer/docs/EmployerHndbk.pdf*** for a complete guide to complying with child support orders.

Table 62. Wage Garnishment and Back Taxes *(continued)*

Other Wage Garnishments	The amount of wages exempt from garnishment is higher under the California standard than the federal standard. In California, a withholding order can't exceed the lesser of: • 25 percent of an individual's weekly disposable earnings; or • 50 percent of the amount by which the disposable earnings for the week exceed 40 times the state (or local, if higher) minimum hourly wage in effect. The Consumer Credit Protection Act prohibits you from terminating employees for having their wages garnished. You must comply with garnishment orders as written until directed otherwise by the issuing agency or the court. When you receive the court order: • Mark the date received on the notice and retain the postmarked envelope in case you need to prove timely compliance. • Keep a copy of the court order in the employee's personnel file as the legal basis for making the payroll deduction. • Advise the employee of the court order within 10 days of receiving the order, as well as the date you will make the first deduction. The first deduction must be made within 10 days of your receipt of the order, unless the order specifies otherwise. Employers can withhold $1.50 for each payment made, in compliance with an earnings withholding order that enforces payment of support obligations. You must notify the appropriate agency if an employee subject to wage garnishment leaves your company.
Back Taxes	The amount deducted depends on how many dependents the employee has. The more dependents, the less the IRS can deduct.

Deductions and Repayment for Employee Related Items

You can make deductions from an employee's paycheck for certain items, such as meals, lodging or other facilities, because these deductions are for the employee's benefit. You can consider it part of the employee's wages and include it in your calculations to ensure that you're meeting minimum wage requirements if:

• The employee entered into a voluntary agreement.

• The amounts credited do not exceed the limits specified in the applicable Wage Order.

As a result of updates to the Division of Labor Standards Enforcement's (DLSE) manual, consider the following before deducting from an employee's paycheck:

- If you loan money to an employee, ask that individual to sign a promissory note guaranteeing repayment and get the repayment by personal check or other form of payment — never through a payroll deduction.

- Discuss automatic enrollment in your 401(k) or other retirement plan with your benefits provider. Not all providers follow the automatic enrollment process.

- Review your policies and procedures regarding loans or advances, including advances on vacation and PTO, to ensure you aren't repaid by payroll deduction.

For more information, see "Wages and Salaries" on page 165.

Impermissible Employer Deductions

You can't deduct for any cash shortages (for example, if a cashier's drawer doesn't match the record), breakage or loss of equipment from employees' wages. You can't make deductions for ordinary wear and tear to uniforms and equipment. You can't deduct the cost of a uniform from employees' wages.

You also can't require them to purchase the uniform on their own, unless it would be generally worn in an occupation — for example, a nurse's uniform, or basic wardrobe items, such as white shirts, dark pants and black shoes and belts (of an unspecified design) for waitstaff.

If you require tools and equipment, you must furnish and maintain them, except for customary hand tools required of employees making at least twice the minimum wage. Be sure to consult the Wage Order applicable to your industry relating to uniforms, tools and equipment.

Voluntary Deductions

Employees can authorize the following deductions from their paycheck:

- 401(k)/IRA contributions.

- Health insurance plans.

Some voluntary deductions can be taken out before taxes, thus reducing the employee's taxable income. For more information, visit the IRS website at **www.irs.gov**.

Deductions from an Exempt Employee's Salary

Exempt employees receive a full week's salary for any week in which they perform any work, except in the following situations:

- If the employee is hired and begins work in the middle of the week.

- If the employee is terminated in the middle of the week.

- If the employee's absences are covered under the federal Family and Medical Leave Act and/or the California Family Rights Act.

- If the employee's absence meets the criteria described in this section.

Deductions may be made from an exempt employee's accrued vacation or paid time off (PTO) bank for partial-day absences, in accordance with your policy or practice. Never make a partial day deduction from an exempt employee's salary.

Deductions for Partial Day Absences Caused by Sickness or Injury

Partial day absences caused by sickness or injury can be charged to an exempt employee's sick pay bank, provided the employee has such sick pay available at the time of the absence.

Deductions for Absences from Vacation Pay/PTO

If the employee has accrued vacation pay/PTO:

- You may make a deduction for a complete day of absence.

 You can't require employees to use vacation/PTO for a partial week's absence for convenience only (for example, for a plant shutdown).

- You may make a deduction for a partial day of absence from accrued vacation pay/PTO in whatever increment your policy specifies. You may not make a deduction for a partial day of absence from the employee's *salary*.

For employees with no vacation/PTO accrued or who have used up all of their vacation pay/PTO:

- You may make a deduction for a complete day of absence from their salary if they're absent for personal reasons and have no accrued benefit or used all accrued time.

- You may not make a salary deduction if the employee is sick. Deductions from pay for full day increments if an employee is sick may be made only if the employer has a bona fide sick leave plan, the employee has exhausted all sick leave available and the employee is absent for a full day.

- You may *not* make a deduction for a partial day of absence from an exempt employee's salary.

You should give reasonable notice to exempt employees before you require them to take PTO or vacation during a business closure or plant shutdown.

Pay and Scheduling Violations

Employee pay is a serious matter. You face steep penalties if you fail to pay employees in the proper manner and do not make required withholding deductions.

The Labor Commissioner enforces wage-and-hour laws and has the power to:

- Issue levies and liens on employer property to enforce a judgment;
- Issue a "stop order" to satisfy a final judgment for unpaid wages; or
- Deny a license to an employer in the long-term care industry for failing to pay a judgment for unpaid wages.

California law also:

- Imposes personal liability on individuals acting on the behalf of the employer who violate wage and hour provision in the Labor Code; and
- Creates joint liability for wage and hour violations when employers use staffing agencies or labor contractors to supply workers.

Failing to Pay the Minimum Wage

The California Labor Commissioner can:

- Assess fines.
  - First offense: $100 per employee per pay period.
  - Subsequent offenses: $250 per employee per pay period.
- File charges with the district attorney.

If found guilty of a misdemeanor (a criminal offense that's less serious than a felony), you will have to pay the difference between the minimum wage and the wage paid during the period of violation, and pay court costs. You may also have to pay a fine of $100 or more; go to jail for 30 days; or both.

Failing to Pay Overtime

The California Labor Commissioner can assess civil penalties against you or any other person acting on your behalf:

- First offense — $50 fine per underpaid employee, plus the amount of underpaid wages.

- Subsequent offenses — $100 fine per underpaid employee, plus the amount of underpaid wages.

Failing to Pay Wages Due

A law effective January 1, 2020, gives employees the ability to bring a private action to either:

- Recover statutory penalties against the employer in a hearing before the Labor Commissioner; or

- Seek to enforce civil penalties under the Private Attorneys General Act.

They may not do both.

If an employee files a complaint with the Labor Commissioner to recover unpaid wages, the Labor Commissioner will:

- Investigate the complaint.

- Hold hearings and take action to recover wages (the Labor Commissioner will notify the parties whether a hearing will be held within 30 days after a complaint was filed).

- Assess penalties and make demands for compensation.

Also effective January 1, 2020, the Labor Commissioner may now issue citations and recover amounts owed by an employer who has paid less than the wages set by contract, even if it was more than minimum wage.

The Labor Commissioner can assess fines of up to $200 per employee per pay period, plus 25 percent of the wages not paid to each employee each pay period. All awards made by the Labor Commissioner accrue interest on all due and unpaid wages. In the event of a dispute over wages, you must pay, without condition, all of the undisputed wages.

If you don't pay the disputed wages within 10 days after the Labor Commissioner resolves the dispute, you will have to pay triple the amount due to the employee.

If you must comply with the federal Fair Labor Standards Act, employees may initiate claims with the U.S. Department of Labor (DOL). Employers should contact legal counsel if the DOL begins an investigation. For details about the FLSA and the DOL, see "Glossary of Terms, Laws and Agencies" on page 339.

Labor Contractor Violations

Under state law, an employer who contracts for labor may be held accountable for wage-and-hour violations committed by the labor contractor.

 The law covers any business entity with 25 or more workers that obtains or is provided at least six (6) workers to perform labor within the usual course of business from one labor contractor or various labor contractors.

If a labor contractor fails to pay its employees properly or fails to provide workers' compensation coverage for those employees, the client employer is legally responsible.

Alternative Workweek Schedules and Pay Violations

The Labor Commissioner can invalidate an alternative workweek schedule for a number of reasons, including improper implementation, improper payment of overtime and changing the schedule without the required procedure, among others.

Failing to Provide a Statement of Wage Deductions

If you don't provide the paycheck information, the employee can recover $50 per employee for the initial violation and $100 per employee for subsequent violations, up to $4,000.

If you don't provide the statements in writing or fail to keep the records for three years, you must pay a civil penalty of $250 per employee for the first violation and $1,000 per employee for each subsequent violation. If you make a clerical error or inadvertent mistake on the first violation, the Labor Commissioner has discretionary power not to penalize you.

Paychecks Returned for Insufficient Funds

The penalty for issuing a nonsufficient funds (NSF) check is one day's pay for each day the wages remain unpaid, not to exceed 30 days of wages:

- The penalty applies to any wages paid with a nonsufficient funds instrument.
- If the NSF check is provided for payment of final wages owed, the employer would face penalties both for payment by NSF check and for late payment of final wages.
- The penalty provided for NSF is not applicable if the employee recovers the service charge authorized by law.

Late Paychecks

You are liable for a penalty of one day's wages for each day the check is late, up to a maximum of 30 days. Any penalty awarded by the Labor Commissioner is paid to the employee who was not paid on time.

Wage Claims

Employees who believe they haven't been paid correctly may file a wage claim with the state Labor Commissioner or pursue a civil claim. When a claim is filed with the Labor Commissioner and a decision rendered, either party can file an appeal to a trial court.

If the party seeking the review is not successful, the court could award the non-appealing party monetary damages for court costs and attorneys' fees. The party that appealed would have to pay these costs. An employee's claim is considered successful if the individual recovers a judgment in any amount greater than zero.

Private Attorneys General Act (PAGA) Claims

Under the Private Attorneys General Act of 2004 (PAGA), an individual aggrieved employee, acting in a personal capacity and/or on behalf of other current and former employees, can bring a civil action for Labor Code violations.

An aggrieved employee can recover the applicable civil penalty on behalf of himself/ herself and other current or former employees against whom one or more of the alleged violations was committed. Employees must comply with specific procedural and notice requirements before filing a civil suit. Employers have the opportunity to "cure" violations before the lawsuit proceeds. The law includes civil penalties of:

- $100 per aggrieved employee per pay period for the initial violation
- $200 per aggrieved employee per pay period for subsequent violations

Twenty-five percent of the penalties goes to the employee(s). If the employee prevails in the civil action, that individual is also entitled to an award of reasonable attorneys' fees and costs.

Minimum Compliance Elements

1. Hang your *2020 California and Federal Labor Law Poster* (available from *store.calchamber.com*), which includes mandatory postings that all employees and applicants must be able to see, in a prominent place (such as a break room). It includes the current California Minimum Wage Order.

    If you have employees working in a city or county with a local minimum wage and/or paid sick leave ordinance, you may also need to post required local notices and provide additional notices to employees at the time of hire.

2. Require your nonexempt (hourly) employees to keep accurate records of time worked.

3. Require that your nonexempt (hourly) employees follow meal and rest break requirements.

4. Calculate overtime for nonexempt employees after eight hours worked in a day and after 40 hours in a workweek (see "Overtime Pay" on page 184).

5. Make sure you don't treat your exempt employees like nonexempt workers — remember, your exempt employees get paid to get the job done, not to work a set number of hours.

6. Get to know the Wage Order for your industry and post it in a conspicuous place (see "California Wage Orders" on page 161).

7. Comply with payday rules and notice requirements.

8. Distribute required notices and pamphlets.

Forms and Checklists

The following table describes forms and checklists associated with paying employees.

 TIP You can find these forms in your forms download, described in detail in "Online Forms" on page 9.

Table 63. Forms and Checklists

Notice or Form	What Do I Use It For?	When Do I Use It?	Who Fills It Out?	Where Does It Go?
Absence Request	Give this form to employees when requesting future time off or reporting previous time off. This form also gives your employees the opportunity to indicate a Family and Medical Leave absence, although it is not required.	When an employee requests time off or reports time off taken.	The employee.	In the employee's personnel file; and a copy should go to payroll.
Absence Request - Spanish	Give this form to employees when requesting future time off or reporting previous time off. This form also gives your employees the opportunity to indicate a Family and Medical Leave absence, although it is not required.	When an employee requests time off or reports time off taken.	The employee.	In the employee's personnel file; and a copy should go to payroll.
Makeup Time Checklist	To help you figure out if, when and how to offer the time.	When you plan your pay policies.	The employer.	Keep the checklist in your own employee pay records.
Makeup Time Request	To document requests for the time.	When an employee requests the time.	The employee.	Keep it in the employee's personnel file.

Table 63. Forms and Checklists *(continued)*

Notice or Form	What Do I Use It For?	When Do I Use It?	Who Fills It Out?	Where Does It Go?
Makeup Time Request - Spanish	To document requests for the time.	When an employee requests the time.	The employee.	Keep it in the employee's personnel file.
Meal Break Waiver - Employee Shift 6 Hours or Less	Written documentation of a worker's waiver of the 30-minute meal break.	When a nonexempt employee works a shift of six hours or less; use this form when both you and the worker wish to waive the required 30-minute meal break.	You and the employee.	In the employee's file; a copy to payroll.
Meal Break Waiver - Employee Shift 6 Hours or Less - Spanish	Written documentation of a worker's waiver of the 30-minute meal break.	When a nonexempt employee works a shift of six hours or less; use this form when both you and the worker wish to waive the required 30-minute meal break.	You and the employee.	In the employee's file; a copy to payroll.
Meal Break - On Duty	Written documentation of an on-duty meal break.	When a nonexempt employee's work prevents the employee from taking a meal break and both you and the worker wish to have the worker work through the required 30-minute meal break, use this form. On-duty meal breaks are enforceable in very limited circumstances. Please consult with legal counsel before using this form.	You and the employee.	In the employee's file; a copy to payroll.

Table 63. Forms and Checklists *(continued)*

Notice or Form	What Do I Use It For?	When Do I Use It?	Who Fills It Out?	Where Does It Go?
Meal Break Waiver - Second Meal	Written documentation of a second meal break waiver.	When a nonexempt employee's shift will be more than 10 hours but less than 12 hours, the worker has not waived his first meal break, and the worker wishes to waive the second required 30-minute meal break, use this form.	You and the employee.	In the employee's file; a copy to payroll.
Overtime Request	To document in writing employee requests to work overtime hours.	Provide these forms to supervisors, managers and employees and train all employees in using this form whenever overtime work is needed or performed.	You and the employee.	In the employee's file; a copy to payroll.
Overtime Request - Spanish	To document in writing employee requests to work overtime hours.	Provide these forms to supervisors, managers and employees and train all employees in using this form whenever overtime work is needed or performed.	You and the employee.	In the employee's file; a copy to payroll.
Wage and Employment Notice to Employees (Labor Code section 2810.5)	To notify nonexempt employees of their hourly or piece rate of pay, pay dates and other information required by law.	At the time of hire, or on an employee's first day of employment.	The employer.	Give a copy to the new employee and keep a copy in the employee's personnel file.

Where Do I Go for More Information?

CalChamber and federal and state government agencies offer a variety of resources to help you learn more about issues related to wages and hours.

Table 64. Additional Resources

For Information On	Check Out These Resources
General	From CalChamber: • The *2020 California Labor Law Digest*, the most comprehensive, California-specific resource to help employers comply with complex federal and state labor laws and regulations • *Employee Handbook Creator* • *HRCalifornia.com* • *store.calchamber.com*
Child Support Wage Garnishments	State Department of Social Services, Office of Child Support (866) 249-0773 *www.childsup.ca.gov* Franchise Tax Board *www.ftb.ca.gov/pay/collections/withholding-orders/wage-garnishments.html*

TIP CalChamber also provides many ongoing and comprehensive educational opportunities for small business owners, HR beginners and experienced HR professionals alike. These include online training, and special HR seminars and webinars. For more information, please visit the CalChamber store website at *store.calchamber.com*.

Chapter 6

Ensuring Workplace Safety

You must provide a safe working environment for all your workers. The law requires you to reasonably protect your employees from work-related illness and injuries and workplace violence.

In this chapter, you can find answers to questions about:

- Basic standards.

- Injury and Illness Prevention Program (IIPP).

- OSHA inspections.

- Heat illness.

- The new wildfire smoke regulation.

Basic Standards

Every employer must follow regulations created by the U.S. Occupational Safety and Health Administration (OSHA) and the California Division of Occupational Safety and Health, better known as Cal/OSHA (see "Glossary of Terms, Laws and Agencies" on page 339). These regulations set standards for workplace safety.

The Cal/OSHA standards you must comply with vary on the size of your company and whether your company is deemed high- or low-hazard. Six basic standards apply to just about every company:

- IIPP (see page 218).

- Emergency Action Plan (see page 221).

- Fire Prevention Plan (see page 222).

- Work Surfaces, Control Devices and Emergency Equipment (see page 223).

- Hazard Communication Program (HAZCOM) (see page 223).

- Repetitive Motion Injuries (Ergonomics) (see page 225).

- Hotel Housekeeping Musculoskeletal Injury Prevention Program (see page 227).

Individual standards require more detailed plans, such as the Emergency Action Plan, that describe how you will help your employees stay safe on the job. Knowing which safety standards apply to your company and communicating them clearly to your employees is essential for avoiding inspections and, more importantly, preserving the welfare and safety of your workplace and employees.

If your company is exempt from complying with part or all of a standard, you should consider establishing a plan or program for handling potential situations, especially if the information can be added to your employee handbook or employee manual. You can get copies of the exact standards from Cal/OSHA. See "Where Do I Go for More Information?" on page 255.

California employers face Cal/OSHA inspections, citations and compliance schedules. Cal/OSHA's inspection program targets workplaces where there is a likelihood of health and safety hazards and/or violations of standards. Cal/OSHA must have reasonable cause to conduct an inspection, but court decisions have granted Cal/OSHA broad discretion in determining what is reasonable cause.

Following Standards

If you don't follow these standards and don't create appropriate safety plans or programs, Cal/OSHA can cite you for violating the applicable standard. In addition, documenting your plans for compliance can help you prove your intentions of complying if you receive a citation, which can help reduce the citation.

Sharing the information in these standards with your employees also helps you provide them with the knowledge they need to avoid or respond to potential dangers. For example, advise them on the best escape route in case of a fire, where you store the first aid kit, what health dangers they might be exposed to at work and how they can communicate their safety concerns to you.

Self-Inspections

It's a good practice to perform your own inspections of your site and equipment, your employees' safety practices and your safety documents:

- Internal inspections present the best defense against and preparation for inspections by outside agencies.

- Many OSHA standards require you to document periodic inspections for compliance.

- During an inspection, you may identify a potential hazard, find a broken safety guard or determine that your employees need refresher safety training.

- Inspections keep you familiarized with your site, processes and operations so you can evaluate your workplace's efficiency and productivity.

Smoking in the Workplace

California has a uniform statewide ban on smoking in the workplace that applies to all employers. You cannot knowingly or intentionally permit the smoking of tobacco products at a place of employment or in an enclosed space. This prohibition includes permitting nonemployees to smoke in an enclosed workplace and the use of e-cigarettes and other nicotine-delivery devices, such as vaporizers.

There are only a few limited exemptions from the requirement, consult legal counsel to determine if your business falls within an exemption.

Marijuana and Workplace Policies

In 2016, California joined several other states in legalizing recreational use of marijuana by adults. Proposition 64, also known as the Adult Use of Marijuana Act, legalized the recreational use of marijuana for adults 21 years old and over.

However, Proposition 64 maintains the status quo for employers seeking to maintain a drug- and alcohol-free workplace that includes marijuana use in the workplace. Prop. 64 explicitly states that it is intended to "allow public and private employers to enact and enforce workplace policies pertaining to marijuana."

Even with the passage of Prop. 64, employers may continue to prohibit use, possession and impairment at work and may continue to test for use when appropriate. Prop. 64 is not intended to interfere with these workplace policies or practices.

Injury and Illness Prevention Program

Every company must create an effective Injury and Illness Prevention Program (IIPP) to keep its workforce free from work-related injuries and illnesses.

The IIPP essentially contains a generalized plan for keeping the workforce free from work-related injuries and illnesses, including workplace violence. The forms download that comes with this book contains an approved *Injury and Illness Prevention Program for Non-High Hazard Employers*.

No single law governs how all organizations should address the issue of workplace violence. The steps you should take to prevent violence in the workplace depend on the risk factors present in your particular workplace. However, an increasing amount of legislation is enacted to protect against violence in certain highly charged and vulnerable workplaces. California laws might play a role in how your organization prepares for or responds to acts of violence in the workplace.

Cal/OSHA requires specified types of hospitals, including general acute care hospitals or acute psychiatric hospitals, to adopt workplace violence prevention plans as part of the hospitals' injury and illness prevention plans. The intent is to protect health care workers and other facility personnel from aggressive and violent behavior.

Table 65. Injury and Illness Prevention Plan

Question	Answer
Does the law require me to comply with this standard?	Yes, every employer must have a program, but some establishments may be exempt from some of the written record keeping requirements. Visit "Fire Prevention Plan" on page 222 for details.
Does the law require me to create a written program?	Yes. "Creating a Written Program" on page 225 lists what it must include.
Does the law require me to provide training?	Yes. Training is required when you implement your IIPP, assign a new employee to a position, transfer an existing employee to a new position, or make changes to workplace conditions. Provide refresher training as necessary. You can use the *Individual Safety Training Certificate*, *Initial Safety Training Certificate* and *Training Sign-In Sheet*, described in Table 74 on page 250, to document training sessions.
Does the law require me to provide PPE?	Only if other standards, such as those governing chemical use or certain types of machinery, require you to supply equipment to protect your employees. PPE includes items such as gloves, masks and special clothing used to protect against hazardous, toxic or infectious materials.

Table 65. Injury and Illness Prevention Plan *(continued)*

Question	Answer
Does the law require me to perform inspections?	Yes. You can choose the frequency, depending on how hazardous your work environment is.
Does the law require me to record and/or report anything?	Yes. Any injury that requires medical treatment beyond first aid and all occupational illnesses must be investigated, recorded and reported. You can use the *Accident, Injury and Illness Investigation* form described in Table 74 on page 250, to help you document the incident. For more information on knowing what to record and when, see "Reporting and Recording Work-Related Injuries and Illnesses" on page 240.

Legal Requirement

Every employer must have an IIPP. You may be exempt from some of the written recordkeeping requirements if you are an establishment:

- With fewer than 20 employees during the calendar year and in an industry not on the designated high hazard list and you have a workers' compensation Experience Modification Rate (ExMod) of 1.1 percent or less; or

- With fewer than 20 employees during the calendar year on a designated list of Low Hazard Industries.

If you fall into one of these two categories, you can limit written documentation of the IIPP to the following requirements:

- The identity of the person(s) with authority and responsibility for program implementation as required by Title 8 of the California Code of Regulations, section 3203(a)(1;)

- Scheduled periodic "inspections" to identify unsafe conditions and work practices as required by Title 8 of the California Code of Regulations, section 3203(a)(4); and

- Training and instruction provided to employees as required by Title 8 of the California Code of Regulations, section 3203(a)(7).

Local government entities are not required to keep records of the steps taken to implement and maintain their IIPPs. These include:

- Counties, cities and districts;

- Public or quasi-public corporations;

- Public agencies; and

- Any public entity, other than a state agency, that is a member of, or created by, a joint powers agreement.

Creating a Written Program

You can use the *Injury and Illness Prevention Program for Non-High Hazard Employers*, described in Table 74 on page 250, to help you get started with your written program.

Your plan must specify:

- Management approval of the plan and the person(s) responsible for implementing it;

- A company safety policy statement;

- A system to identify workplace hazards;

- A plan for periodic scheduled inspections;

- A plan for investigating injuries;

- A plan for safety training;

- How you will communicate with employees about safety; and

- The recordkeeping and posting requirements and any exceptions to these.

Emergency Action Plan

The Emergency Action Plan standard requires you to create and follow a plan for handling emergencies, including evacuating employees, providing emergency medical attention and reporting emergencies to employees and community agencies.

Table 66. Emergency Action Plan

Question	Answer
Does the law require me to comply with this standard?	Yes, every employer must have a program, but you are exempt from the written plan requirements if you employ 10 or fewer workers.
Does the law require me to create a written program?	Yes, if you have more than 10 employees. You can use the Emergency Action Plan, described in Table 74 on page 250, to help you document your program. Your plan must specify: • Person(s) responsible for implementing the plan or portions of the plan. • How to communicate emergencies to employees. • Fire and emergency evacuation policies. • Personnel assigned to provide first aid and emergency medical attention.
Does the law require that I provide training?	Yes, you must provide training. Train employees when you establish or change your plan, and when you hire new employees. Conduct emergency training and drills periodically. You can use the *Individual Safety Training Certificate, Initial Safety Training Certificate* and *Training Sign-In Sheet*, described in Table 74 on page 250, to document training sessions.
Does the law require me to provide PPE?	You must comply with blood-borne pathogens exposure regulations and exposure prevention requirements for any employee who provides emergency first aid, and you must provide any other equipment employees need to handle emergencies. See "Where Do I Go for More Information?" on page 266 for links to helpful websites.
Does the law require me to perform inspections?	The law does not require inspections, but you should cover this as part of your periodic IIPP inspections.
Does the law require me to record and/or report anything?	Recordkeeping is required for your IIPP, but not for the Emergency Action Plan. Follow those requirements in case of an incident.

Fire Prevention Plan

The Fire Prevention Plan standard requires you to know what fire hazards your employees are exposed to and to create and follow a plan for handling fires. For companies with more than 10 employees, the plan must be in writing.

Table 67. Fire Prevention Plan

Question	Answer
Does the law require me to comply with this standard?	Yes, every employer must have a plan.
Does the law require me to create a written program?	Yes, If you employ more than 10 employees. You can use the *Fire Prevention Plan*, described in Table 74 on page 250, to help you document your program. Your plan must specify: • Person(s) responsible for implementing the fire prevention program; • Known fire hazards in the area; • Your fire prevention practices; • What fire control measures you put in place (i.e. sprinkler systems); • The frequency of inspection and maintenance of fire control devices; • Alarm systems; and • Special employee responsibilities.
Does the law require that I provide training?	Yes. Train employees on fire prevention and safe work practices, either as part of your IIPP training or as a separate fire prevention program. You can use the *Individual Safety Training Certificate*, *Initial Safety Training Certificate* and *Training Sign-In Sheet*, described in Table 74 on page 250, to document training sessions.
Does the law require me to provide PPE?	No, PPE is not required. But standard fire protection equipment, such as fire extinguishers, sprinkler systems and alarms, is required.
Does the law require me to perform inspections?	Yes, inspections are required. Use the *Fire Prevention Checklist*, described in Table 74 on page 250, to help you determine what and when you should inspect.
Does the law require me to record and/or report anything?	Yes. Record employee training in fire prevention, and document periodic inspections and fire protection equipment maintenance.

Work Surfaces, Control Devices and Emergency Equipment

The Work Surfaces, Control Devices and Emergency Equipment standards cover employee-occupied areas and set minimum safety limits for lighting, flooring, housekeeping, entrances and exits.

Table 68. Work Surfaces, Control Devices and Emergency Equipment

Question	Answer
Does the law require me to comply with this standard?	Yes, every employer must comply with the standards. Use the *Safety Inspection for Work Spaces and Surfaces Checklist*, described in Table 16 on page 260, to help you comply.
Does the law require me to create a written program?	No. Include general information about potential hazards in your written IIPP.
Does the law require that I provide training?	Training is required only if you use engineered controls, such as guard rails. Include the training as part of your IIPP training.
Does the law require me to provide PPE?	Personal protective equipment is not required, unless another standard also applies, such as working with chemicals, projectiles or machinery.
Does the law require me to perform inspections?	Inspections are not required. IIPP inspections cover most situations.
Does the law require me to record and/or report anything?	Record employee training and document any inspections.

HAZCOM

The Hazard Communication Program (HAZCOM) standard requires all employers to communicate workplace hazards to employees, particularly when employees handle, or may be exposed to, hazardous substances during normal work or foreseeable emergencies.

Cal/OSHA modified the California HAZCOM standard to include:

- Revised criteria for classifying chemical hazards;

- Revised labeling provisions that include requirements for use of standardized signal words, pictograms, hazard statements and precautionary statements;

- A specified format for safety data sheets (previously referred to as "Material Safety Data Sheets");

- Revisions related to definitions of terms used in the standard; and

- Requirements for employee training on labels and safety data sheets.

Cal/OSHA made the modifications to the state standard because the federal OSHA made revisions to federal hazardous communications rules.

Manufacturers of designated cleaning products are required to disclose the chemicals in those products and create product safety data sheets. Designated cleaning products include general cleaning, air care, automotive, or polish or floor maintenance products used primarily for janitorial, industrial or domestic cleaning purposes. Employers must obtain information from manufacturers about the cleaning products and make those safety data sheets available.

Table 69. HAZCOM

Question	Answer
Does the law require me to comply with this standard?	All employers must comply, except in a few, limited situations. See "Where Do I Go for More Information?" on page 266 for a link to the federal Standard Industry Code (SIC) website.
Does the law require me to create a written program?	Yes. See "Creating a Written Program" on page 225 for details.
Does the law require that I provide training?	Yes. Train all new employees and provide refresher training when you receive new information on hazards and standards. New training is required whenever a new chemical hazard is introduced into the employees' work area.
	Employers must provide training on new labels and safety data sheets, as well as Proposition 65 warnings. You can use the Individual Safety Training Certificate and Training Sign-In Sheet, described in Table 16 on page 260, to document training sessions.
Does the law require me to provide PPE?	You are not required to provide personal protective equipment unless another standard, such as working with chemicals, projectiles or machinery, also applies.
Does the law require me to perform inspections?	Inspections are optional as long as you properly maintain all standard documents, such as safety data sheets, labels and warnings.
Does the law require me to record and/or report anything?	Yes, you must develop and maintain an inventory of all hazardous substances, and document employee training and compliance with the standard. Ensure that hazardous substances in the workplace have safety data sheets. You must document employee training and compliance with the standard.

Creating a Written Program

You are required to create a written program. Use the *Hazard Communication Program* form, described in Table 74 on page 250, to help you document the program.

You must explain how you will meet requirements for labeling hazardous substances and other forms of warning that you will provide to employees.

You must obtain and maintain safety data sheets from manufacturers for all labeled containers and items on your inventory of hazardous substances. Your suppliers must provide the safety data sheets.

Safety data sheets contain information provided by a product's manufacturer that describes the product's chemical properties, potential hazards and instruction in safe handling. Inspections are optional as long as you properly maintain all standard documents, such as safety data sheets, labels and warnings.

All labels will be required to have pictograms, a signal word, hazard and precautionary statements, the product identifier and supplier identification. Labels cannot be removed or defaced. A pictogram "quickcard" is currently available on this OSHA webpage at ***https://www.osha.gov/Publications/HazComm_QuickCard_Pictogram.html***.

Repetitive Motion Injuries (Ergonomics)

The Repetitive Motion Injuries Standard, commonly referred to as the Ergonomics Standard, requires employers to address workplace injuries due to repetitive motion hazards, which are work tasks that require repeated actions with the additional stress of improper ergonomics or work-station design.

 Ergonomics is the scientific study of the relationship between people and their work environments.

Table 70. Repetitive Motion Injuries

Question	Answer
Does the law require me to comply with this standard?	Yes, all employers must do what they can to prevent repetitive motion injuries (RMIs). See "Legal Requirement" on page 226for formal requirements.
Does the law require me to create a written program?	No, but a written procedure can assist you in properly implementing the standard. See "Creating a Written Program" on page 227 for details.

Table 70. Repetitive Motion Injuries

Question	Answer
Does the law require that I provide training?	You must provide initial training. But refresher training is not required. The standard itself specifies training program content and implementation. See the Office and Commercial Establishment Safety, Including Ergonomics and Office Chemical Safety form, described in Table 16 on page 260, for an example of the required training elements.
Does the law require me to provide PPE?	Only as a supplement to engineering controls (workstation redesign, adjustable fixtures, etc.) and administrative controls (job rotation and work pacing).
Does the law require me to perform inspections?	Yes, you need to evaluate a representative number of jobs, processes or operations for proper ergonomic design and to determine if they involve certain motions, positions or other bodily movements hazardous to muscles and joints.
Does the law require me to record and/or report anything?	Yes, you must keep records of all worksite evaluations conducted, control measures taken, training provided and Cal/OSHA *Form 300* reporting completed.

Legal Requirement

All employers must do what they can to prevent repetitive motion injuries (RMIs). The formal requirements of the standard apply only when:

- More than one employee suffers an RMI.

- The RMIs are musculoskeletal injuries diagnosed by a licensed physician.

- The RMIs were predominantly caused by a repetitive job, process or operation.

- The affected employees performed a job, process or operation of identical work activity.

- The reports of the two RMIs occurred within 12 months of each other.

Creating a Written Program

Employers are not required to create a written program. But a written procedure can assist you in properly implementing the standard. You can use the *Office and Commercial Establishment Safety, Including Ergonomics and Office Chemical Safety* form, described in Table 74 on page 250, as a guide. Your written program should describe:

- How the standard applies and step-by-step instructions for compliance;

- Any interim actions you will take to prevent RMIs;

- How you will verify the diagnosis of an RMI;

- How you will conduct worksite evaluations; and

- How to implement controls of RMI hazards.

Hotel Housekeeping Musculoskeletal Injury Prevention Program

The Hotel Housekeeping Musculoskeletal Injury Prevention Program requires employers in the hotel and lodging industry to establish, implement and maintain an effective, written musculoskeletal injury prevention program (MIPP) that addresses hazards specific to housekeeping. Musculoskeletal injuries are injuries of a muscle, tendon, ligament, bursa, peripheral nerve, joint, bone or spinal disc that can limit or prevent someone from working.

The written MIPP must be incorporated into the employer's written Injury and Illness Prevention Program, or may be maintained as a separate program.

The MIPP must include:

- Procedures to identify and evaluate housekeeping hazards through worksite evaluations;

- Procedures to investigate musculoskeletal injuries to housekeepers;

- Methods to correct identified hazards; and

- Training of employees and supervisors on safe practices and controls, and a process for early reporting of injuries to the employer.

When evaluating worksite hazards, investigating injuries and identifying corrective measures, input from the housekeepers and their union representatives is required.

More information can be found on the Cal/OSHA website at ***https://www.dir.ca.gov/dosh/dosh1.html***.

Heat Illness

Exposure to conditions of extreme heat and high humidity can subject employees to physical conditions that can range from inconvenient to life-threatening. Cal/OSHA's heat illness regulations apply to all outdoor places of employment. The heat illness prevention measures required by the regulation may be included in an employer's written IIPP, or in a separate document.

Employers subject to all provisions of the regulations, including the high-heat procedures, include agriculture, construction, landscaping, oil and gas extraction, and transportation or delivery of agricultural products, construction materials or other heavy materials.

Cal/OSHA revised the state's heat illness prevention standard. The revisions detail exactly what needs to be in an employer's heat illness prevention plan and include changes to:

- When employees must be permitted access to shade;

- What is considered "potable water" that must be made available to employees;

- The monitoring of employees taking a "preventative cool-down rest;" and

- High heat procedures.

 The revised heat illness regulations significantly change the obligations of employers with outdoor places of employment. Employers with outdoor workplaces will need to review their compliance obligations.

Cal/OSHA created a chart to provide guidance on the new requirements. The *Heat Illness Prevention Regulation Amendments Guidance* chart can be downloaded free of charge from HRCalifornia at **www.hrcalifornia.com** and from Cal/OSHA's heat illness information page at **www.dir.ca.gov/dosh/heatillnessinfo.html**. Cal/OSHA also updated its Heat Illness Prevention Enforcement Q&A webpage and revised educational materials on its website.

Employers with outdoor workforces are advised to review the guidance document and consult legal counsel with any questions.

 Cal/OSHA had until January 1, 2019, to propose a heat illness and injury prevention standard for indoor workplaces that equals or exceeds protections that already exist for outdoor workplaces. As of the time of publication, Cal/OSHA was preparing rulemaking documents, but final documents had not yet been released.

Employers with indoor workplaces that reach or exceed 80 degrees — which can include warehouses, restaurants, laundry operations, delivery drivers and many more

— are advised to keep apprised of Cal/OSHA's draft standard and consult legal counsel with any questions.

For updates on this standard, visit ***https://www.dir.ca.gov/dosh/doshreg/Heat-illness-prevention-indoors/.***

Providing Water

Employees must have access to potable drinking water meeting certain requirements. The water must be "fresh, pure, suitably cool, and provided to employees free of charge."

The water must be fit to drink and free from odors that would discourage workers from drinking the water. Containers provided to employees must be clean and water provided from non-approved, non-tested water sources (e.g. untested wells) is unacceptable, according to the guidance.

Where drinking water is not plumbed or otherwise continuously supplied, it must be provided in sufficient quantity at the beginning of the work shift to provide one quart per employee per hour for drinking for the entire shift.

Access to Shade

Shade is required to be present when the temperature exceeds 80 degrees Fahrenheit. The employer must maintain one or more shaded areas at all times while employees are present. These shaded areas must be open to the air or ventilated or cooled by other safe means.

The amount of shade must be enough to accommodate the number of employees on recovery or rest periods and those taking onsite meal breaks (the prior standard stated that the shade must accommodate at least 25 percent of the employees on the shift at any time).

Employees must be able to sit in a normal posture fully in the shade without physically touching other employees. The shaded area must be located as close as possible to the areas where employees are working.

When the outdoor temperature in the work area does not exceed 80 degrees Fahrenheit, employers must either provide shade as described in the preceding paragraph or provide timely access to shade upon an employee's request. Employees must be allowed and encouraged to take a cooldown rest in the shade when they feel the need to do so to protect themselves from overheating. Such access to shade must be permitted at all times.

Except for employers in the agricultural industry, cooling measures other than shade (e.g., use of misting machines) may be provided in lieu of shade if the employer can demonstrate that these measures are at least as effective as shade in allowing employees to cool.

Recovery Periods Protected

An employer with employees who work outside cannot require an employee to work during any "recovery period" taken to avoid heat-related illness, as required under Cal/OSHA's heat illness standard. A "recovery period" is defined as a "cooldown period afforded an employee to prevent heat illness."

A worker who takes a preventative cooldown rest must be monitored and asked if he/she is experiencing heat illness symptoms; must be encouraged to remain in the shade; and must not be ordered back to work until any sign or symptoms have abated, **but in no event less than five (5) minutes in addition to the time needed to access the shade**.

If an employee exhibits signs or reports symptoms of heat illness during the rest, the employer is required to provide first aid or emergency response. According to Cal/OSHA's guidance, first aid should be initiated without delay due to the fact that progression to more serious illness can be rapid. If heat illness is suspected, emergency medical personnel should be immediately contacted.

Employers must be aware of other "preventative cooldown rest periods" requirements, which are a separate set of requirements that apply to the high-heat procedures described in "High Heat Procedures."

An employer who does not provide an employee with a rest and recovery period must pay a one-hour-of-pay premium penalty for each day that the recovery period is not provided. This mirrors the meal and rest period requirements. Rest and recovery periods are paid breaks and count as hours worked.

High-Heat Procedures

Under the heat illness prevention standard, employers in the agriculture, construction, landscaping, oil and gas extraction, and certain transportation and delivery industries must implement high-heat procedures when temperatures equal or exceed 95 degrees.

These procedures must include the following, to the extent practicable:

1. Ensuring that effective communication by voice, observation or electronic means is maintained so that employees at the work site can contact a supervisor when necessary. An electronic device, such as a cell phone or text messaging device, may be used for this purpose only if reception in the area is reliable.

2. Observing employees for alertness and signs or symptoms of heat illness. Under the revised standard, employers are required to ensure effective employee observation and monitoring of signs or symptoms of heat illness. According to the guidelines, whichever method is used the employer must be able to ascertain the condition of employees at regular intervals. Under the regulations, the employer must implement one or more of the following:

   – Direct observation of 20 or fewer employees by a supervisor/designee;

   – Mandatory buddy system;

   – Regular communication with employees working alone; or

   – Other effective means of observation.

3. Designating one or more employees on each worksite as authorized to call for emergency medical services, and allowing other employees to call for emergency services when no designated employee is available.

4. Reminding employees throughout the work shift to drink plenty of water.

5. Holding pre-shift meetings before work begins to review high heat procedures, encourage employees to drink plenty of water and remind employees of their right to take a cool-down rest when necessary. This is a new obligation for covered employers. According to the guidance, the meetings are meant to briefly remind supervisors and employees of the high-heat procedures and not meant to review every element covered in the training. Topics to be covered include staying hydrated, taking cool-down rests, identifying employees who should call for emergency medical services, and how employees will be observed.

For employees employed in the agriculture industry, when temperatures reach 95 degrees or above, the employer must ensure that the employees take a minimum 10-minute preventative cooldown rest period every two hours.

Acclimatization

Acclimatization is a process by which the body adjusts to increased heat exposure. The body needs to adapt when working in hotter environments.

According to Cal/OSHA, employees are more likely to develop heat illness if they don't take it easy when a heat wave strikes or when starting a job that newly exposes them to heat. Most people are usually acclimated within four to 14 days of regular work involving at least two hours per day in the heat.

The revised heat illness standard sets new acclimatization procedures that apply to **all** outdoor places of employment. All employees must be closely observed by a supervisor during a "heat wave" — defined as any day in which the "predicted" high temperature will be at least 80 degrees and at least 10 degrees higher than the average high daily temperature in the preceding five days.

Employers are also required to be extra vigilant with new employees — close observation by a supervisor or designee is required for the first 14 days of employment.

Emergency Response Procedures

The heat illness standard contains more detailed requirements regarding emergency response procedures. Employers must implement effective emergency response procedures, including:

- Ensuring effective communication so that employees can contact a supervisor or emergency medical services when necessary;

- Responding to signs and symptoms of possible heat illness, including first aid measures and how emergency medical services will be provided;

- Implementing procedures for contacting emergency responders and, if necessary, transporting employees to a place where they can be reached by a medical provider; and

- Ensuring that clear and precise directions to the work site are available to be provided to emergency providers, when needed.

When signs or symptoms of heat illness appear, additional burdens on the employer apply:

- If a supervisor observes, or an employee reports, signs or symptoms of heat illness, the supervisor must take immediate action commensurate with the severity of the illness.

- If the signs and symptoms indicate severe heat illness (such as decreased consciousness, staggering, vomiting, disorientation, irrational behavior or convulsions) the employer must implement emergency response procedures.

- Any workers who display or report any signs or symptoms of heat illness must not be left alone or sent home without being offered on-site first aid or emergency medical services.

Employers are not required to provide medical personnel on site and supervisors and employees are not expected to have medical expertise.

Training Requirements

Employee training must be provided before an employee or supervisor begins outdoor work. Effective training in the following topics shall be provided to all supervisory and non-supervisory employees:

- The environmental and personal risk factors for heat illness, as well as the added burden of heat load on the body caused by exertion, clothing and personal protective equipment;

- The importance of frequently consuming small quantities of water, up to four cups per hour, when the work environment is hot and employees are likely to be sweating more than usual while performing their duties;

- The importance of acclimatization;

- The different types of heat illness and the common signs and symptoms of heat illness;

- The importance to employees of immediately reporting to the employer, directly or through the employee's supervisor, symptoms or signs of heat illness in themselves or in co-workers; and

- The employer's procedures for contacting emergency medical services, and if necessary, for transporting employees to a point where they can be reached by an emergency medical service provider.

Employers must ensure that workers are adequately trained on employer responsibilities and how to recognize and react to heat illness signs or symptoms, including appropriate first aid and/or emergency responses.

Training must be understood by employees and provided in a language the employees understand. Inspectors will look for indicators that the employer has made a good faith effort to communicate all the essential information to employees.

Supervisor Training

Before supervising employees working in the heat, the supervisor(s) must receive training on the following topics:

- The information required to be provided by employee training requirements above;

- The procedures the supervisor is to follow to implement the applicable provisions in this section;

- The procedures the supervisor is to follow when an employee exhibits symptoms consistent with possible heat illness, including emergency response procedures; and

- How to monitor weather reports and how to respond to hot weather advisories.

Employers must compile and maintain written procedures for:

- Employee training;

- Employer procedures for compliance;

- Employer procedures for responding to symptoms of possible heat illness; and

- Procedures for ensuring that, in the event of an emergency, directions to the worksite can be provided.

Employers must ensure that supervisors are adequately trained on employer responsibilities and how to recognize and react to heat illness signs or symptoms, including appropriate first aid and/or emergency responses.

Wildfire Smoke Regulation

On July 29, 2019, the California Occupational Safety and Health Standards Board's emergency regulation to protect outdoor workers from the harmful effects of wildfire smoke became effective. Under the new regulation, affected employers must take steps to protect workers who could be exposed to wildfire smoke.

Smoke Exposure Reduction Methods

Employers must monitor the Air Quality Index (AQI) at their worksites for fine particulate matter (PM 2.5). If the AQI for PM 2.5 is greater than 150 and the employer "reasonably anticipates" that employees will be exposed to wildfire smoke, then employers must reduce exposure to the smoke. You may do this in using one of two methods, depending on the worksite and conditions:

Table 71. Smoke Exposure Reduction Methods

Method	Definition
Engineering Control Method	Reduce workers' exposure to wildfire smoke by relocating them to enclosed buildings with filtered air.
Administrative Control Method	Reduce workers' exposure by relocating them to another outdoor location where the AQI for PM 2.5 is 150 or lower.

If it's not feasible to reduce smoke exposure using engineering or administrative control methods, then employers must give employees the option to use air respirators, such as N95s.

If the AQI exceeds 500, then respirator use is mandatory, and employers must also comply with burdensome respiratory protection requirements that include fit testing and medical evaluations.

Certain workplaces are exempt, but all employers with a worker who could spend a cumulative hour or more outside over the course of a shift — which could include employers whose employees are intermittently exposed to outside air — must comply with the regulation.

Even an employer with no outdoor employees should be cautious, as the regulation could also apply to high traffic indoor worksites such as restaurants or banks where doors are consistently opened and allow in outside air. Employers should consult with legal counsel to determine if they fall into an exemption.

Other Standards

In certain designated high-hazard industries, other specific Cal/OSHA standards may apply to your company. This table will help you determine which may apply.

Table 72. Other Standards

If Employees ...	This Standard Applies
May be exposed to an airborne contaminant.	Permissible Exposure Limits
Use or are exposed to a certain level or concentration of hazardous chemicals, such as lead, benzene, formaldehyde and other carcinogens.	Chemical Protection
Use any respirator, except for voluntary filtering dust masks.	Respiratory Protection
Are exposed to hazardous substances in a laboratory operation, except for test kits, and manufacturing and process simulations.	Exposure to Hazardous Substances in Laboratories
Are assigned to provide an emergency medical response, or may potentially be exposed to blood borne pathogens.	Blood Borne Pathogens
Must work in a facility that contains a confined space, such as a tunnel, underground storage tank or utility vault, that presents or contains a hazard.	Permit Required Confined Space Entry
May be exposed to hazardous machinery motion during normal operations or servicing.	Lockout/Tagout and Machinery Guarding
Operate a forklift or industrial truck, or if onsite materials are handled in volume.	Forklifts and Material Handling
Are exposed to noise averages over 85 dBA during a work shift.	Occupational Exposure to Noise
Are exposed to certain highly dangerous chemicals at or above the specified threshold quantities.	Process Safety Management (PSM) of Acutely Hazardous Materials (also known as the "Access Standard")
Lift/transfer patients in a health care facility.	Patient Protection and Health Care Worker Back and Musculoskeletal Injury Prevention Plan adopted as part of the IIPP. The plan must include a safe patient handling policy reflected in professional occupational safety guidelines for the protection of patients and health care workers in health care facilities.

For additional information on high-hazard industries, visit the Department of Industrial Relations (DIR) Model IIPP website at ***www.dir.ca.gov/dosh/dosh_publications/iiphihzemp.html***.

Creating a Written Program

Employers should consider establishing a plan or program for handling potentially dangerous situations. Know which safety standards apply to your organization and communicate these standards to your employees. Understanding the safety standards is essential to avoiding Cal/OSHA fines and preserving the safety of your employees and workplace.

When you create a written program, either for your IIPP or for any other standard, base it on processes and policies you put in place for your company. The following section guides you through the process of developing a written program.

Research and Prepare

Gather any existing documents you have that can help you fill in the information (such as a fire escape plan, local emergency contact information, safety data sheets or workplace violence policies).

Find out if Cal/OSHA considers your company to belong to a high-hazard industry. For general guidelines on high hazard employers, see the Cal/OSHA's Model IIPP website at ***www.dir.ca.gov/dosh/dosh_publications/iiphighhaz.html***.

Find out if Cal/OSHA considers your workplace to be at-risk for workplace violence. For workplace violence guidelines, visit Cal/OSHA's Workplace Security website at ***www.dir.ca.gov/dosh/dosh_publications/worksecurity.html***.

Identify lacking or missing processes or policies, and what else you need to implement. Create two levels of information; general and detailed. The general information will go in your IIPP and your employee handbook. The detailed information will go in the appropriate document for each specific standard.

Compile Information

Use the *Injury and Illness Prevention Program for Non-High Hazard Employers*, described in Table 74 on page 250, to create your IIPP and to determine what information you need to supply.

Keep in mind that your IIPP doesn't need to cover every detail. The IIPP is only an outline of your entire compliance plan.

Use the detailed information to complete the written programs for all other standards. Consider adding text for standards that don't require written programs to your employee handbook or safety manual.

Maintain the Plan

The easiest way to help your company avoid violations, injuries and lawsuits is to keep your compliance information up-to-date and to communicate changes to your employees.

Safety Training

Most Cal/OSHA standards require training, which is an effective way for you to keep employees informed of your policies and procedures. The regulations don't specify the type of training or the frequency. The following section describes the essentials of developing a training program.

Table 73. Safety Training

Question	Answer
Who?	Designate an internal or external resource qualified to provide training, based on the requirements of the standard. Remember that you must also provide training to independent contractors.
What?	Determine which standards require you to train your employees. You can also refer to the Cal/OSHA Training Requirements, described in Table 16 on page 260, for information on training requirements for all Cal/OSHA standards. ❗ Keep in mind that even when a particular standard doesn't require training, the IIPP often does. Compile all the subjects into a list to determine if you can combine subjects to cover multiple standards. You can use this list as a foundation for selecting your method of training.

Table 73. Safety Training

Question	Answer
When?	Provide the training: • To all new employees and existing employees who transfer to new positions; • After an incident or change of process (e.g., when you install new equipment or if you move certain operations to a new site); and • As an annual refresher.
How?	The method you use to provide training is up to you, depending on how complex the training needs to be, the number of employees you need to train and your budget. Keep in mind that supervisors may need separate training. In addition, always document the training employees receive to show your compliance with the IIPP and that you take safety seriously.

Providing Personal Protective Equipment to Employees

Providing PPE (for example, gloves, lead aprons, hard hats and keyboard wrist rests) to your employees, if required, helps prevent injuries and illnesses. Use the following guidelines to help you determine what your employees need to work safely.

1. Evaluate your workplace for the need for PPE. Consider all the jobs, processes and operations (day-to-day and emergency) employees will perform. Some examples of evaluation questions might be:

    • Do your employees handle, or are they exposed to, chemicals or blood borne pathogens?

    • Do your employees perform tasks that require the same bodily motions to be repeated?

    • Do your employees work in areas with falling items, flying projectiles or heavy machinery?

    • Do your employees lift heavy or cumbersome objects, or work in areas that require forceful exertion to perform tasks?

2. Document the situations that require your employees to use PPE, and identify which PPE items you will supply.

3. Provide and maintain PPE for all employees exposed to hazards.

4. Perform periodic inspections: Make sure the PPE is in good working order and is readily accessible, and verify that employees use PPE properly and consistently.

 You can't charge employees for the use and cost of PPE.

Reporting and Recording Work-Related Injuries and Illnesses

Recording and reporting work-related fatalities, injuries and illnesses are two separate processes required by Cal/OSHA's *Form 300* regulations. You don't always have to do both.

 To determine if you must comply with *Form 300* requirements, use CalChamber's Log 300 Wizard at ***https://hrcalifornia.calchamber.com/forms-tools/wizards/log300***.

Reporting includes notifying Cal/OSHA of a serious work-related injury or death. For more information, see ""Serious" Injury, Exposure Defined" on page 241. All employers must report fatal or serious incidents within eight hours of the incident or fatality. Report fatal or serious incidents to the Cal/OSHA district office nearest to your business. To find the nearest Cal/OSHA district office, go to this DIR website at ***www.dir.ca.gov/DOSH/DistrictOffices.htm***.

Recording involves creating and maintaining records of work-related injuries, both to keep documents as references, and to prepare in case an inspection requires you to present your records.

You are exempt from recording if you employ 10 or fewer staff or if your company is classified in a specific low hazard Standard Industry Code (SIC) category. SICs classify businesses by their primary activity, and get used for a variety of statistical purposes.

As of July 1, 2018, all affected employers must electronically submit injury and illness data in the federal OSHA Injury Tracking Application (ITA) online portal. For specific instructions, go to federal OSHA's ITA website at ***https://www.osha.gov/injuryreporting***.

Certain California employers must electronically submit their *Form 300A* information to a federal OSHA database annually, which is in compliance with federal OSHA requirements.

 Form 300A summary data is due by March 2 of the year after the calendar year covered by the forms, which means the data from 2019 is due March 2, 2020.

On January 25, 2019, federal OSHA issued a final rule amending the recordkeeping regulation, effective February 25, 2019. To protect worker privacy, OSHA rescinded the requirement for employers with 250 or more employees to electronically submit *Form 300* and *Form 301*. These establishments must still retain *Form 300* and *Form 301* records on-site, and OSHA will obtain them as needed through inspections and enforcement actions. On May 1, 2019 California adopted emergency regulations consistent with these federal regulations. Permanent regulations regarding Form 300A electronic submissions are still pending. Information on the status of the regulations can be found on the Cal/OSHA website at ***https://www.dir.ca.gov/dosh/calosha-updates/log300-reporting.html***.

"Serious" Injury, Exposure Defined

Effective January 1, 2020, the definitions of "serious injury" and "serious exposure" were changed to align with the federal Occupational Safety and Health Administration (OSHA) standards, effectively removing the requirement that inpatient hospitalization last at least 24 hours.

Under the new definition, a serious injury is a work-related incident that results in the:

- Death of an employee;

- Hospitalization of an employee for treatment other than observation; or

- Loss or serious disfigurement of any body part.

This means employers must report all inpatient hospitalizations, regardless of the length of stay.

"Serious exposure" is defined as exposure to a hazardous substance that has a "realistic possibility" of death or serious physical harm.

Reporting an Incident

You must submit incident reports in two situations:

- When an employee is seriously or fatally injured; and

- When you receive an annual survey form from the Bureau of Labor Statistics or a specific request from Cal/OSHA.

Effective January 1, 2020, California employers are required to immediately report a serious occupational injury, illness or death to the DIR either by telephone or through an online portal created by the DIR. Until the online portal is created, employers may continue to submit reports via email.

 California law mandates a fine of $5,000 for employers who don't report a serious injury or death. Individual employees serving in supervisory, management or similar roles may be individually liable for up to one year in jail and/or a $15,000 fine. Corporations face fines up to $150,000.

Employers' liability for workplace injury recordkeeping violations is five years. Cal/OSHA may issue citations for recordkeeping violations until violations are corrected or discovered by Cal/OSHA, or until any recordkeeping duty is eliminated — for up to the entire five-year mandatory record retention period.

Keeping Records

You must save the *Form 300* for five years after the end of the year the records cover.

During the storage period, you must update the *Form 300* to include newly discovered recordable injuries or illnesses and to show changes that occurred in the classification of previously recorded injuries and illnesses.

The *Form 300* is available in the forms download for this product.

Cal/OSHA

Cal/OSHA oversees the protection of workers from health and safety hazards on the job through its research and its standards, enforcement and consultation programs. Employers face inspections, citations and compliance schedules. A limited appeals process for employers is in place, but the best way to comply is simply to maintain a safe workplace.

The Cal/OSHA Inspection Process

Cal/OSHA inspections follow a process governed by the Labor Code and the Cal/OSHA Policy and Procedure Manual:

1. **Unannounced Inspections**. You receive no advance notice, except:

   • When apparent imminent danger requires prompt correction.

- To ensure availability of essential personnel or access to the site, equipment or specific process.

- When the Cal/OSHA chief or the chief's designee decides that giving advance notice would help achieve a thorough inspection.

2. **Opening conference**. The Cal/OSHA inspector presents credentials and provides the reason for the inspection to someone with the authority to consent to the inspection.

   You can ask for a postponement of the inspection but only for a good reason, such as:

   - All essential personnel are not available.

   - The inspector's credentials or the stated reasons for the inspection lack credibility.

   The inspector can obtain a search warrant if you refuse the inspection.

3. **Document request**. The inspector usually asks to review the following documents:

   - Cal/OSHA *Form 300* for the current year and for the five previous years.

   - Your written IIPP.

   - Any written programs required by a standard that your business must follow.

   - Codes of safe practice at a construction site.

   - A copy of any permit issued by Cal/OSHA.

4. **Walk-through**. The inspector conducts a walk-through of the premises subject to the inspection, accompanied by key personnel from your company.

   This can take the form of a wall-to-wall inspection or involve only the limited area defined by the inspector's represented reasons for the inspection (such as an employee complaint about the warehouse). It's good practice to restrict the inspector's access to the areas specifically designated for inspection.

   During a wall-to-wall inspection, the inspector may stop to examine machinery, interview employees and observe working situations. Your personnel accompanying the inspector may be asked to explain an operation or answer questions.

5. **Exit and closing conferences**. When the inspection is over, the inspector:

   - Summarizes the results of the inspection.

   - Makes any pertinent observations.

- Discusses findings and conclusions.

- Requests information, documents or further inspections.

If the inspector issues no citations, this is considered an exit conference and nothing else follows. If the inspection results in a citation or another action (such as a Special Order), the exit conference is followed by a formal closing conference, approximately one month after the issuance of any citations.

Reasons for Cal/OSHA Inspections

Cal/OSHA's inspection program targets workplaces with a likelihood of health and safety hazards and/or violations of standards. Due to constitutional limitations on government searches and seizures, the agency must have reasonable cause to conduct an inspection. However, court decisions have granted Cal/OSHA broad discretion in determining what is reasonable cause.

Cal/OSHA inspects when:

- An employer reports a fatality or serious injury or illness.

- An employee complains.

- The issuance of a permit requires a follow-up inspection.

- The Cal/OSHA general administrative plan calls for inspections for a certain type of employer (the targeted group shifts periodically based on injury/illness statistics for that industrial classification).

- An industry has been selected as part of the TICP.

- A Cal/OSHA inspector sees a violation from a location readily available to the general public or a casual observer.

The **TICP**, or Targeted Inspection and Consultation Program, is a Cal/OSHA program that identifies certain high-hazard employers and requires them to pay a fee to fund a special inspection unit. Cal/OSHA also offers other consultation services to help businesses avoid investigations and costly fines. You can find more information on these programs on this DIR website at *www.dir.ca.gov/dosh/consultation.html*.

Preparing for an Inspection

You should develop policies for handling an inspection, designate key personnel to participate, train them in procedures to follow and advise them on handling potential issues that may emerge as the inspection progresses. Your policy can be formal or informal but should cover the key phases of an inspection. See "The Cal/OSHA Inspection Process" on page 242.

To find resources that can help you develop these procedures, check out "Where Do I Go for More Information?" on page 255.

Penalties for Violations

You could receive a citation with civil penalties based on the violation's severity, extent, likelihood and size of your business. In addition to penalties for non-serious or minor violations, repeat or willful violations, serious violations, and failure to correct or abate a violation — all of which may increase annually based on the Consumer Price Index — you may also incur or receive:

- Substantial fines if you fail to report a fatal or serious incident. For details, see "Reporting an Incident" on page 241.

- A "Special Order" forcing you to remedy any unsafe condition, device or other workplace hazard to employee safety and health not covered by any existing standard. In a sense, this creates a special standard for you.

- A "Notice to Comply" if the violation is a general or regulatory offense and doesn't immediately relate to employee safety and health.

- An "Information Memorandum" to direct your attention to a workplace condition with the potential of becoming a hazard to the safety or health of employees.

- An "Order to Take Special Action" in situations where an unsafe workplace condition, covered by an existing standard, requires specific instruction.

- Cal/OSHA issuing an "Order Prohibiting Use" ("yellow tagging") when any condition, equipment or practice poses an imminent hazard to employees that could cause death or serious physical harm immediately or before you can eliminate the hazard.

Whatever the result of your violation, you must:

- Post the citation, order or notice of violation in a place where employees working nearby can easily read it.

- Correct the problem within a specified amount of time and notify Cal/OSHA of the correction.

Cal/OSHA can require an employer to abate (fix) serious workplace safety violations and can also issue civil penalties. An employer can appeal the citation.

In a 2018 case, the California Supreme Court expanded employer liability for workplace safety violations by permitting civil suits under the Business and Professions Code to proceed against employers who endanger worker health.

The Court also held that an employer may face a civil lawsuit and penalties due to alleged unfair and fraudulent business practices, as well as false and misleading statements intended to gain a competitive edge.

The state Occupational Safety and Health Appeals Board (OSHAB) is prohibited from modifying civil penalties for abatement or credit for abatement unless the employer:

- Fixed the violation at an initial inspection or a subsequent inspection prior to issuance of the citation; or

- Submitted a signed statement and supporting evidence within 10 working days after the date fixed for abatement showing that the violation has been fixed.

In cases of serious, repeat serious or willful serious violations, California law generally prohibits a stay or suspension of an abatement requirement while an appeal or petition for reconsideration is pending, unless the employer can demonstrate that a stay or suspension will not adversely affect the health and safety of employees.

Make sure to review the content of the citation or order for accuracy in terms of its statement of the violated standard's requirements, your observations of the inspection and your understanding of the inspector's findings.

If you object to the citation and can produce enough evidence, you can appeal. For more information, see "Appealing a Citation or Order" on page 247.

Appealing a Citation or Order

You can appeal to the OSHAB within 15 business days of receiving a citation or order.

How the Appeals Process Works

1. Because the time allotted to appeal is so short (15 business days), you should start the decision-making process immediately upon receiving an order or citation. You should identify issues that you can appeal, and consider:

   - The size of the penalty;

   - The cost and time allowed for correction, as compared to an appeal;

   - The potential for a repeat citation; and

   - Your likelihood of success, given the strength of your defenses.

2. Communicate your desire to appeal to the OSHAB by hand delivery, mail, fax or telephone.

   The OSHAB provides you with information on the appeal process and an appeal form. If you return the form within 10 business days, the appeal form is considered complete.

   After the appeal process begins, OSHAB's assignment of a docket number may take up to six months. When the docket number is issued, the OSHAB sends a copy of the form to you with a docket number and OSHAB stamp affixed.

 You must post a copy of the docketed appeal form at or near the site of the already posted citation. The posting must remain in place until the appeal hearing begins or you receive an order disposing of the appeal.

3. Since notification of docketing can be a lengthy process, begin preparing your defense for the hearing while the incident/inspection/facts are current and fresh.

   Hearings typically happen no more than six months from the docketing of the appeal. You can investigate Cal/OSHA's information by filing a discovery letter on the agency, with copies sent to the OSHAB and any other interested party. You can subpoena witnesses or physical evidence.

   You can't communicate with the OSHAB unless all parties to the appeal receive notification. You may serve a document on another party by personal delivery, first-class mail, overnight delivery or fax. You can do this by a declaration, a written statement or by a letter of transmittal.

4. You can request an informal conference.

   This meeting between you, your representatives, Cal/OSHA's district manager and the inspector responsible for the citation allows you to discuss any evidence in an attempt to resolve any disputes and avoid the need to continue with the appeal.

   District managers must hold the conference no more than 10 business days after issuing citations. If you already filed an appeal, the conference can occur any time up to the date of the hearing.

 You must notify employees of the conference, its date and location. The usual way to do this is to post this information near the already posted citation and a copy of the conference confirmation issued by Cal/OSHA.

   At this stage, the district manager, based on new evidence or a new interpretation, can withdraw or amend citations, including the existence of the violations, proposed penalties and correction methods and schedules.

5. If you don't reach a settlement, you will make your defense in an official hearing before an Administrative Law Judge (ALJ).

   At least 30 days prior to the hearing, the OSHAB will send the parties a notice of hearing, advising them of the location, date and time. A hearing is postponed only if an emergency arises, or if a party or witness has a pre-existing scheduling conflict. If either party fails to appear at the hearing, the OSHAB will send a notice of intent to dismiss. To reinstate the matter, the absent party must establish just cause within 10 business days for the failure to appear.

 You must notify employees of the pending hearing, usually by posting this information near the already posted citation.

6. At the close of the hearing, all the proceedings are considered submitted for decision. The ALJ summarizes the evidence received, makes findings and files a proposed decision along with his/her reasons for the decision within 30 business days of the hearing's close.

   The OSHAB may confirm, adopt, modify or set aside the proposed decision. The OSHAB then sends copies of its decision to each party. If no one files a petition for reconsideration, the decision is final and can't be reviewed by any court or agency.

7. Either party can take up to 30 business days to file a petition for reconsideration. The petition must set forth, specifically and in full detail, every issue to be considered by the OSHAB. Anything not raised in the petition is waived and can't be re-examined. If the OSHAB does not act upon a petition within 45 business days, the petition is considered denied.

Upon reconsideration, the OSHAB can make another decision or let the original one stand. If no one requests a judicial review, the decision is final.

8. Any party that disagrees with a decision after reconsideration or the denial of a petition must apply to the Superior Court for a writ of mandate within 30 business days of the OSHAB's decision or denial.

Minimum Compliance Elements

1. Hang your *2020 California and Federal Labor Law Poster* (available from *store.calchamber.com*), which includes mandatory postings and Cal/OSHA postings that all employees and applicants must be able to see, in a prominent place (such as a break room).

    If you have employees working in a city or county with a local minimum wage and/or paid sick leave ordinance, you may also need to post required local notices and provide additional notices to employees at the time of hire.

2. Create and follow an Injury and Illness Prevention Program (IIPP) (see "Injury and Illness Prevention Program" on page 218), and make sure your employees know about the workplace safety practices it covers (see "Basic Standards" on page 215).

Forms and Checklists

The following table describes forms and checklists associated with workplace safety.

 TIP You can find these forms in your forms download, described in detail in "Online Forms" on page 9.

Table 74. Forms and Checklists

Notice or Form	What Do I Use It For?	When Do I Use It?	Who Fills It Out?	Where Does It Go?
Accident, Injury and Illness Investigation	To help you document information about a workplace incident that involves an accident, injury or both.	As soon as possible after an incident occurs.	The employer.	If you don't have to report the incident, keep the document for at least one year (longer if you are documenting compliance). If you must record the incident on the *Form 300*, keep the document for five years.
Cal/OSHA Training Requirements	To determine which standards require you to provide safety training for your employees.	Use the form for reference when planning your safety training program.	No filling out needed.	Incorporate the information in the document into your training program.
Emergency Action Plan	To help you create a written plan for handling emergency situations, and to satisfy Cal/OSHA compliance.	Before your business opens, or as soon after as possible.	The employer.	Make the information in your plan available to your employees through training and in your employee handbook or safety manual. Keep and maintain the document as long as the company operates.

Table 74. Forms and Checklists *(continued)*

Notice or Form	What Do I Use It For?	When Do I Use It?	Who Fills It Out?	Where Does It Go?
Ergonomics Checklist - Computer and Keyboard Issues	As an inspection tool to help you identify potential ergonomic problems related to computers and keyboards.	Annually and as needed.	The employer.	N/A
Ergonomics Checklist - Hand Tool Use	As an inspection tool to help you identify potential ergonomic problems related to hand tool use.	Annually and as needed.	The employer.	N/A
Ergonomics Checklist - Manual Handling	As an inspection tool to help you identify potential ergonomic problems related to manual handling.	Annually and as needed.	The employer.	N/A
Ergonomics Checklist - Task-Work Methods	As an inspection tool to help you identify potential ergonomic problems related to task/work methods.	Annually and as needed.	The employer.	N/A
Ergonomics Checklist - Workstation Layout	As an inspection tool to help you identify potential ergonomic problems related to workstation layout.	Annually and as needed.	The employer.	N/A
Fire Prevention Checklist	To determine which fire hazards are present in your workplace so you can create and maintain a written plan for preventing and handling workplace fires.	Before your business opens, or as soon after as possible.	The employer.	Use the checklist as an inspection tool. Keep and maintain the document as long as the company operates.

Table 74. Forms and Checklists *(continued)*

Notice or Form	What Do I Use It For?	When Do I Use It?	Who Fills It Out?	Where Does It Go?
Fire Prevention Plan	To help you create a written plan for preventing and handling workplace fires and to satisfy Cal/OSHA standard compliance.	Before your business opens, or as soon after as possible.	The employer.	Make the information in your plan available to your employees through training and in your employee handbook or safety manual. Keep and maintain the document as long as the company operates.
Hazard Assessment and Correction Record	To document hazard identification and correction, and to assure compliance with applicable Cal/OSHA standards.	When an unsafe working condition is brought to your attention.	The employer.	In your files.
Hazard Communication Program	To document training provided to an employee and to satisfy Cal/OSHA standard compliance.	Before your business opens, or as soon after as possible.	The employer.	Make the information in your plan available to your employees through training and in your employee handbook or safety manual. Keep and maintain the document as long as the company operates.
Heat Illness Prevention Plan - Outdoor Employees	To develop your company's plan and procedures for complying with Cal/OSHA regulations on heat illness prevention for outdoor workers.	Before your business opens, or as soon after as possible.	The employer.	Make the information in your plan available to your employees through training and in your employee handbook or safety manual. Keep and maintain the document as long as the company operates.

Table 74. Forms and Checklists *(continued)*

Notice or Form	What Do I Use It For?	When Do I Use It?	Who Fills It Out?	Where Does It Go?
Initial Safety Training Certificate	To document the first training provided to an employee.	When you hire someone, reassign someone or identify a previously unknown hazard.	The employer.	Keep this document in the employee's personnel file. Provide a copy of this document to the employee if requested.
Individual Safety Training Certificate	To document training provided to an employee and to satisfy Cal/OSHA standard compliance.	When the employee successfully completes the training.	The employee.	Keep the certificate in the employee's personnel file. Provide a copy of the certificate to the employee if requested.
Injury and Illness Prevention Program for Non-High Hazard Employers	To outline your plan for compliance with all OSHA standards, including a detailed plan for: • Handling emergency situations; • Preventing and handling workplace fires; • Addressing ergonomic issues; and • Documenting information about workplace hazards.	Before your business opens, or as soon after as possible.	The employer.	Make the information in your plan available to your employees through training and in your employee handbook or safety manual. Keep and maintain the document as long as the company operates.
Office and Commercial Establishment Safety, Including Ergonomics and Office Chemical Safety	To identify and address office hazards.	Before your business opens, or as soon after as possible.	The employer.	Keep and maintain the document as long as the company operates.

Table 74. Forms and Checklists *(continued)*

Notice or Form	What Do I Use It For?	When Do I Use It?	Who Fills It Out?	Where Does It Go?
Safe Practices for Construction Workplaces - Sample Code	The sample code in this form was developed by the California Department of Occupational Safety and Health. It is a suggested code, general in nature and is intended as a basis for preparing a code that fits the specific contractor's operations more exactly.	Use this form to assist you in preparing a code of safe practices.	N/A	N/A
Safety Inspection for Work Spaces and Surfaces Checklist	To help you identify and prevent work space and surface hazards in your workplace and to satisfy Cal/OSHA standard compliance.	During periodic inspections, and after incidents or a change in process.	The employer.	Keep the checklist as a record of periodic inspections for five years after you fill it out.
Safety Program Self Audit Checklist	To help ensure that your workplace safety program complies with state requirements and is well tailored to reducing risks and claims in your workplace.	Before your business opens, or as soon after as possible.	The employer.	Keep and maintain the document as long as the company operates.
Training Sign-In Sheet	To record and track employee attendance at training courses.	Before or after completing a training course.	You prepare the form and employees sign it.	Keep the documents as proof that an employee attended mandatory training for five years after the training.

Table 74. Forms and Checklists *(continued)*

Notice or Form	What Do I Use It For?	When Do I Use It?	Who Fills It Out?	Where Does It Go?
Training Sign-In Sheet - Spanish	To record and track employee attendance at training courses.	Before or after completing a training course.	You prepare the form and employees sign it.	Keep the documents as proof that an employee attended mandatory training for five years after the training.
Worker Training and Instruction Record	To document and track all training provided to an employee.	Whenever an employee attends or completes training.	The employer.	Maintain in your training files and a copy in the employee's personnel file.

Where Do I Go for More Information?

CalChamber and federal and state government agencies offer a variety of resources to help you ensure safety in your workplace.

Table 75. Additional Resources

For Information On	Check Out These Resources
General	From CalChamber: • **store.calchamber.com** • **HRCalifornia.com**
Workers' Compensation	From CalChamber: • **2020 California Labor Law Digest**

Table 75. Additional Resources *(continued)*

For Information On	Check Out These Resources
State Government	• California Department of Industrial Relations at ***www.dir.ca.gov*** • California Division of Occupational Safety and Health at ***www.dir.ca.gov/DOSH/dosh1.html*** • California's Occupational Safety and Health Standards Board at ***www.dir.ca.gov/oshsb/oshsb.html*** • Model Injury and Illness Prevention Program for High Hazard Employers at ***www.dir.ca.gov/dosh/dosh_publications/iiphighhaz.html*** • Cal/OSHA Guidelines for Workplace Security at ***www.dir.ca.gov/dosh/dosh_publications/worksecurity.html*** User's Guide to Cal/OSHA at ***http://www.dir.ca.gov/dosh/dosh_publications/osha_userguide.pdf*** • For contact information for various Cal/OSHA offices, see the *Cal/OSHA Poster* (located in the ***2020 California and Federal Labor Law Poster*** and the ***Required Notices Kit with Poster***) • HAZCOM regulations; ***www.dir.ca.gov/title8/5194.html*** • Repetitive motion (ergonomics); ***www.dir.ca.gov/title8/5110.html*** • *Form 300/300A* at ***www.dir.ca.gov/dosh/dosh_publications/RecKeepOverview.pdf***
Federal Government	OSHA's SIC manual at ***www.osha.gov/pls/imis/sic_manual.html***

CalChamber also provides many ongoing and comprehensive educational opportunities for small business owners, HR beginners and experienced HR professionals alike. These include safety posters and special HR seminars and webinars. For more information, please visit the CalChamber website at ***store.calchamber.com***.

Chapter 7

Discrimination

Employment discrimination happens in many ways, some of which may not be intentional. For example, a supervisor doesn't usually decide to overlook a person for promotion because of the person's race or gender. But certain acts can constitute unlawful discrimination due to their effect, regardless of their motivation. You can begin to protect yourself by understanding discrimination, taking steps to avoid situations that would inspire lawsuits and by knowing how to handle complaints when they do arise.

In this chapter, you can find answers to questions about:

- Protected classes.
- The Americans with Disabilities Act (ADA).
- California's Fair Employment and Housing Act (FEHA).

Discrimination

The word "discrimination" is often used as a synonym for anything an employee may personally believe is unfair. In employment law, however, the word "discrimination" is more narrowly defined.

Discrimination, legally speaking, covers only actions taken against people because they belong to certain protected classes as outlined in applicable state and federal laws. See "Protected Characteristics and Activities" on page 261.

Discrimination means treating those people differently, and disadvantageously, compared with other people not in the same class. Remember, everyone is part of a protected class because everyone belongs to a race, has a marital status, is perceived as one gender or another, and associates with people in protected classes.

Discrimination can occur in two ways:

Table 76. Disparate Treatment vs. Impact

Type	Definition
Disparate (unequal) treatment	When an employee or applicant is treated differently, specifically because of that individual's protected class status.
Disparate (unequal) impact	An employment practice that appears neutral on its face but discriminates against protected classes in practice (for example, height and weight requirements may unequally impact women).

Discrimination Laws Overview

Several state and federal laws prohibit employment discrimination.

California's Fair Employment and Housing Act (FEHA) prohibits discrimination against employees and applicants on the basis of race or color, religious creed, national origin or ancestry, physical disability, mental disability, medical condition, genetic information, marital status, sex (including pregnancy, childbirth, breastfeeding or related medical condition), gender, gender identity, gender expression, age (40 plus), military and veteran status, and sexual orientation. Retaliating against individuals for asserting rights under these laws is also prohibited.

FEHA further requires reasonable accommodation of an employee's religion and/or disability, absent an undue hardship.

 You are covered by FEHA's anti-discrimination protections and reasonable accommodation obligations if you employ, or have employed, five or more individuals during 20 or more calendar weeks within the calendar year preceding an alleged violation of FEHA.

 California's anti-harassment laws cover **all employers** who regularly employ one or more people or regularly receive services of one or more independent contractors. For more information, see Chapter 8, "Preventing Harassment."

California also has several other laws, such as whistleblower laws, immigration protections, workers' compensation protections and the California Fair Pay Act, that cover all employers.

Several federal laws also prohibit discrimination. The following federal laws apply if you have 15 or more employees:

- Title VII of the Civil Rights Act prohibits discrimination against applicants and employees on the basis of race, color, religion, sex, or national origin.

- The Pregnancy Discrimination Act prohibits discrimination on the basis of pregnancy, childbirth or related medical conditions.

- The Americans with Disabilities Act prevents discrimination against the disabled and requires reasonable accommodation.

- The Genetic Information Nondiscrimination Act (GINA) prohibits discrimination on the basis of Genetic Information.

 The federal Age Discrimination in Employment Act prohibits employment discrimination against persons 40 years of age or older.

 California law covers more employers and provides more protections than federal law. Take steps to prevent both discrimination and harassment in your workplace.

Discrimination and Employment Practices

You commit a discriminatory employment practice if you, among other things:

- Base any employment decision regarding hiring, benefits, promotion or discipline in whole or in part on an individual's protected class status.

- Rely on stereotypes about the competence, appearance, health, interest or qualifications of individuals in protected classes.

- Engage in any employment practice that adversely impacts the hiring, training, classification, promotion or retention opportunities of individuals in a protected class.

- Engage in, or permit your employees to engage in, harassment of any member of any protected class.

- Act on the perception or assumption of a disability without evaluating the individual's fitness for the job.

- Retaliate against an employee, applicant or independent contractor for opposing sexual harassment or other unlawful discrimination, or for filing a complaint, testifying, assisting or participating in an investigation, proceeding or hearing, etc.

- Refuse to honor an otherwise eligible employee's request for pregnancy disability leave, leave under the New Parent Leave Act, or leave under CFRA or FMLA (see "Glossary of Terms, Laws and Agencies" on page 339 for more details).

- Refuse to reasonably accommodate disabilities, religious requirements, etc.

Retaliation

Both federal and state laws protect employees and applicants from employer retaliation for engaging in activity that's protected by anti-discrimination laws. Retaliation claims consistently top the list of workplace discrimination charges filed against employers.

California law defines retaliation as any adverse employment action taken against an individual who opposed a legally prohibited practice or who filed a complaint, testified, assisted or participated in an investigation or proceeding conducted by California's Department of Fair Employment and Housing or by the federal Equal Employment Opportunity Commission (EEOC).

Government agencies and the courts will look for a causal link between the protected activity and the adverse action. Timing is everything. If retaliation is established, you will have to show the legitimate, nondiscriminatory business reason for the adverse action.

Federal and California law protects applicants and employees from retaliation. California law also protects unpaid interns and volunteers.

Protected Characteristics and Activities

You may not discriminate against persons because they belong to certain protected classes. In addition, California's FEHA protects not only actual membership in the classes that FEHA specifies, but also perceived membership in one or more of those classes. For example, individuals could file a sexual orientation discrimination charge claiming they were discriminated against because they were perceived as homosexual even if they are not, in fact, homosexual. You may not discriminate against a person on the basis of:

Table 77. Protected Characteristics at a Glance

Characteristic	Discrimination
Age	Be careful how you treat employees over the age of 40. For specific things to avoid, turn to page 263.
AIDS/HIV+ Status	These conditions are considered protected disabilities. Turn to page 263 for activities to avoid.
Disability	You can't discriminate against a disabled person or someone you perceive to be disabled. For more information, turn to page 263.
Gender	You can't discriminate or allow harassment on the basis of gender. For additional details, including pay and gender and transgender employees in the workplace, turn to page 264.
Genetic Information/ Genetic Characteristics	Different levels of protection exist for a person's genetic information/ genetic characteristics based on state and federal law. For those details, turn to page 266.
Height/Weight	You can't establish height and weight standards unless you can show that such restrictions relate directly to, and are an essential function of, the job. Turn to page 267for details.
Immigration Status	Many state laws affect immigrants. For information about those laws, including retaliation and unfair immigration practices, and license revocation and criminal extortion for threatening to report immigration status, see page 267.
Language	You can't base personnel actions on a person's accent or English proficiency except in specific circumstances. For details, turn to page 269.
Lawful, Off-Duty Conduct	You can't discriminate against applicants or employees for lawful conduct they engage in during nonworking hours away from the company premises. For more details, turn to page 270.
Marital Status	This is an individual's state of marriage, non-marriage, divorce or dissolution, separation, widowhood, annulment or other marital status. For further information, see page 270.

Table 77. Protected Characteristics at a Glance *(continued)*

Characteristic	Discrimination
Medical Condition	You can't base employment decisions on an employee's or applicant's medical condition. See page 271 for more details.
National Origin	You can't discriminate against applicants and employees based on their national origin. For details, turn to page 271.
Pregnancy	You can't discriminate in any way against an employee due to that employee's pregnancy, perceived pregnancy, or potential to become pregnant. For additional details, turn to page 272.
Race/Color	You can't base employment decisions on an employee's or applicant's race. **New** Effective January 1, 2020, the law expands the definition of "race" to prohibit discrimination against employees based on their natural hairstyles. This includes "traits historically associated with race, including, but not limited to, hair texture and protective hairstyles," such as "braids, locks, and twists."
Religion	California's FEHA protects employees against religious discrimination. For details, turn to page 274.
Sex	You can't base employment decisions on an employee's or applicant's sex or gender. Turn to page 274 for details.
Sexual Orientation	Employees in California are protected from employment discrimination based on their actual or perceived sexual orientation. For more information, turn to page 275.
Union Membership	Employees enjoy the right to organize and form unions. Consult with counsel when working with unions.
Unpaid Interns, Volunteers, Apprentices	Discrimination against unpaid interns, volunteers, apprentices or individuals participating in unpaid work experience is prohibited.
Veteran Status	You can't base employment decisions on an employee's or applicant's status as a veteran. See page 275 for details.
Whistleblower	Several protections exist for whistleblowers. Turn to page 276 for details.

Age

You may not:

- Use age as a consideration for employment decisions, unless it is a bona fide occupational qualification (BFOQ).

- Discriminate against someone who opposed, filed a charge against, testified or participated in an investigation of unlawful employment practice under the Age Discrimination in Employment Act (ADEA) (see "Glossary of Terms, Laws and Agencies" on page 339 for more information on the ADEA).

- Place an employment notice or advertisement indicating a preference, limitation or specification based on age, unless it is a BFOQ.

- Terminate employees based on salary if the terminations create a disproportionate impact on older workers.

- Force employees to retire because they reached a certain age.

- Discriminate on the basis of age with regard to the terms, conditions or privileges of employment; for example, denying an employee aged 40 or over the educational opportunities that you give to younger employees.

AIDS/HIV+ Status

These conditions are considered protected disabilities. You may not:

- Use blood tests as a condition of employment or to determine insurability.

- Terminate, deny insurance coverage or refuse to hire individuals exposed to the AIDS virus.

 There may be limited exceptions in the medical field.

Disability

You can't discriminate against a disabled person or someone you perceive to be disabled. You may face serious consequences if you discriminate against persons with disabilities in your employment decisions, or if you fail to make reasonable accommodation for an applicant's or employee's disability.

Federal and state laws create significant protections for people with disabilities. The federal Americans with Disabilities Act (ADA) covers employers with 15 or more employees, and California's FEHA covers employers with five or more employees.

For more information about the ADA, FEHA and how disabilities are defined, see "Disability Discrimination" on page 277.

 In California, a **disability** is a physical or mental impairment that limits one or more of the major life activities.

Gender

You can't discriminate or allow harassment based on gender, which is defined as an individual's actual sex or as the employer's perception of that individual's sex. This includes your perception of an employee's/applicant's identity, appearance or behavior, regardless of whether that identity, appearance or behavior is different from the sex associated with the employee/applicant at birth.

"Gender" includes both "gender identity" and "gender expression," and discrimination on either basis is prohibited.

Table 78. Gender Identity vs. Expression

Term	Definition
Gender Identity	A person's identification as male, female or a gender different from the person's sex at birth; it specifically includes transgender persons.
Gender Expression	A person's gender-related appearance or behavior, whether or not stereotypically associated with the person's assigned sex at birth.

Laws relating to gender-based discrimination do not affect the employer's ability to require an employee to adhere to reasonable workplace appearance, grooming and dress standards. But, employers must allow an employee to appear or dress consistently with the employee's gender identity or gender expression.

Transgender Employees in the Workplace

Transgender employees are specifically protected under the FEHA gender identity protections. Transgender is a "general term that refers to a person whose gender identity differs from the person's sex assigned at birth. A transgender person may or may not have a gender expression (meaning a person's gender-related appearance or behavior regardless of person's sex at birth) that is different from the social expectations of the sex assigned at birth."

The FEHA prohibits discrimination against applicants and employees on the basis of gender expression or gender identity, or because an individual is transgender, is transitioning, has transitioned or is perceived to be transitioning.

Employers are generally prohibited from asking questions that identify an individual on the basis of sex, gender, gender identity or gender expression, and may not require individuals to provide proof of sex, gender, gender identity or gender expression.

You must honor an employee's request to be referred to by a particular name, gender or pronoun, including gender-neutral pronouns. You can use the gender or legal name that appears on an employee's government-issued identification document only if necessary to meet a legally mandated obligation.

You must provide all employees with safe, comparable and adequate facilities without regard to the sex of employees. An employee must be allowed to use the facility that corresponds to the employee's gender identity or gender expression. You cannot require an employee to use a particular facility, such as a unisex or single-user restroom. If you have single-user facilities, such as restrooms, you must have gender-neutral signs.

In addition, all single-user toilet facilities in any business establishment, place of public accommodation or government agency must be identified as "all-gender" toilet facilities.

For additional guidance on how to address this sensitive workplace topic, employers can refer to the U.S. Occupational Safety and Health Administration's *A Guide to Restroom Access for Transgender Workers* at ***https://www.osha.gov/Publications/ OSHA3795.pdf***, which the agency developed in alliance with the National Center for Transgender Equality.

In addition, the DFEH has prepared *Transgender Rights in the Workplace* which can be found at ***www.dfeh.ca.gov/wp-content/uploads/sites/32/2017/11/DFEH_E04P-ENG-2017Nov.pdf***.

Pay and Gender

Under California's Fair Pay Act, employers are prohibited from paying any employees less than employees of another gender, race or ethnicity for "substantially similar work."

In addition, a person's prior salary cannot justify any disparity in compensation.

Employers are prohibited from asking about a job applicant's salary history, and may not rely on salary history information as a factor in determining hiring and compensation decisions. For more information, see "Salary History Questions Prohibited" on page 20.

Genetic Information/Genetic Characteristics

State and federal law create different levels of protection for a person's genetic information/genetic characteristics.

State Law (Genetic Information)

Under California's FEHA, employers are prohibited from discriminating against employees on the basis of genetic characteristics and genetic information. This means information about any of the following:

- The individual's genetic tests;

- The genetic tests of family members of the individual; or

- The manifestation of a disease or disorder in the individual's family members.

Genetic information includes any request for, or receipt of, genetic services, or participation in clinical research that includes genetic services, by an individual or any family member of the individual. Genetic information does not include information about the sex or age of any individual.

Federal Law (Genetic Characteristics)

Genetic characteristics means any inherited characteristic or scientifically or medically identifiable gene or chromosome or combination or alteration thereof known to be a cause or increase the risk of a disease or disorder in a person or that person's offspring.

GINA prohibits use of genetic information to make decisions about health insurance and employment, and restricts the acquisition and disclosure of genetic information.

GINA generally prohibits employers from requesting, requiring, or purchasing an applicant's or employee's genetic information, even if the employer never uses that information.

According to the EEOC, "genetic information" includes:

- Information about an individual's genetic tests;

- Information about the genetic tests of a family member;

- Family medical history;

- Requests for, and receipt of, genetic services by an individual or a family member; and

- Genetic information about a fetus carried by an individual or family member, or about an embryo legally held by the individual or family member using assisted reproductive technology.

The EEOC published detailed information on GINA and its final regulations on its website at *www.eeoc.gov/laws/types/genetic.cfm*.

Height/Weight

Height and weight standards are prohibited unless you can show that such restrictions are relate directly to, and an essential function of, the job. In addition, height and weight standards can be a form of national origin discrimination if they have an adverse impact on individuals based on their national origin.

Severe obesity may also be a protected disability under the Americans with Disabilities Act or FEHA.

Immigration Status

State law includes protections that address retaliation against immigrant workers who complain about unfair wages or working conditions. All California workers, regardless of whether they are authorized to work in the United States, are protected by California's labor and employment laws.

California law clarifies that these protections extend to child workers. California law pre-empts federal immigration laws protecting immigrant workers and guarantees their access to the same California employment laws as legally authorized workers.

Retaliation and Unfair Immigration Practices

Employers are prohibited from engaging in "unfair immigration-related practices" when an employee asserts protected rights under the Labor Code.

Employers cannot use immigration law to retaliate against employees who exercise their employee rights. An "unfair immigration related practice" includes the following actions when taken for retaliatory purposes:

- Requesting more or different documents than are required under federal immigration law, or refusing to honor documents tendered pursuant to federal law that, on their face, reasonably appear to be genuine.

- Using the federal E-Verify system to check the employment authorization status of a person at a time or in a manner not required under federal law or not authorized under any memorandum of understanding governing the use of the federal E-Verify system.

- Threatening to file or the filing of a false police report.

- Threatening to contact or contacting immigration authorities because employees complained that they were paid less than the minimum wage.

The definition of an unfair immigration-related practice is expanded to include threatening to file or filing a false report or complaint with any state or federal agency.

In addition, an employer cannot discriminate, retaliate or take adverse action against employees who update their personal information based on a lawful change of name, Social Security number, or federal employment authorization document.

Employers who engage in unfair immigration-related practices will face various penalties, including an employee's right to bring a civil action and potential suspension of certain business licenses.

 Workers in California are entitled to the protections of the state Labor Code regardless of whether they are legally authorized to work in the United States. If you hire unauthorized employees, you must pay them and follow the state labor laws.

License Revocation for Threatening to Report Immigration Status

The state may suspend or revoke an employer's business license where that employer reports, or threatens to report, the immigration status of any employee because the employee makes a complaint about employment issues. It also allows for disbarment of attorneys for similar conduct against witnesses or parties in a lawsuit.

This covers reports, or threats to report, employees, former employees, prospective employees or family members, as defined, to immigration authorities. Employers are not subject to the suspension or revocation of a business license for requiring a worker to verify eligibility for employment under the *Form I-9*. For more information on the *Form I-9*, see "Completing the Form I-9" in Chapter 2, page 44.

Criminal Extortion for Threatening to Report Immigration Status

A person may be guilty of criminal extortion if the person threatens to report the immigration status or suspected immigration status of individuals, or their relative or a member of their family.

Language

You can't make employment decisions based on an applicant's or employee's accent unless you can prove that the person's accent interferes materially with that individual's ability to perform the job. You also can't discriminate against an applicant or employee because of the person's English proficiency unless the English proficiency requirement is justified by business necessity.

Language restriction policies, such as English-only policies, are unlawful unless you can show that:

- There is a business necessity for the language restriction;

- The language restriction is narrowly tailored; and

- You have effectively notified employees of the circumstances and time when the language restriction must be observed and of the consequence for violating the restriction.

"Business necessity" means:

- The language restriction is necessary to the safe and efficient operation of the business;

- The language restriction effectively fulfills the business purpose it is supposed to serve; and

- There is no alternative practice to the language restriction that would accomplish the business purpose equally well with a lesser discriminatory impact.

A language restriction that merely promotes business convenience or is based on customer or co-worker preference won't meet the business necessity requirement.

 In addition, you can never require English-only policies during employees' non-work time, such as meal and rest breaks, and unpaid employer-sponsored events.

Lawful, Off-Duty Conduct

You can't discriminate against applicants or employees for lawful conduct they engage in during nonworking hours away from the company premises, including:

- Exercising free speech rights;

- Engaging in political activity;

- Reporting information to the government;

- Moonlighting (working a second job for a different employer); and

- Engaging in conduct you feel to be morally in conflict with your business.

Marital Status

This is an individual's state of marriage, non-marriage, divorce or dissolution, separation, widowhood, annulment or other marital status.

California recognizes same-sex marriages as lawful. In addition, the United States Supreme Court has ruled that it is unlawful to exclude same-sex spouses from the definition of "spouse" under federal law. Employers may not discriminate against an employee in a same-sex marriage.

If you employ even one person, you can't condition benefits or employment decisions on whether the employee is considered a "principal wage earner" or "head of household." You also can't use job responsibilities, such as travel or customer entertainment, as justification for discrimination. You can't impose a "no employment of spouses" rule, but you can establish a policy that outlines how you situate spouses within the company.

State law also prohibits discrimination and/or harassment based on a person's status as a registered domestic partner. California law defines domestic partners as "two adults who have chosen to share one another's lives in an intimate and committed relationship of mutual caring." To become registered domestic partners, each person in the partnership must file a form with the California Secretary of State, as well as meet additional criteria available in California Family Code section 297.

In July 2019, California expanded the domestic partnership criteria to let any straight couple register, an option that previously was only available to same-sex couples or straight couples who were over the age of 62.

State law gives registered domestic partners the same rights as spouses. Conversely, you can't discriminate against someone based on marital status in favor of another person who is in a registered domestic partner relationship.

Medical Condition

This includes any health impairment related to or associated with a diagnosis of a health impairment such as cancer, or a record or history of any health impairment, as well as an individual's genetic characteristics. See "Genetic Information/Genetic Characteristics" on page 266.

If you employ even one person, you can't base employment decisions on an employee's or applicant's medical condition or request any sort of medical examination until after you make an offer of employment.

National Origin

Title VII and the FEHA prohibit employers from discriminating against applicants and employees based on national origin. Under the FEHA, the broad definition of national origin includes, but is not limited to, an individual's or the individual's ancestors' actual or perceived:

- Physical, cultural or linguistic characteristics associated with a national origin group;

- Marriage to or association with persons of a national origin group;

- Tribal affiliation;

- Membership in or association with an organization identified with or seeking to promote the interests of a national origin group;

- Attendance or participation in schools, churches, temples, mosques or other religious institutions generally used by persons of a national origin group; and

- Name associated with a national origin group.

 You can't base employment decisions on an employee's or applicant's national origin.

The FEHA also specifies that an employer discriminating against individuals because they hold or present a driver's license granted under section 12801.9 of the Vehicle Code (so-called AB 60 licenses) is a form of national origin discrimination. For more information, see "California Driver's License" in Chapter 2, page 49.

Pregnancy

You can't discriminate in any way against an employee due to that employee's pregnancy, perceived pregnancy, or potential to become pregnant.

The federal Pregnancy Discrimination Act requires that you treat a pregnant employee the same as any other employee. When an employee becomes unable to work due to pregnancy, childbirth or related medical conditions, you must treat that disability the same as any other disability.

California's FEHA prohibits employment discrimination on the basis of pregnancy, childbirth, breastfeeding or related medical condition. Employers must also provide up to four months of pregnancy disability leave (PDL) to an employee who is "disabled by pregnancy."

 Pregnancy leave does not need to be taken in one continuous period of time. Employees are eligible for up to four months of leave per pregnancy, not per year. For more information, see "Pregnancy Disability Leave" in Chapter 3, page 93.

Lactation Accommodation - Expressing Breast Milk at Work

Both California and federal law require all employers to reasonably accommodate employees who want to express breast milk at work, including to provide a private place and a reasonable amount of break time for employees to express milk.

 Effective January 1, 2020, California law expands lactation accommodation requirements. In addition to requiring that employers provide a location for lactation accommodation other than a bathroom, the room itself must:

- Be in close proximity to the employee's work area, shielded from view, and free from intrusion;

- Be safe, clean and free of toxic or hazardous materials;

- Contain a surface to place a breast pump and other personal items;

- Contain seating; and

- Have access to electricity.

Employers also must provide access to a sink with running water and a refrigerator suitable for storing breast milk close to the employee's workspace. The new law also requires employers to create and implement a lactation accommodation policy, including publishing the policy in the employee handbook and providing the policy when an employee asks about or requests parental leave.

The employee's normal work area can be used if it meets all the requirements above.

 Employers with fewer than 50 employees may be eligible for an undue hardship exemption regarding the lactation accommodation location. The employer must demonstrate that finding a location other than a bathroom is an undue hardship due to the size, nature or structure of the employer's business. If the employer successfully demonstrates an undue hardship, the employer must make reasonable efforts to provide a private and close location other than a toilet stall.

While there is no requirement that an employer provide a permanent location designated solely for lactation accommodation by its employees, if a temporary location is used, it's subject to the following requirements:

- The employer must be unable to provide a permanent lactation location because of operational, financial or space limitations;

- The temporary location must be private and free from intrusion while an employee expresses milk;

- The temporary location must be used only for lactation purposes while an employee expresses milk; and

- The temporary location must otherwise meet the requirements of state law concerning lactation accommodation.

An agricultural employer may comply with the lactation accommodation requirement by providing an employee with a private, enclosed and shaded space to express milk, such as the air-conditioned cab of a truck or tractor.

Employees can be required to use the paid rest break time you have already provided to express milk. If the employee needs a reasonable amount of additional time beyond the normal paid rest breaks for expressing milk, the time must be provided, but it can be unpaid. Employees can also choose to use lunch break time to express breast milk, but this does not relieve you of your responsibility to provide reasonable time in addition to rest breaks.

The Labor Commissioner may issue a citation if you violate this law, subjecting you to a civil penalty of $100 for each violation.

 There are limited circumstances under state and federal law when an employer may be able to deny a lactation accommodation on undue hardship grounds. However, consult legal counsel before you deny a lactation accommodation request.

Local ordinances may also impose requirements related to lactation accommodation.

Employers should also be aware that the definition of "sex" under the state Fair Employment and Housing Act includes breastfeeding and medical conditions related to breastfeeding. Employers are prohibited from discriminating against employees or job applicants because of breastfeeding and related medical conditions.

Religion

California's FEHA protects employees against religious discrimination. The FEHA also sets forth religious accommodation requirements for employers.

All aspects of religion, religious belief, observance and practice, including dress and grooming practices, are protected:

- "Religious dress practice" is construed broadly to include the wearing or carrying of religious clothing, head or face coverings, jewelry, artifacts, and any other item that is part of the observance by an individual of his or her religious creed.

- "Religious grooming practice" includes all forms of head, facial and body hair that are part of individuals observing their religious creed.

You must also accommodate the known religious creed (such as allowing the person time off for religious observance) of an applicant or employee unless you can demonstrate that such accommodation imposes undue hardship. You can't discriminate against or retaliate against an employee for requesting an accommodation, regardless of whether you provide the accommodation.

Religious corporations and associations are generally exempt from laws governing this protected class. The absence of a religion (atheism and agnosticism) is also a protected class.

In addition, religious belief protections and religious accommodation requirements are extended to anyone in an apprenticeship training program, an unpaid internship or any other program to provide unpaid experience for a person in the workplace or industry.

Sex

You can't base employment decisions on an employee's or applicant's sex or gender. "Sex" also includes pregnancy, childbirth and medical conditions related to pregnancy and childbirth.

The definition of "sex" under the FEHA specifically includes "breastfeeding and medical conditions related to breastfeeding." Employers are clearly prohibited from discriminating against employees or job applicants because of breastfeeding and related medical conditions.

Both state and federal law prohibit discriminatory compensation decisions based on sex. For more information about California law and pay discrimination, see "Wages and Salaries" in Chapter 5, page 165.

Sexual Orientation

Employees in California are protected from employment discrimination based on their actual or perceived sexual orientation. "Sexual orientation" is defined as "heterosexuality, homosexuality and bisexuality."

Employers of four or fewer employees and religious nonprofit organizations are exempt from state sexual orientation anti-discrimination laws.

Federal Title VII bars sex and gender discrimination in employment but does not explicitly prohibit workplace discrimination based on sexual orientation. However, the federal EEOC has stated its position that discrimination against an individual because of that person's sexual orientation is a violation of Title VII's prohibition of sex discrimination in employment.

Veteran Status

You can't base employment decisions on an employee's or applicant's status as a veteran. Military personnel also enjoy limited protection from termination for a period of time after returning to work.

A new law expands protections for members of the armed services by prohibiting discrimination in all "terms, conditions, or privileges" of employment. This law protects servicemembers from hostile work environments in their civilian jobs.

"Military and veteran status" has been added to the list of categories protected from employment discrimination under the Fair Employment and Housing Act. The law provides an exemption for an inquiry by an employer regarding military or veteran status for the purpose of awarding a veteran's preference as permitted by law. Legislation from prior years required veteran preference on civil service employment lists.

Whistleblowers

You can't:

- Retaliate against an employee who discloses information to a government or law enforcement agency if your employee has reasonable cause to believe that the information discloses a violation of state or federal statute; or a violation of or noncompliance with a state or federal rule or regulation;

- Retaliate against an employee who refuses to participate in an activity that would result in a violation of law; or

- Retaliate against an employee if the employee's action occurred when that individual worked for a former employer.

Whistleblower protections:

- Include reports alleging a violation of a local rule or regulation.

- Protect an employee who discloses, or may disclose, information regarding alleged violations internally "to a person with authority over the employee or another employee who has authority to investigate, discover or correct the violation."

- Prohibit retaliation when the employer simply believes that the employee may disclose information even if the employee has not actually done so.

These protections also apply to an employee who is a family member of a person who engaged in, or was perceived to engage in, the protected conduct or made a complaint protected by these provisions.

Fines for retaliation are up to $10,000 for each violation. The Attorney General of California maintains a whistleblower hotline to receive calls from individuals with knowledge about possible violations of state or federal statutes.

You must display a posting that details employees' rights and responsibilities under the whistleblower laws and includes the telephone number of the whistleblower hotline. The posting is included on the *2020 California and Federal Labor Law Poster* available from *store.calchamber.com*.

Disability Discrimination

Disability discrimination laws protect qualified individuals with disabilities from disparate treatment by employers. A qualified individual with a disability is a person who meets legitimate skill, experience, education or other requirements, and can perform the essential functions of the position with or without reasonable accommodation. Individuals aren't unqualified simply because they can't perform marginal or incidental job functions.

"Disabilities" Defined Under Federal and California Laws

The federal Americans with Disabilities Act (ADA) prohibits employers from discriminating against qualified individuals with disabilities. The ADA also requires an employer to provide reasonable accommodation for a qualified applicant's or employee's known disability, unless it would impose undue hardship on the employer's business, or unless the applicant or employee would cause a direct safety threat to others.

Person are considered disabled under federal law if they:

- Have a physical or mental impairment that substantially limits one or more of the "major life activities," which include working, caring for oneself, sleeping, learning, walking, interacting with others, working, and other physical, mental and social activities;

- Have a record of such an impairment;

- Are regarded as having such an impairment;

- Are regarded by the employer as having some condition that has no present disabling effect but may become a physical disability; or

- Have any health impairment that requires special education or related services.

California's FEHA provides greater protection from disability discrimination than the ADA. Under the FEHA, persons are considered disabled if they are "limited" in one or more of the major life activities, rather than "substantially limited" in those activities as required under the ADA. The FEHA covers employers of five or more employees and requires employers to reasonably accommodate people with disabilities.

You can't ask questions during a job interview that would be likely to lead to information about a disability unless the questions are job-related and consistent with business necessity. You can't request a medical examination until after you make an offer of employment.

Drug or Alcohol Abuse as a Disability

The federal ADA and California's FEHA do not protect individuals who currently use drugs. You can terminate, discipline or refuse to hire any individual who currently uses controlled substances or who is addicted to them.

There are exceptions. The ADA and FEHA protect people who:

- Formerly abused alcohol or illegal drugs;

- Successfully rehabilitated themselves, either through a supervised rehabilitation program or through their own program; and

- No longer use illegal drugs.

This protection extends to individuals participating in a drug or alcohol rehabilitation program. Although individuals with a record of drug use who successfully completed a rehabilitation program and no longer use illegal drugs may be protected, addiction-related misconduct that violates company policy or performance standards is not protected under the ADA or FEHA.

Reasonable Accommodation Defined

A "reasonable accommodation" is any modification or adjustment in a job, an employment practice or the work environment that allows a qualified individual with a disability to enjoy an equal employment opportunity. Examples of reasonable accommodations include:

- Modifying a work schedule.

- Providing an interpreter.

- Making facilities accessible.

- Acquiring accessibility equipment.

- Providing an extended leave of absence.

 Employers with 50 or more employees who provide leave under FMLA/CFRA also have an additional duty to comply with FEHA to engage in the interactive process and determine whether additional leave is an appropriate reasonable accommodation after FMLA/CFRA leave is exhausted.

The reasonable accommodation obligation is an ongoing duty, and may arise any time a person's disability or job changes. You must engage in a timely, good faith interactive process to determine and provide effective, reasonable accommodations. You should document this process.

 You can't retaliate against an employee for requesting reasonable accommodation.

The Interactive Process

The FEHA requires that you engage in a timely, good-faith interactive process to determine effective reasonable accommodations for an employee.

The interactive process is a collaborative effort between the employer and the employee to determine what accommodation, if any, can help the employee perform the essential functions of that person's position. The employer and the employee must exchange essential information during the interactive process.

The law does not explain to what extent you must go in engaging in a timely, good-faith interactive process. At a minimum, you should meet with the employee to discuss possible reasonable accommodations and ask the employee for a note from the treating physician stating that the employee has a medical condition and, preferably, any of the physician's proposed accommodations.

Be open to the employee's suggestions, and be willing to try various accommodations in an attempt to find one that is successful. Document the process that you and the employee go through.

Employer Responsibilities

To comply with FEHA, an employer may either grant the employee or applicant's requested accommodation or reject the initial accommodation and initiate discussion regarding alternatives.

In consultation with the employee and in conjunction with a review of the employee's job description, the employer should identify potential accommodations for the employee, and consider the effectiveness of the accommodations to allow the employee to perform essential functions and to the employee's preference in implementing an accommodation.

If the employer considers reassigning the employee to another position, the employer may ask an employee about his/her qualifications for that position. This does not mean that an employer must put an employee into a position that he/she is not qualified for. Also, an employer is not required to continue to employ the person on an open-ended leave of absence while waiting for an appropriate vacant position to arise.

For more information on accommodations related to pregnancy, see "Pregnancy Disability Leave" in Chapter 3, page 93.

Employee Responsibilities

Employees must cooperate in good faith in the reasonable accommodation process and provide medical documentation where a disability or need for accommodation is not obvious and the documentation is requested by the employer.

Employees must also give their employers information about education or work history that might qualify them for alternative positions.

Essential Functions

Essential functions are fundamental job duties of the position or the reason the job exists. You don't have to alter the essential functions of a job — that's not considered a reasonable accommodation.

You need to establish the essential functions of a job to determine whether an individual with a disability is able to perform the job with or without reasonable accommodation, and as a defense against any subsequent claim of discrimination.

When determining essential functions; document all important job functions, be accurate and realistic, stay current, be flexible and review job descriptions with the employee in that job.

The law doesn't require you to reasonably accommodate a qualified individual with a disability if you can prove that the accommodation would cause undue hardship. The EEOC and the California Department of Fair Employment and Housing (DFEH) determine undue hardship on a case-by-case basis, taking into consideration the size of your business and the availability of tax incentives and assistance from the government.

 The concept of **undue hardship** includes any accommodation that is unduly costly, extensive or substantial, or an accommodation that would fundamentally alter the nature of the operation of your business. This is a difficult standard to meet. Consult legal counsel before making any determination.

You don't need to hire or retain a person who poses a direct threat to the health and safety of co-workers. The risk must be current, not speculative, not remote, not lessened by accommodation and based on reasonable medical judgment or other objective evidence.

Responding to a Discrimination Complaint

Because of the serious nature of discrimination claims, you need to know what to do ahead of time. If an employee files a discrimination complaint, properly handling the complaint could prevent the situation from escalating into a lawsuit.

You should take all discrimination complaints very seriously. When an employee makes a complaint, you must be prepared to conduct an investigation. Follow this basic process:

1. Interview the complainant and document the complaint.

2. Determine if a formal investigation is necessary.

3. Decide on interim actions.

4. Conduct a formal investigation.

5. Take quick corrective action.

For a complete discussion of these steps and conducting a thorough investigation, see "Responding to a Complaint" in Chapter 8, page 302.

Penalties Related to Discrimination

The penalties for engaging in unlawful employment discrimination differ based on the law that was violated and the agency or court that assesses the penalty. All discrimination cases can have a substantial financial impact and lay the groundwork for similar claims by other employees. Under California law, liability for a discrimination claim belongs solely to you, the employer.

Remedies Under California's FEHA

If you are found to have engaged in an employment practice that is unlawful under the FEHA, you can be required to:

- Pay actual damages for injuries or losses that the complainant suffered, including loss of back pay and front pay for lost future wages where reinstatement is inappropriate.

- Pay compensatory damages — for pain, suffering, humiliation and embarrassment.

- Pay punitive damages.

- Pay attorneys' fees.

- Pay costs.

- Conduct training for all employees, supervisors and management on FEHA and your internal grievance procedures.

- Pay expert witness fees to the prevailing party.

- Pay fines of up to $25,000 for perpetrators of hate crime violence.

The California DFEH may bring a civil action directly to court if the agency determines an employer has failed to eliminate an unlawful employment practice.

Remedies Under Title VII

The federal Civil Rights Act of 1991 expanded the right of plaintiffs to compensatory and punitive damages. It allows those who claim intentional discrimination or harassment based on sex, race, religion, national origin or color under Title VII, or disability under the ADA or Rehabilitation Act, to obtain compensatory and punitive damages.

The compensatory and punitive damages are measured by the size of the employer's workforce, up to a maximum of $300,000:

- 1 - 14 employees: no damages recoverable (employers with fewer than 15 employees are not covered by these federal acts, but are covered by FEHA).

- 15 - 100 employees: $50,000.

- 101 - 200 employees: $100,000.

- 201 - 500 employees: $200,000.

- 500+ employees: $300,000.

Front Pay and Title VII

The $300,000 cap on damages awarded under Title VII does not apply to "front pay" (money that an employee would have continued to earn if he/she was not illegally fired). In federal courts hearing employment discrimination lawsuits, employers face the possibility of employees being awarded unlimited amounts of front pay.

Minimum Compliance Elements

1. Hang your ***2020 California and Federal Labor Law Poster*** (available from ***store.calchamber.com***), which includes mandatory postings that all employees and applicants must be able to see, in a prominent place (such as a break room). It includes the required federal and California anti-discrimination posters.

    If you have employees working in a city or county with a local minimum wage and/or paid sick leave ordinance, you may also need to post required local ordinances and provide additional notices to employees at the time of hire.

2. Create and follow a written policy forbidding harassment, discrimination and retaliation in your workplace, and enforce it consistently for all employees (see "Establish a Policy" on page 293).

3. Take every discrimination complaint seriously — establish a complaint procedure, tell your employees about it and follow it faithfully if you learn of suspicious behavior (see "Responding to a Discrimination Complaint" on page 281).

4. Hold a training session so all your employees and managers can learn about discrimination. If you have five or more employees, harassment prevention training is mandatory (see "Harassment-Prevention Training" in Chapter 8, page 296).

5. Accommodate employees with disabilities so they can work equally with their non-disabled colleagues (see "Reasonable Accommodation Defined" on page 278).

Forms and Checklists

The following table describes forms and checklists associated with discrimination and harassment.

 TIP You can find these forms in your forms download, described in detail in "Online Forms" on page 9.

Table 79. Forms and Checklists

Notice or Form	What Do I Use It For?	When Do I Use It?	Who Fills It Out?	Where Does It Go?
Harassment Complaint Procedure	To explain your company's harassment complaint procedure.	Distribute the procedure along with your non-harassment policy to new employees and perhaps annually to all employees.	N/A	Give a copy to all employees or incorporate in your employee handbook that's distributed to all employees.
Harassment Complaint Procedure - Spanish	To explain your company's harassment complaint procedure.	Distribute the procedure along with your non-harassment policy to new employees and perhaps annually to all employees.	N/A	Give a copy to all employees or incorporate in your employee handbook that's distributed to all employees.
Harassment Discipline Checklist	Not required. This form will help you decide how to discipline a harasser.	Before and after an investigation.	N/A	N/A
Harassment Investigation Credibility Assessment Guidelines	Not required. This form will help you evaluate the people involved in your investigation.	Before and after an investigation interview.	N/A	N/A
Harassment Investigation Interview Guidelines	Not required. This form will help you conduct a legal, useful investigation interview.	When preparing for an investigation interview.	N/A	N/A

Table 79. Forms and Checklists *(continued)*

Notice or Form	What Do I Use It For?	When Do I Use It?	Who Fills It Out?	Where Does It Go?
Manager's Checklist to Avoid Discrimination	Not required. This form will help your managers and supervisors avoid discriminatory behavior.	In any situation where a discrimination complaint could be filed.	N/A/	Just read it as a guideline and give it to your managers.
Sexual Harassment Investigation Checklist	Not required. This form will help you run your investigation smoothly and legally.	When considering an investigation interview.	N/A	N/A
Sexual Harassment Hurts Everyone pamphlet (available in the **2020 Required Notices Kit**)	Required. This pamphlet describes the problem and the penalties of sexual harassment, and what an employee with a complaint should do.	Whenever you hire a new employee, or engage an independent contractor, etc.	N/A	Give it to your workers and make sure they understand its contents.

Where Do I Go for More Information?

CalChamber and federal and state government agencies offer a variety of resources to help you prevent discrimination and harassment.

Table 80. Additional Resources

For Information On	Check Out These Resources
General	From CalChamber: • The ***2020 California Labor Law Digest***, the most comprehensive, California-specific resource to help employers comply with complex federal and state labor laws and regulations • ***Sexual Harassment Hurts Everyone*** pamphlets, sold separately or as part of CalChamber's ***Required Notices Kit*** • ***store.calchamber.com*** • ***HRCalifornia.com***
EEOC	Equal Employment Opportunity Commission (EEOC) (415) 625-5600 or (800) 669-4000 ***www.eeoc.gov***
DFEH	Department of Fair Employment and Housing (DFEH) (916) 478-7251 or (800) 884-1684 ***www.dfeh.ca.gov***

TIP CalChamber also provides many ongoing and comprehensive educational opportunities for small business owners, HR beginners and experienced HR professionals alike. These include online sexual harassment prevention training, special HR seminars and webinars. For more information, please visit our website at ***store.calchamber.com***.

Chapter 8

Preventing Harassment

Sexual harassment remains a serious area of concern for employers. Sexual harassment lawsuits spur record settlements and damage awards to victims. Employers bear liability for harassing acts that supervisors and employees commit.

Sexual harassment is not the only type of unlawful harassment prohibited in the workplace. It is illegal to harass an employee based on the employee's race, national origin, religion or any other protected characteristic.

Emergency legislation effective August 30, 2019, addressed issues raised after California passed its mandatory harassment prevention training law in 2018. For complete details, see "Mandatory Sexual Harassment Prevention Training" on page 296.

You can begin to protect yourself by understanding harassment, taking steps to avoid situations that would inspire lawsuits and by knowing how to handle complaints when they do arise.

In this chapter, you can find answers to questions about:

- The definition of harassment.
- Liability.
- Defamation protection.
- Effective harassment-prevention policies.
- Harassment-prevention training.
- Investigations.

Harassment Defined

Sexual harassment is the most common type of workplace harassment and gets the most attention, but the law shields all workers in any size company from any type of harassment.

It's your duty as an employer to create a work environment free from harassment for all your workers, whatever their gender, age, race or other protected class status might be.

Types of Harassment

Sexual harassment can include behaviors such as asking for sexual favors, sexual touching or offensive language. Not all sexual conduct in the workplace rises to the level of unlawful "sexual harassment." Generally, the conduct must be so frequent or severe that it creates a hostile or offensive work environment.

Generally, harassment is a pattern of unwelcome behavior. If an individual indicates that advances, attentions, remarks or visual displays are unwanted and should stop but the behavior continues, that constitutes harassment.

 Though most unlawful harassment is a pattern of conduct, a single incident may constitute unlawful harassment if the conduct is sufficiently severe.

Harassment can include several behaviors:

Table 81. Types of Harassment

Type of Harassment	Definition
Sexual	Courts and government enforcement agencies define two broad categories of sexual harassment: • **Quid pro quo**: this conditions job continuance, benefits, promotions, etc., on receiving sexual favors; and • **Hostile environment**: a pattern of unwelcome sexual comments, touching or visual displays of a supervisor or co-worker creates an offensive working environment that inhibits the employee's ability to work.
Verbal	Epithets, continued requests for dates, derogatory comments, slurs, obscenities, sexually explicit or racial jokes, graphic commentary about someone's body, verbal abuse, questions about personal practices, use of patronizing terms or remarks or threats and demands to submit to sexual advances.

Table 81. Types of Harassment *(continued)*

Type of Harassment	Definition
Physical	Assault, unwanted touching, grabbing, brushing against or interfering with a person's movement.
Visual	Offensive cartoons, posters, drawings, gestures or staring. Emojis and internet postings are increasingly prevalent forms of visual harassment.

Federal and State Law

Both federal and California law prohibit sexual harassment, as well as other forms of harassment based upon race, color, religion, and national origin. California law also prohibits harassment based upon several additional protected classes. For a complete list of protected classes, see "Protected Characteristics and Activities" in Chapter 7, page 261

The U.S. Equal Employment Opportunity Commission (EEOC) enforces federal prohibitions against sexual harassment, which it defines as "unwelcome sexual advances, requests for sexual favors and other verbal or physical conduct of a sexual nature."

Conduct may constitute sexual harassment when:

- It's an employment condition (submitting to harassing conduct is made a term of employment).

- It's an employment consequence (submitting to or rejecting harassing conduct is used as the basis for employment decisions).

- It's an offensive job interference (harassing conduct unreasonably interferes with an employee's work performance or creates an intimidating, hostile or offensive work environment).

The Department of Fair Employment and Housing (DFEH) enforces California prohibitions against sexual harassment. Under California law, sexually harassing conduct doesn't need to be motivated by sexual desire. Hostility based on someone's gender can amount to unlawful sexual harassment regardless of whether the treatment was motivated by any sexual desire.

California courts use a "reasonable victim" standard to determine if a particular situation constitutes harassment. Though any person of any gender can be subject to unlawful harassment, courts ask whether a reasonable person in the victim's position would consider the conduct sufficiently severe or pervasive to create a hostile or abusive working environment.

Liability for Sexual Harassment

In most cases, the employer will be held responsible for harassment that occurs in the workplace or in connection with the employment relationship. The degree to which the employer will be held liable depends, in part, on the source of the unlawful conduct.

Employees who believe they are being harassed can file a claim against your company and against any supervisors engaging in harassing behavior. If you fail to take action to stop harassment, you and any supervisors involved may be liable for damages if an employee files a complaint.

Employers are prohibited from requiring an employee, in exchange for a raise or bonus, or as a condition of employment or continued employment to:

- Agree not to sue or bring a claim against the employer under the FEHA, including claims for harassment; or

- Sign a non-disparagement agreement preventing the employee from disclosing information about unlawful acts in the workplace, including but not limited to sexual harassment.

Harassment by Supervisors

Under California law, employers are strictly liable for harassment by a supervisor. Strict liability means that the employer has absolute legal responsibility for any harm — the employer does not have to be found careless or negligent.

Because employers can be strictly liable for the harassing acts of their supervisors, how state and federal law define a "supervisor" matters.

Under federal law, a "supervisor" is defined as a person who has the power to hire and fire or to cause another significant change in employment status. California's FEHA provides a broader definition of who is a "supervisor" under state law:

- "Supervisor" means any individual having the authority, in the interest of the employer, to hire, transfer, suspend, layoff, recall, promote, discharge, assign, reward or discipline other employees, or the responsibility to direct them, or to adjust their grievances, or effectively to recommend that action, if, in connection with the foregoing, the exercise of that authority is not of a merely routine or clerical nature, but requires the use of independent judgment.

Although the company can be held legally responsible for the conduct, the supervisor's personal assets may also be at risk in some circumstances.

Harassment by Co-Workers

You're liable for harassment between co-workers only if you knew (or should have known) about the conduct and fail to take immediate and appropriate corrective action.

Example: An employee informed a supervisor about harassing behavior, but the supervisor's response was to tell the employee to "relax and not be so sensitive."

Example: An HR representative's friend told the HR person "off the record" that he felt he was being harassed, but the HR representative did nothing.

If you didn't know about the conduct but should have known it was going on, you must show that you took reasonable steps to prevent harassment from occurring. These steps include distributing sexual harassment pamphlets, creating a harassment-prevention policy and providing effective sexual harassment training.

Harassment by Third Parties

If people not under your employ harass employees, applicants or independent contractors in your workplace, you are liable for the conduct if you, your agents or supervisors knew or should have known of the conduct and failed to take immediate and appropriate action.

These third parties could include customers, vendors or employees of service companies called to your workplace.

 Any workplace relationship is subject to a harassment complaint: employee/independent contractor, vendor/employee, employee/employee or supervisor/employee, among others.

Other Forms of Harassment

Under California's Civil Code, certain professionals can be liable to their clients for sexual harassment, including doctors, attorneys, bankers and accountants, elected officials, lobbyists, investors, directors and producers, among others.

In addition, liability for harassment is expanded to include persons who hold himself/themselves as being able to help someone establish a business, service or professional relationship, whether with that individual or with a third party. Although the law used to require a showing that the relationship could not be easily terminated, that requirement has been eliminated, ensuring that responsibility remains with the harassing party regardless of whether the other party could have walked away.

Defamation Protection

Employers and sexual harassment victims are protected from liability for defamation by an alleged harasser after a sexual harassment complaint has been made.

California's Civil Code Section 47 ensures that victims of sexual harassment and employers won't be sued for defamation — a claim for injury to one's reputation resulting from a false written or oral statement — by the alleged harasser. This means that:

- Employees who report harassment aren't liable for injury to the alleged harasser's reputation;

- Communications between the employer and victims/witnesses are protected;

- An employer is now permitted to reveal in a job reference whether the individual isn't eligible for rehire because the employer determined that the individual engaged in sexual harassment; and

- Employees who report harassment, based on credible evidence and without malice, won't be liable for injury to the alleged harasser's reputation.

Harassment-Prevention Policies

California employers must implement harassment-prevention policies and are required to inform employees about their protections against harassment in the workplace. The purpose of a harassment-prevention policy, beyond complying with the law, is to ensure employees are notified of their rights and responsibilities.

Harassment-prevention policies can also protect you. In one case, a court found that an employer's stated "zero tolerance" policy requiring investigation and documentation of every report of sexual harassment, posting anti-harassment posters in the workplace, requiring all employees to review training videos and consistent implementation of these requirements was sufficient to avoid liability.

Your policies should also outline the complaint process and discipline plan, point out that retaliation will not be tolerated and explain that harassers may be held personally liable in a lawsuit. Review the *Workplace Harassment Guide for California Employers* for recommended employer practices for preventing and addressing all forms of workplace harassment.

Establish a Policy

You must maintain written policies that explain your commitment to protecting your employees from harassment. Your employee handbook should include your harassment, discrimination and retaliation prevention policy. Use the appropriate *Harassment, Discrimination and Retaliation Prevention Policy* (described in Table 88 on page 312).

Your policy must meet 10 different requirements:

1. Be in writing.

2. List all protected categories covered under the FEHA (not just sex/gender, but race, religion, national origin, etc.). You should also clearly describe the types of conduct that constitute harassment under state and federal laws.

3. Indicate that the law prohibits supervisors, managers, co-workers and third parties with whom the employee comes into contact from engaging in prohibited conduct.

4. Include a complaint process. The process that you develop must ensure that complaints receive all of the following:

   – A designation of confidentiality to the extent possible;

- A timely response;

- An impartial and timely investigation by qualified personnel;

- Documentation and tracking for reasonable progress;

- Appropriate options for remedial actions and resolutions; and

- Timely closure.

5. Make clear that an employee has the right to complain about harassment or participate in any workplace investigation without fear of retaliation.

6. State that confidentiality will be kept by the employer to the maximum extent possible. However, the policy should not indicate that the investigation will be kept completely confidential. For more information, see Harassment Investigations.

7. Explain that employees need not complain directly to their immediate supervisor and provide an alternative complaint mechanism, including but not limited to:

- Direct oral or written communication with a designated company representative, such as an HR manager, EEO officer or other supervisor;

- A complaint hotline;

- Access to an ombudsperson; and/or

- The DFEH or the EEOC.

8. Instruct supervisors to report any complaints of misconduct to a designated company representative (such as an HR manager) so that the company can try to resolve the claim internally.

9. Explain your process for investigating all complaints of misconduct — whether it's harassment or other prohibited conduct. Indicate that you will conduct a fair, timely and thorough investigation that provides all parties appropriate due process and reaches reasonable conclusions based on the evidence collected.

10. Include a statement that if misconduct is found at the end of the investigation, your company will take appropriate corrective and remedial measures (which can include discipline and other measures such as future training).

You may disseminate the policy to employees in one or more of the following ways:

- Printing and providing a copy of the policy to all employees with a form for the employee to sign and return acknowledging receipt.

- Sending the policy via e-mail with an acknowledgment return form.

- Posting the current version of your policy on a company intranet with a tracking system documenting that all employees have read and acknowledged receipt of the policy.

- Discussing policies upon hire and/or during new hire orientation.

- Any other way that ensures employees receive and understand the policy.

Policy Limitations

Simply maintaining a harassment-prevention policy and creating internal complaint procedures doesn't completely insulate you from liability for harassment. You must consistently follow those policies and procedures to better protect yourself against liability.

If your harassment-prevention policy doesn't specifically prohibit harassment or if your investigation procedure requires employees to first report an incident to a supervisor (who might actually be the harasser), your policies and procedures aren't effective.

Update your policies and procedures as often as needed. For details, see "Responding to a Complaint" on page 302.

Policies in a Multilingual Workforce

You must translate your harassment, discrimination and retaliation prevention policy into any language that is spoken by at least 10 percent of your workforce. It is a good practice to translate all policies and communicate them in the language(s) spoken by your workforce.

If possible, provide a complaint mechanism that identifies an official who speaks the language(s) of your workforce, or explain that an interpreter will be provided, if necessary.

Harassment-Prevention Training

Training is the best way for you to communicate your expectations to your employees, including those relating to harassment in the workplace. Putting a training program in place can save you time, money and stress. If training can prevent one angry employee from filing a lawsuit, it's worth it.

Harassment prevention training is mandatory for all employers with five or more employees.

Mandatory Sexual Harassment Prevention Training

Previously, only employers with 50 or more employees were required by law to provide harassment training and only to their supervisors. But as of January 1, 2019, virtually all California employers must provide sexual harassment training to all employees

5+ Specifically, by January 1, 2021, all employers with **five or more** employees must provide two hours of sexual harassment training to supervisors and one hour of training to nonsupervisory employees. The training must be provided within six months of hire or promotion, and every two years thereafter. Also beginning January 1, 2021, temporary and seasonal employees must be trained within 30 days of hire or 100 hours worked, whichever is earlier. Temporary services employers will be responsible for training employees placed with clients.

 Emergency legislation effective August 30, 2019, extended the sexual harassment prevention training deadline under the 2018 law from January 1, 2020, to January 1, 2021.

Table 82. Harassment Prevention Training Timetable

Year You Last Trained	Next Required Training Year	Explanation
2019	2021	Employers who trained their employees in 2019 aren't required to provide refresher training until two years from the time the employee was trained.
2018	2020	Employers who trained employees in 2018 to maintain their two-year cycle and still comply with the new January 1, 2021, deadline.
2017	2019	Employers who trained supervisors in 2017 under prior law, known as AB 1825, should have trained those employees in 2019 in order to maintain their two-year cycle.

This legislation also clarifies that employers who train their employees in 2019 aren't required to provide refresher training until two years from the time the employee was trained. The bill included an urgency provision and went into effect immediately upon the governor's signature.

The harassment prevention training must include information and practical guidance about federal and state sexual harassment laws, and it must be interactive. Computer-based training that's provided by qualified organizations, such as CalChamber, and that includes interactive components meets the requirements. CalChamber's California Harassment Prevention Training contains this curriculum, and is available for purchase at ***https://store.calchamber.com/10032185/training/-sexual-harassment-training***. The new law also permits an employer to develop its own compliant course and requires the Department of Fair Employment and Housing (DFEH) to develop an online course.

The DFEH Council's "Employment Regulations Regarding Definitions; Harassment and Discrimination Prevention and Correction; and Training" for employers with five or more employees was approved by the Office of Administrative Law and filed with the Secretary of State on June 24, 2019. The regulations went into effect on October 1, 2019. Information about new or updated regulations can be found on the DFEH website at ***https://www.dfeh.ca.gov/fehcouncil***. Employers should consult with legal counsel concerning any questions related to the new training requirements.

An employer with a multi-lingual workforce should ensure that the training is clearly and effectively communicated to employees who speak a language other than English.

Coverage

California's new training law applies to all employers with **five or more** employees located anywhere, including part-time and temporary employees (including those hired through temporary staffing agencies), and independent contractors. Although you must count all employees located anywhere to determine whether you're covered by the mandatory training law, you only have to train employees and supervisors located in California.

"Supervisory authority" generally includes anyone possessing the authority to exercise independent judgment to:

- Hire, transfer, suspend, lay off, recall, promote, discharge, assign, reward or discipline other employees.

- Direct other employees' work or adjust their grievances.

- Effectively recommend any of these actions.

Employees who make recommendations to managers about such matters must receive supervisory training if those recommendations are likely to result in managers taking employment actions.

Duration of Training

You must provide one hour of training for non-supervisory employees and two hours of training for supervisors. The new law allows the training to be completed in shorter segments as long as the applicable hourly total requirement is met.

Current regulations provide that for classroom training or webinars, the minimum duration of a training segment can't be less than 30 minutes.

Interactive Training Required

The training provided to employees and supervisors must be interactive. The training must include practical examples aimed at instructing individuals in the prevention of harassment, discrimination and retaliation, and must be presented by trainers or educators with knowledge and expertise in those topics. The current regulations state that the training must include questions that assess learning, skill-building activities that assess the trainee's application and understanding of the content, and hypotheticals about harassment — each with one or more discussion questions so individuals remain engaged with the training.

Content of Training

The law requires that the training include information and practical guidance regarding the federal and state statutory provisions concerning the prohibition against and the prevention and correction of sexual harassment, as well as the remedies available to victims of sexual harassment in employment.

The current regulations also contain a list of specific subjects that must be covered in the training. It's unknown whether the required subjects will be changed once the DFEH updates the regulations to reflect the new expanded training law.

The learning objectives of the training, according to the current regulations, are to:

- Assist California employers in changing or modifying workplace behaviors that create or contribute to "sexual harassment," as that term is defined in California and federal law;

- Provide trainees with information related to the negative effects of abusive conduct in the workplace; and

- Develop, foster and encourage a set of values in supervisory employees who complete mandated training that will assist them in preventing and effectively responding to incidents of sexual harassment, as well as implementing procedures that promptly address and correct wrongful behavior.

Types of Harassment Training

The new training law requires employers to provide classroom or other effective interactive training and education to all employees and supervisors. The training can be completed by employees individually or as part of a group presentation.

The current regulations state that the training can take the following forms:

Table 83. Harassment Prevention Training Timetable

Training Type	Details
Classroom Training	Also referred to as in-person training, classroom training features content that was created by a trainer and is provided in a setting that's removed from the individual's daily duties. California law specifically defines the credentials that a qualified trainer must possess, described in "Trainer Qualifications" on page 300.
E-Learning	Individualized, interactive and computer-based training is created by a trainer and an instructional designer. Individuals taking the training must have the opportunity to ask a trainer questions and receive a response within two business days after asking the questions.
Webinar	An Internet-based seminar that features content created and taught by a trainer and is transmitted over the Internet or an intranet in real time. Employers who use a webinar for training must document that each person not physically in the same room as the trainer actually attended the training and actively participated in the training's interactive content, discussion questions, hypothetical scenarios, polls, quizzes or tests, and activities. Webinars must give users the opportunity to ask questions and receive answers to them, or otherwise seek guidance and assistance.

It is unknown whether these provisions will be changed once the DFEH updates the regulations to reflect the new expanded training law.

The DFEH has been tasked with developing or obtaining an online training course, which it must make available to employers. The 2019 law says that questions resulting from the DFEH's online training course must be directed to the employer's Human Resources Department or equally qualified professional. At the time of publication, the DFEH has not developed or obtained a training course.

Trainer Qualifications

The current regulations also contain specific trainer qualifications. The trainer must be one of the following:

- An attorney who has been admitted for two or more years to the bar of any U.S. state and whose practice includes employment law under FEHA and/or Title VII of the federal Civil Rights Act of 1964;

- A human resources professional or harassment prevention consultant who has a minimum of two years of practical experience in sexual harassment prevention training; responding to sexual harassment complaints; conducting harassment complaint investigations; and advising employers or employees about discrimination, retaliation and sexual harassment; or

- A professor or instructor at a law school, college or university who has a post-graduate degree or California teaching credential and 20 instruction hours or two or more years of experience teaching employment law under FEHA and/or Title VII of the federal Civil Rights Act of 1964.

The current regulations also require that the trainers have knowledge of and ability to train on several specific topics.

It's unknown whether the trainer requirements will be changed once the DFEH updates the regulations to reflect the new training law.

Tracking Harassment Training

The current regulations permit employers to use individual tracking or training year tracking, or a combination of both:

Table 84. Types of Tracking

Training Type	Details
Individual Tracking	You track your training requirement on an individual calendaring basis, measuring two years from the date the training was last completed by each individual.
Training Year Tracking	You designate a "training year" in which you conduct training, and then conduct training every two years by the end of the designated training year, even for those who received training in the prior year because they were newly hired or promoted.

The current regulations allow employers to accept a supervisor's training from a previous employer as valid and place the supervisor on a two-year tracking schedule based on the prior training date. However, if you do so, you must prove that the training the supervisor received from the prior employer meets the legal requirements of the mandatory training law. In addition, the supervisor must read and acknowledge receiving your anti-harassment policy within six months of being hired or promoted.

Documentation and Recordkeeping Requirements

Regulations related to the prior law require employers to track compliance and keep documentation for a minimum of two years. You must be able to provide copies upon request.

The current regulations require that the training record must include all of the following information:

- The name of the supervisor trained;

- The training date;

- The sign-in sheet;

- A copy of all certificates of attendance or completion issued;

- The training type;

- A copy of all written or recorded materials that comprise the training; and

- The training provider's name.

In addition, additional documentation is required for e-learning and webinar training:

Table 85. Additional Training Documentation

Training	Required Documentation
E-Learning	The trainer must maintain all written questions received and all written responses or guidance provided for a period of two years after the date of the response.
Webinars	The employer must maintain a copy of the webinar, all written materials used by the trainer and all written questions submitted during the webinar. The employer must also document all written responses or guidance the trainer provided during the webinar.

The DFEH also must provide a method for employees to save and print a certificate of completion if the employer utilizes the DFEH's training course.

It's unclear whether the current documentation and recordkeeping requirements will be changed once the DFEH updates the regulations to reflect the new training law.

Responding to a Complaint

Harassment in the workplace is a serious area of concern. Harassment lawsuits can spur record settlements and damage awards to victims. You must take harassment allegations very seriously, and you must prepare the appropriate staff to correctly respond to these allegations.

When an employee makes a sexual harassment complaint, you must conduct a thorough, impartial investigation. If performed properly, the investigation:

- Reassures employees that complaints will be heard and resolved within the company.

- Explains to all parties that company policy prohibits any retaliatory behavior.

- Minimizes the chance of disciplining or terminating an employee for something that individual didn't do.

- Makes it less likely that an outside agency and/or attorney will become involved.

You may find that the allegations can be resolved after only an informal investigation, or you may discover that a full, formal investigation is warranted. Always document the process you followed, take corrective action as necessary — such as disciplining employees, rewriting policies or providing additional training — and follow up with the appropriate parties to ensure the issue was adequately resolved.

Time Limits for Filing Sexual Harassment Claims

Previously, an employee who wanted to file a harassment lawsuit against an employer had to file a claim with California's DFEH within one year of the alleged act(s) of harassment.

 Starting January 1, 2020, the statute of limitations to file a complaint with the DFEH **extends to three years**, which means it's especially important for employers to keep detailed, accurate and contemporaneous employment-related documentation.

Employees who want to file such a claim with the federal Equal Employment Opportunity Commission (EEOC) must do so within 180 days of the alleged violation.

The time limit for filing claims is generally measured from when the harassment occurred. If harassment occurred over a long period of time, the time limit is generally measured from the last unlawful act.

If an employee first files a charge with the DFEH, the employee can then file a charge with the EEOC within 300 days of the alleged violation or within 30 days of receiving notice that the DFEH terminated its proceedings, whichever is earlier.

 Employees are not required by law to share their complaints with a manager or other employer representative first before filing a claim with the DFEH.

Plan Your Investigation

When an employee files a complaint or you become aware that an employee may have violated your policies, follow this basic process:

Table 86. Investigation Process

1.	Interview the complainant and document the complaint (see page 303).
2.	Determine the level of investigation necessary (see page 304).
3.	Decide on interim actions (see page 305).
4.	Conduct an investigation (see page 306).
5.	Take quick corrective action (see page 310).

Interview the Complainant and Document the Complaint

After finding out the general nature of the complaint, make sure the employee feels comfortable that you can objectively address the complaint or that you will identify an investigator who can. Then:

- Arrange for a private, comfortable setting.

- Provide ample time and opportunity to gather the facts. Make sure employees know they can take as much time as needed, and can come back if they recall other facts later.

- Encourage them to speak freely and make all complaints known.

- Re-state your policies against both harassment and retaliation for having filed a complaint, and ask them to report any retaliation to you immediately.

- Tell them your procedure for resolving complaints.

- Instruct them to keep information about the complaint as confidential as possible, given the particular circumstances.

- Tell them that you will only disclose information on a need-to-know basis.

- Ask for any suggestions for a resolution to the problem. Stress that you may not be able to follow these suggestions, but you will take them into consideration.

- Ask if they would like to recommend anyone else you could speak with, or if any documents exist related to the complaint.

- Review the interview notes and prepare a formal statement. Although complainants aren't required to, request that they sign the statement.

Taking Notes

When you take notes on the interview(s):

- Document the date, and beginning and ending times of the interview.

- Record only the facts and descriptions of what occurred during the interview, not your interpretations of the interview, the employee or the situation.

- Keep these notes in a separate place from notes regarding other business issues, and don't record them in a bound notebook or format that might contain information outside of the particular complaint.

- Keep notes about different employees on separate pieces of paper.

 Accurate, consistent note-taking plays a critical role in your investigation.

Determine the Level of Investigation Necessary

Certain situations automatically trigger your duty to investigate:

- A formal complaint, written or oral.

- A subtle verbal or written complaint that a co-worker makes the concerned employee feel uncomfortable.

- A charge from the EEOC or DFEH.

- A civil lawsuit.

- An observation of harassment.

- An anonymous note stating that prohibited or questionable behavior is occurring.

In other situations, you may need to determine if you need additional information to resolve an employee's concerns. Consider whether:

- The problem has a simple, straightforward solution or if it is more complex.

- It involves more people than just this complainant.

- It stems from a single incident or a pattern of conduct.

- You need more facts than the employee can provide.

- You need the help of other experts (legal counsel, security personnel or risk management professionals).

If you need more information, conduct an investigation.

Decide on Interim Actions

You may need to take action during the investigation to protect the health and safety of employees and the integrity of your company's policies or guidelines.

Leave of Absence

If you suspect an employee of ongoing harmful behavior, you may place the individual on a leave of absence pending the completion of an investigation. Give the employee a leave of absence notice that states:

- The person's name;

- The estimated time required for the investigation;

- Who to contact if the individual has any questions or concerns; and

- Any expectations of yours, such as:

    - Full cooperation and complete honesty during the investigation.

    - All information and documentation relevant to the investigation.

    - Confidentiality.

    - How the employee's return to work will be handled.

Conduct an Investigation

Carefully plan how to conduct the formal investigation. A poor investigation may expose both the company and the investigator to liability.

Select the Investigator

Select someone who employees view as fair, objective, reasonable, and able to make difficult decisions.

 If the complaint progresses to legal action, the investigator may be called as a witness. If you want your attorney to defend you during litigation, find a third party to conduct the investigation instead. Make sure the complainant feels comfortable with the investigator. If you choose an outside third party to perform investigations, that individual must be a private investigator or attorney licensed to practice in California. An HR consultant who's not a licensed attorney or private investigator can't legally perform these investigations. Using an outside HR consultant, as opposed to in-house HR staff, could negatively affect the validity of any investigation.

Gather Supporting Documents

Identify all documents relevant to an investigation. They may:

- Provide background information to help verify facts;
- Identify people to interview; and
- Identify which questions to ask.

Throughout the investigation, ask repeatedly for any documentation that might be helpful.

Interview Appropriate People

Interview the appropriate people in this specific order:

Table 87. Investigation Interviewees

Person	Details
1. The Complainant	For guidance on conducting this interview, see "Interview the Complainant and Document the Complaint" on page 303.
2. The Person Named by the Complainant 🛇 The law requires that you conduct an objective, thorough investigation. If you make assumptions before talking to the person who's being accused of misconduct, you aren't being objective.	Start by stating that you're investigating a complaint of workplace misconduct. Then: • Review the allegations in their entirety, and give the employee the opportunity to respond generally. This allows you to get the employee's emotional response to the allegations. • Give the employee an opportunity to tell their side of the story. • Ask questions that provide chronological answers. You can use the *Harassment Investigation Interview Guidelines*, described in Table 88 on page 312, to help you form questions.Remind the employee of the company policy against retaliation, and make sure they understand that this applies to retaliation against them as well as retaliation against the complainant. • Tell the employee that they should not do anything to impede or interfere with the investigation. • Review the interview notes and prepare a formal statement. Although the employee is not required to, request that they sign the statement.
3. Any Witnesses 🛇 Divulge only enough information necessary to learn what information this witness has to offer.	Since being interviewed as part of an investigation can be quite stressful for an interviewee, make an effort to put witnesses at ease. • Emphasize that they are only witnesses and not a subject of the investigation. • Tell witnesses that you will only share the information they provide with people who have a need to know, and stress to them that they shouldn't do anything to impede or interfere with the investigation. • Reiterate the company policy against retaliation against witnesses, as well as the alleged harasser or the complainant. • Use the *Harassment Investigation Interview Guidelines*, described in Table 88 on page 312, to structure your interview. Go through events chronologically, and ask for any information witnesses have to confirm or refute what you were told. • Ask witnesses if they're aware of any other workplace misconduct. • Ask if they know whether the complainant harbors any bias against the alleged harasser, and vice-versa.

Examine Facts and Assess Credibility

You must determine whether the information you gathered is credible before relying on it to reach a conclusion. You need to make credibility assessments while conducting interviews. Ask yourself:

- Did the person raise the complaint in a timely manner? If not, why not? And why raise the complaint now?

- Did similar things happen in the past that didn't result in a complaint? If so, why?

- Did any person you interviewed say something that you found later to be untrue?

- Did anyone change their story or withdraw an allegation?

- Is the complainant's story consistent and plausible? Does it make sense? Does it correspond with the information learned from other witnesses?

- Does any evidence exist to corroborate the complaint?

- What would motivate the complainant to fabricate facts?

- Did you observe any indications of bias, hostility or self-interest? Part of this involves observing body language, tone of voice, eye contact, reactions to questions, and word selection (for example, "girl" vs. "woman").

Don't fear making decisions on credibility, but make sure you can back them up with a reasonable explanation. For additional questions to consider, see the *Harassment Investigation Credibility Assessment Guidelines*, described in Table 88 on page 312.

Reach a Conclusion

After analyzing the facts and assessing credibility, you should determine only whether company policy was or was not violated.

 You should not attempt to make a determination as to whether the law was violated. Only legal counsel should make legal conclusions.

Document the Findings and Conclusions

Write an investigation summary that includes:

- The sequence and process followed for the investigation;

- The key facts relied on to make the final decision, such as interviews and any relevant support documentation;

- The criteria used to assess credibility;

- The bottom-line, factual conclusions: for example, "The alleged harasser did touch [name of complainant], and this touch was unwanted and offensive;" and

- Any complaints not resolved in the investigation and why.

Keep this summary and other relevant documentation, interview notes, etc., in a file labeled as "Need-to-Know, Confidential." Limit access to this file to only those with a legitimate business reason to know the information. Neither the complainant nor the alleged harasser need access to this file in the normal course of business.

Communicate Results

1. Notify the complainant of the results. Discuss:

   - The conclusion you reached;

   - How you reached the conclusion;

   - What actions you will take that affect the individual;

   - What to do if the complainant experiences any retaliation; and

   - That you expect the complainant to keep all aspects of the investigation confidential.

 Though you shouldn't divulge the nature of the disciplinary action against the person being accused, you may want to indicate that you will take action consistent with your company policy.

2. Notify the alleged harasser of the results. Discuss:

   - The complaint(s) raised;

   - The steps you took to investigate;

   - How you reached the conclusion;

   - Any complaints that weren't resolved and why;

   - The actions you will take as a result of the investigation; and

   - Whom to contact if the alleged harasser wants to ask questions or wants information in the future.

Take Quick, Corrective Action

You need to move quickly in determining what action to take. Consider the following:

- Do any federal, state or local laws require you to take certain actions?

- What did the company do in the past for similar violations of policy?

- How serious was the policy violation?

- Did the employee violate any other policies in the past?

- How long has the employee been employed with your company? What is the employee's performance history?

After weighing these factors, determine the amount of discipline this situation warrants. Some of your options include:

- No action;

- Verbal discussion/counseling;

- Written warning;

- Training;

- Transfer;

- Suspension; and/or

- Termination.

You can use the *Harassment Discipline Checklist*, described in Table 88 on page 312, to help make sure you cover all the issues. Terminating a harasser is acceptable when, after an investigation, you have reasonable grounds for believing that the employee engaged in sexual harassment.

 Be careful not to give information about allegations, investigations or resulting discipline to anyone but those with a legitimate business need to know.

Penalties Related to Harassment

The important thing for employers to remember about workplace harassment is that employees or supervisors can be held personally liable for harassing behaviors — in addition to any liability imposed on your company.

The amount of liability you may face varies on the type and severity of the claim, repeat offenses and whether you can provide a relevant defense. The penalties include reinstatement, payment of back wages and payment of damages and attorneys' fees. Damages can total enormous sums of money. Courts have levied damages large enough to destroy small businesses. Typically, courts base fines on a business's assets.

For more, see "Penalties Related to Discrimination" in Chapter 7, page 281.

Minimum Compliance Elements

1. Hang your *2020 California and Federal Labor Law Poster* (available from **store.calchamber.com**), which includes mandatory postings that all employees and applicants must be able to see, in a prominent place (such as a break room). It includes the California and federal anti-discrimination/harassment poster.

   If you have employees working in a city or county with a local minimum wage and/or paid sick leave ordinance, you may also need to post required local ordinances and provide additional notices to employees at the time of hire.

2. Pass out the mandatory *Sexual Harassment* pamphlets (located in the *Required Notices Kit* available from **store.calchamber.com**), forbidding unlawful harassment at your company.

3. Create and follow a written harassment, discrimination and retaliation prevention policy in your workplace, and enforce it consistently for all employees (see "Establish a Policy" on page 293).

4. Take every harassment complaint seriously — establish a complaint procedure, tell your employees about it and follow it faithfully if you learn of suspicious behavior (see "Responding to a Complaint" on page 302).

5. If you have five or more employees, provide two hours of mandatory harassment prevention training to supervisors and one hour of training to nonsupervisory employees by January 1, 2021, and every two years thereafter, as specified by law (see "Mandatory Sexual Harassment Prevention Training" on page 296). If you have less than five employees, consider providing harassment training to all employees.

Forms and Checklists

The following table describes forms and checklists associated with discrimination and harassment.

 TIP You can find these forms in your forms download, described in detail in "Online Forms" on page 9.

Table 88. Forms and Checklists

Notice or Form	What Do I Use It For?	When Do I Use It?	Who Fills It Out?	Where Does It Go?
Harassment Complaint Procedure	To explain your company's harassment complaint procedure.	Distribute the procedure along with your harassment, discrimination and retaliation prevention policy to new employees and perhaps annually to all employees.	N/A	Give a copy to all employees or incorporate in your employee handbook that's distributed to all employees.
Harassment Complaint Procedure - Spanish	To explain your company's harassment complaint procedure.	Distribute the procedure along with your harassment, discrimination and retaliation prevention policy to new employees and perhaps annually to all employees.	N/A	Give a copy to all employees or incorporate in your employee handbook that's distributed to all employees.
Harassment Discipline Checklist	Not required. This form will help you decide how to discipline a harasser.	Before and after an investigation.	N/A	N/A
Harassment Discrimination and Retaliation Prevention Policy - Five or More Employees	To tell your employees that your company prohibits harassment, discrimination and retaliation in the workplace.	You must distribute the policy to all employees.	You and the employee.	Give a copy to all employees and incorporate in your employee handbook that's distributed to all employees.

Table 88. Forms and Checklists *(continued)*

Notice or Form	What Do I Use It For?	When Do I Use It?	Who Fills It Out?	Where Does It Go?
Harassment Discrimination and Retaliation Prevention Policy - Five or More Employees - Instructions	To understand your obligations related to the *Harassment, Discrimination and Retaliation Prevention Policy - Five or More Employees.*	Download and read these instructions prior to using the *Harassment, Discrimination and Retaliation Prevention Policy - Five or More Employees.*	N/A	N/A
Harassment Discrimination and Retaliation Prevention Policy - Less Than Five Employees	To tell your employees that your company prohibits harassment, discrimination and retaliation in the workplace.	You must distribute the policy to all employees.	You and the employee.	Give a copy to all employees and incorporate in your employee handbook that's distributed to all employees.
Harassment Discrimination and Retaliation Prevention Policy - Less Than Five Employees - Instructions	To understand your obligations related to the *Harassment, Discrimination and Retaliation Prevention Policy - Less Than Five Employees.*	Download and read these instructions prior to using the *Harassment, Discrimination and Retaliation Prevention Policy - Less Than Five Employees.*	N/A	N/A
Harassment Discrimination and Retaliation Prevention Policy - Spanish - Five or More Employees	To tell your Spanish-speaking employees that your company prohibits harassment, discrimination and retaliation in the workplace.	You must distribute the policy to all employees.	You and the employee.	Give a copy to all employees and incorporate in your employee handbook that's distributed to all employees.

Table 88. Forms and Checklists *(continued)*

Notice or Form	What Do I Use It For?	When Do I Use It?	Who Fills It Out?	Where Does It Go?
Harassment Discrimination and Retaliation Prevention Policy - Spanish - Less Than Five Employees	To tell your Spanish-speaking employees that your company prohibits harassment, discrimination and retaliation in the workplace.	You must distribute the policy to all employees.	You and the employee.	Give a copy to all employees and incorporate in your employee handbook that's distributed to all employees.
Harassment Investigation Credibility Assessment Guidelines	Not required. This form will help you evaluate the people involved in your investigation.	Before and after an investigation interview.	N/A	N/A
Harassment Investigation Interview Guidelines	Not required. This form will help you conduct a legal, useful investigation interview.	When preparing for an investigation interview.	N/A	N/A
Manager's Checklist to Avoid Discrimination	Not required. This form will help your managers and supervisors avoid discriminatory behavior.	In any situation where a discrimination complaint could be filed.	N/A	Just read it as a guideline and give it to your managers.
Sexual Harassment Investigation Checklist	Not required. This form will help you run your investigation smoothly and legally.	When considering an investigation interview.	N/A	N/A
Sexual Harassment Hurts Everyone pamphlet (available in the **2020 Required Notices Kit**)	Required. This pamphlet describes the problem and the penalties of sexual harassment, and what an employee with a complaint should do.	Whenever you hire a new employee, or engage an independent contractor, etc.	N/A	Give it to your workers and make sure they understand its contents.

Table 88. Forms and Checklists *(continued)*

Notice or Form	What Do I Use It For?	When Do I Use It?	Who Fills It Out?	Where Does It Go?
Workplace Harassment Guide for California Employers	This guide provides recommended employer practices for preventing and addressing all forms of workplace harassment, including harassment based on sex.	When assessing your harassment prevention practices.	N/A	N/A

Where Do I Go for More Information?

CalChamber and federal and state government agencies offer a variety of resources to help you prevent discrimination and harassment.

Table 89. Additional Resources

For Information On	Check Out These Resources
General	From CalChamber: • The **2020 California Labor Law Digest**, the most comprehensive, California-specific resource to help employers comply with complex federal and state labor laws and regulations • **Sexual Harassment Hurts Everyone** pamphlets, sold separately or as part of CalChamber's **Required Notices Kit** • **store.calchamber.com** • **HRCalifornia.com**
EEOC	Equal Employment Opportunity Commission (EEOC) (415) 625-5600 or (800) 669-4000 **www.eeoc.gov**
DFEH	Department of Fair Employment and Housing (DFEH) (916) 478-7251 or (800) 884-1684 **www.dfeh.ca.gov**

TIP CalChamber also provides many ongoing and comprehensive educational opportunities for small business owners, HR beginners and experienced HR professionals alike. These include online sexual harassment prevention training, special HR seminars and webinars. For more information, please visit our website at **store.calchamber.com**.

Chapter 9

Terminating Employment

Ending an employment relationship, often called "termination" or "separation," involves more than just an employee leaving your business. You must:

- Manage the termination process to avoid liability;
- Make sure the relevant paperwork is completed;
- Provide the appropriate forms and notices to the employee; and
- Properly calculate and deliver the employee's final paycheck.

Protect yourself from an overly complicated separation or even lawsuits with good preparation and by using a consistent approach in the separation process.

In this chapter, you can find answers to questions about:

- Types of separation.
- Ending the employment relationship.
- Calculating a final paycheck.
- Wrongful termination.

Types of Separation

Several distinct types of separation exist, and different laws and guidelines apply to each. This section provides required processes and best practices to guide you through each of these separation events.

Table 90. Separation Types

Type	Definition
Voluntary Quit	When an employee quits, either with or without notice, the separation is called a "voluntary quit."
	You may wish to confirm the voluntary quit by asking for a letter of resignation. Or you may using the *Notice to Employee as to Change in Relationship*, described in Table 94 on page 330, because it contains all the important information.
	Be sure to provide the final paycheck:
	• Within 72 hours of the employee giving notice (if you received less than 72 hours' notice).
	• On the employee's last day of work (if you received 72 hours' notice or more).
Discharge (In-voluntary Term-ination)	California is an at-will employment state. Unless there's an employment contract, employers may discharge employees at any time as long as the discharge isn't unlawful. Follow the parameters of your company policy or collective bargaining agreement to avoid possible wrongful termination lawsuits.
	A termination should never be a surprise to an employee. Document all attempts at addressing workplace performance and other issues, and review the questions in the *Termination Decision Checklist*, described in Table 94 on page 330. When necessary, consult legal counsel regarding steps to take prior to terminating an employee.
	You must provide written notice for involuntary termination. Use the *Notice to Employee as to Change in Relationship*, described in Table 94.
Layoff	A layoff occurs when available work ends either temporarily or permanently and through no fault of the employee.
	Your policy will dictate whether employees who are laid off have preferential return rights or other rights that terminated employees don't have. Part of your layoff procedure should include a discussion with legal counsel as to whether these employees have additional benefits or rights and how this information will be communicated to the employees.
	Document the layoff with a *Notice to Employee as to Change in Relationship*, described in Table 94. Provide the employee with any information about severance packages that you offer. Follow the basic process described in "Ending the Employment Relationship" on page 321.

Table 90. Separation Types *(continued)*

Type	Definition
Mass Layoff	Under federal law, a mass layoff is: • For a period of 30 days. • Of 50 or more full-time employees (provided it affects at least 33 percent of the workforce). • If 500 or more employees will be affected, then the 33 percent requirement does not apply. Under state law, a mass layoff is: • For a period of 30 days. • Of 50 or more full- or part-time employees who've been employed by an employer for at least six of the 12 months preceding the date on which the notice is required for lack of funds or lack of work. The California law defines "mass layoff" more broadly than the federal law as it neither specifies "full-time" employees nor excludes part-time employees. Consequently, a layoff of any 50 or more employees (full-time or part-time) can trigger the state notice requirements. You must provide advance notice of the layoff. Consult legal counsel before taking any action. If you need to lay off an employee on a certain statutory leave (pregnancy disability leave, family and medical leave, workers' compensation related leave or disability leave), the employee has no greater rights than having been at work. You may want to consider alternatives to layoffs, including job sharing. See "Where Do I Go for More Information?" on page 337 for helpful agencies and websites. ❗ Under the state and federal Worker Adjustment and Retraining Notification (WARN) acts, if you employ 75 or more staff and the layoff will affect 50 or more of them, you must provide advance notice of the layoff. Temporary layoffs also are covered by the California WARN Act. Consult with legal counsel prior to implementing a mass layoff of any duration, even temporary ones.

Table 90. Separation Types *(continued)*

Type	Definition
Job Abandon- ment	This means an employee stops showing up to work. You can set a policy that limits the number of days an employee can fail to show up for work without contacting you before you consider the job abandoned and terminate the employment relationship. If you maintain an established and objective job-abandonment policy and you deviate from it, you could be challenged in cases where you apply it. Make certain that you don't count absences protected by law such as time taken under California's paid sick leave law. ❗ Specify in your policy that job abandonment amounts to a "voluntary quit" under company policy. This gives you 72 hours to prepare the final paycheck. Prepare the final paycheck immediately upon determining that the job was abandoned, unless your policy specifies that job abandonment is a voluntary quit ("Voluntary Quit" on page 318).
Refusal to Accept Available Work	This means the employee refused to perform work that is: • Appropriate to the individual's health, safety, morals and physical condition; • Consistent with the individual's prior experience and earnings; and • A reasonable distance from the individual's residence. This type of separation is likely to occur when something about the work changes; for example, your management changes, you reassign an employee to a new work unit or you begin a new project. When the employee refuses appropriate, available work, you can exercise your option to terminate the employee. You can choose to either offer other work or put the employee on a temporary leave of absence. If you maintain an established and objective policy and you deviate from it, you could be challenged in cases where you apply it.

Ending the Employment Relationship

There are several ways to end an employee-employer relationship, but all types require you to perform essentially the same group of tasks. This section will provide guidelines to help you make a sound termination decision.

 See "Protecting Against Wrongful Termination Lawsuits" on page 327 for information on how to protect your company against potential lawsuits.

Finally, if the former employee makes an unemployment insurance (UI) claim, use the *Unemployment Insurance - Responding to a Claim Checklist*, described in Table 94 on page 330.

Table 91. Basics of Ending the Employment Relationship

Before	1. Use the information in Table 90 on page 318 to determine what type of separation applies to the situation.
	2. For a list of the important legal issues to consider when terminating an employee, review the *Termination Decision Checklist*, described in Table 94 on page 330.
	3. Maintain an established termination procedure and follow it consistently.
	4. For a list of the forms you must fill out or provide to the departing employee, review the *Termination Checklist*, described in Table 94 on page 330.
	5. Gather the relevant documentation, including the employee's personnel file, disciplinary notices and forms required at separation.
	If you terminate an employee by phone or letter, the final paycheck rules apply. For information, see "Calculating a Final Paycheck" on page 322.
During	1. Provide the Employment Development Department's *For Your Benefit, California's Program for the Unemployed* pamphlet located in CalChamber's **Required Notices Kit** available from **store.calchamber.com**.
	2. If the employee receives health benefits, fill out and provide the appropriate health insurance and COBRA forms. See COBRA and Cal-COBRA in the "Glossary of Terms, Laws and Agencies" on page 339, for more details. California employers also must provide information relating to extension of benefits under Cal-COBRA. California employers should use the modified California versions of the federal COBRA notices which contain information about Cal-COBRA for California employees. The federal model versions do **not** contain information specific for California employers.
	3. Prepare the employee's final paycheck, including all wages and accrued, unpaid vacation. You can use the *Final Paycheck Worksheet* form to help you prepare the paycheck.

Table 91. Basics of Ending the Employment Relationship *(continued)*

	4. Provide the final paycheck to the employee in the appropriate manner within the required time period, based on the type of separation. In most circumstances, you must provide the final paycheck on the employee's last day of work. For more details, see "Calculating a Final Paycheck" on page 322. **5. Optional:** Ask the employee to sign the *Final Paycheck Acknowledgment* form to document that you met the last paycheck deadline, as required. It also gives you an opportunity to clarify with the employee that proper payment was received. **6. Optional:** Conduct an exit interview on the employee's final day of employment or allow him/her to take the *Exit Interview* form home and return it by mail. The exit interview gives you a chance to learn the employee's thoughts about employment with your company, and to document any employee claims.
After	The terminated employee may be eligible for UI benefits, but he/she must file a claim to the EDD to seek the benefits: **1.** The employee contacts the EDD to apply for benefits. **2.** The EDD mails a notice to you, advising you whether the claimant is eligible and whether your account will be charged for benefits paid to the former employee. Respond to correspondence from the EDD promptly. The EDD strictly enforces deadlines in its correspondence. **3.** You can use the *Unemployment Insurance - Responding to a Claim Checklist*, to determine how to respond to the EDD notice that a claim was filed. **4.** To appeal a claim, see "Unemployment Insurance" in Chapter 4, page 140. Follow your company's policy on references for former employees. See "References and Former Employees" on page 324.

Calculating a Final Paycheck

When preparing a final paycheck, gather all time cards and documentation regarding the employee's unpaid work period or outstanding advances or expenses. Calculate the paycheck through the final day of work, based on the employee's:

- Rate of pay (see Chapter 5, "Paying Employees");

- Hours worked, including overtime;

- Earned bonuses or commissions; and

- Accrued vacation/PTO.

If you can't determine commission wages owed at the time of termination, you must pay the commission owed as soon as the amount is determined — follow your policy and the employee's commission agreement regarding the payout of commissions, even after employees leave your employment.

You can use the *Final Paycheck Worksheet*, described in Table 94 on page 330 to help you. After determining the amount due to the employee, make proper calculations for any deductions, following the guidelines in "Deductions from Employee Pay" in Chapter 5, page 199.

 You can't make deductions from an employee's final paycheck if the employee doesn't return property to you. You face fines if you do so.

To document that the last paycheck deadline was met as required, ask the employee to sign a document acknowledging receipt of the final paycheck. Use this opportunity to verify that the employee received proper payment. You can use the *Final Paycheck Acknowledgment* form for this purpose.

Final Paycheck Time Requirement

Failing to provide a terminating employee with a final paycheck for all wages owed in a timely manner can subject you to waiting time penalties.

The time requirement to pay the employee depends on several factors, such as whether the employee quit with less than 72 hours' notice, quit with 72 hours' notice or more, or was terminated or laid off.

- Termination: The employee must be paid at the time of termination. **You may not** require the employee to wait until the next regular payday. **You may not** withhold a final paycheck.

- Voluntary quit (less than 72 hours' notice): The employee must be paid no later than 72 hours after giving notice. The employee is entitled to receive the final wage payment via mail by request and designation of a mailing address. For purposes of the 72-hour requirement, the mailing date is considered the payment date. Unless the employee specifically requests payment by mail, you may hold the final paycheck until it is picked up.

- Voluntary quit (72 hours' notice or more): The employee must be paid on that individual's last day of work.

- For employees who have authorized direct deposit of paychecks, California's Labor Code allows employers to pay final wages by direct deposit without receiving a separate authorization from the employee to do so, provided that the wages are paid in a timely manner pursuant to the final paycheck time requirements above. Note, however, that the Labor Commissioner's Office has not updated the guidance contained on its website and states that a voluntary authorization is still required.

References and Former Employees

The law makes it clear that you can communicate information on the job performance or qualifications of a current or former employee upon the request of a prospective employer.

A communication indicating if you would rehire a current or former employee is protected under California law. The law specifically provides protection from claims of libel or slander when you respond to an inquiry as to whether you would rehire a current or former employee. In all cases, to avoid liability, make sure to communicate in a non-malicious way and provide only credible information. Effective January 1, 2019, an employer may state whether its decision to rehire is based upon the employer's determination that the current or former employee engaged in sexual harassment.

Some companies set a policy of not providing references at all. This may not be a wise decision because it could lead to liability if, for example, a former employee was terminated for violence or is known to be violent. If that employee is hired by another company and commits a violent act on the job, your company could be liable for failing to provide information that could have prevented the incident.

Policy Guidelines

Develop a company policy for handling employee references and follow it consistently. Consider these guidelines when developing your policy on reference checks:

- Determine who in your company will respond to reference requests.

- Be consistent when providing employee references.

- Create a waiver for former employees to sign at the time employment ends if they want you to release information to potential future employers.

- Do not provide standardized letters of reference to former employees.

- Determine what information will be provided.

- Determine if you will allow oral references or if you will require all references to be in writing.

- State that references will be provided only to those with a need to know the information.

- Provide only truthful job-related information, rather than personal data.

- Document each request for a reference.

It may be helpful to create a form for terminating employees that shows the type of information commonly requested in reference checks, such as dates of employment, positions held, rates of pay and eligibility for rehire. This will help ensure that the information provided was truthful, relevant and based on proper documentation.

Wrongful Termination

Because of increases in wrongful termination lawsuits, terminating an employee comes with increasing risk. Although you may not prevent a wrongful termination lawsuit after terminating an employee, there are several ways to protect yourself against liability for a wrongful termination.

Common Types of Wrongful Termination Lawsuits

In every employment relationship, an implied covenant of "good faith and fair dealing" exists. An ex-employee may file a wrongful termination suit against you if the ex-employee feels they were treated unfairly.

 Good faith and fair dealing means that you should make decisions on a fair basis, and you should treat similarly situated employees in the same manner.

Ex-employees may file several types of wrongful-termination lawsuits against you.

Table 92. Types of Lawsuits

Discrimination	The employee claims the separation was based on that individual's membership in a protected class rather than for legitimate reasons. For a list of protected classes, see "Protected Characteristics and Activities" in Chapter 7, page 261.
Wrongful Termination in Violation of Public Policy	The employee must show that the public policy involved is derived from an administrative regulation or state or federal statute and is fundamental and of benefit to the general public, rather than just to the employee or employer. You, in turn, must show that you based your decision to terminate the employee on legitimate business reasons. A well-documented separation process can help you against this type of lawsuit. See "Protecting Against Wrongful Termination Lawsuits" on page 327.

Table 92. Types of Lawsuits *(continued)*

Retaliation	You can't terminate an employee in retaliation for the employee exercising a right granted by a federal or state law or by federal or state regulations. Employees may allege that they were wrongfully terminated because they: • Refused to violate the law on the employer's behalf (for example, by disposing of hazardous waste improperly); • "Blew the whistle" to a government agency about employer actions that the employees believed violated the law; or their employer believed that they would do so; or one of the employee's family members blew the whistle; and/or • Participated in an investigation against the employer (for example, a sexual harassment investigation or an investigation of wage-and-hour violations).
Breach of Contract	The employee claims that you didn't comply with the terms of an employment contract. This includes written, oral and implied contracts. The employee must prove that the contract exists, and that the termination was in violation of that contract. Your best defense against this type of suit is to not create a contract in the first place. Confirming the at-will status of employment in an offer letter and having employees sign an employment at-will statement upon hire can defeat claims that an implied/oral contract existed. ❗ A clause in a written contract that allows for termination at-will can protect you from breach-of-contract lawsuits
Constructive Discharge	In this type of suit, the employee claims that you made working conditions so intolerable that a reasonable person would be compelled to resign, effectively terminating the individual and breaching your implied covenant of good faith and fair dealing. This most often happens when the employee claims harassment at work and you did nothing to stop it. **New** A pair of appellate decisions published in July 2019 involving the same employer serve as an important reminder: Employees may bring "wrongful termination" claims despite the lack of an employer-initiated termination. The court found that both plaintiffs presented sufficient evidence to show that their working conditions were so intolerable that any reasonable employee in their position would resign, focusing on their supervisor's continual pattern of demeaning the plaintiffs' accents, insulting their intelligence and criticizing their English skills. An "open door policy" may present your best protection against constructive discharge claims. An open door policy encourages employees to bring employment issues to the attention of the employer rather than going outside the company. Make sure you document and address employee concerns in an appropriate manner.

Protecting Against Wrongful Termination Lawsuits

Avoiding a wrongful termination lawsuit begins long before you terminate an employee. An error or miscommunication in any part of the employment process, including job applications, interviews, employee handbooks, and performance reviews can expose you to a wrongful termination lawsuit. You must take proper actions through the employment process to protect yourself against legal action.

Table 93. Protect Against Wrongful Termination Lawsuits

Document the Disciplinary Process	Nothing creates a stronger defense against an employment claim than a personnel file documenting that you:
	• Consistently followed your established disciplinary process;
	• Gave the employee honest performance evaluations;
	• Tracked any behavior/work problems (use the *Warning Letter Checklist and Sample* as a guide for how to draft a letter of warning);
	• Attempted to accommodate the employee's needs/complaints; and
	• Precisely followed your termination policy and process.
	It's a good idea to keep copies of:
	• Any documentation showing that employment was "at will;"
	• A signed *Notice to Employee as to Change in Relationship*, described in Table 94 on page 330;
	• Job description(s);
	• Performance reviews;
	• Records of pay changes and promotions/demotions;
	• Records of disciplinary actions/warnings; and
	• Written complaints, both by and about the employee (for example, harassment or discrimination charges) and records of each complaint's investigation and resolution.

Table 93. Protect Against Wrongful Termination Lawsuits *(continued)*

Establish Company Policies Ahead of Time	An employee handbook sets forth your rules regarding conduct in the workplace, your performance expectations and creates a fair and simple way to resolve disputes. Once you set forth policies, you need to follow those policies until you discontinue or change them.
	If you need to discontinue a policy or implement a new or updated policy, make sure you communicate the new information to employees and document the distribution of the updated handbook. Be careful when you write your policies that you don't limit your ability to take any type of disciplinary action as needed.
	Example: You may create a disciplinary process that requires a verbal warning, written warning and suspension before terminating an employee. If you terminate an employee without following your own policy, you may face a claim for a breach of contract.
	To avoid this situation, you should describe the disciplinary process in your handbook, but reserve the right to follow whatever course of discipline is warranted in a particular situation.
Watch Your Language	In all communication with employees, be careful to avoid language that could limit your right to terminate an individual employee. California is an at-will state, but certain language or conduct may create a written, oral or implied employment contract that may override the legal presumption that employment is at will. For details, see "Employment Contracts" in Chapter 2, page 61.
Train Supervisors and Managers	No matter how much care you take to avoid a wrongful termination lawsuit, if your managers and supervisors don't follow your guidelines, you will be the one to pay the price.
	Ensure that your managers and supervisors know how to:
	• Avoid creating oral or implied employment contracts;
	• Prevent and deal with harassment or discrimination in the workplace;
	• Manage employee performance; and
	• Consistently implement the company's discipline policy.
Be Aware of Public Policies	State and federal laws create exceptions to at-will employment, including protecting employees from discrimination based upon a protected class (see "Protected Characteristics and Activities" in Chapter 7, page 261). Be sure to properly document the reasons for termination to show that the termination is based upon legitimate, non-discriminatory reasons.

Table 93. Protect Against Wrongful Termination Lawsuits *(continued)*

Be Aware of Protected Activities	In addition to protecting classes of employees, state law also protects certain employee activities. You can't terminate an employee for:
	• Performing service — including serving jury duty, performing military service or acting as a volunteer firefighter.
	• Asserting legal rights — including refusing to commit an illegal act, "whistle- blowing" if the individual believes the company is violating the law or exercising a statutory obligation to report apparent victims of abuse or neglect.
	• Protecting privacy — including refusing to authorize disclosure of medical information or disclosing or refusing to disclose wages.
	• Engaging in lawful behavior — including participating in political activity, enrolling in an adult literacy program, or taking time off for a child's school or day care activities.
Follow a Standardized Method of Separation	To make sure that all employees get treated the same way upon separation, create a standard separation process and don't deviate from the established methods in that process. No specific law requires you to terminate an employee in person, so if you terminate someone by phone or letter, create a standard "script" or form letter that the terminating manager can use.
	The sample *Termination Decision Checklist* can help you decide whether to go forward with the termination and how to proceed. The sample *Termination Checklist* can help you make sure you've done everything you need to during the separation event. For specific guidelines for different types of separation, see "Types of Separation" on page 318.

Minimum Compliance Elements

1. Hang your *2020 California and Federal Labor Law Poster* (available from *store.calchamber.com*), which includes mandatory postings that all employees and applicants must be able to see, in a prominent place (such as a break room).

   If you have employees working in a city or county with a local minimum wage and/or paid sick leave ordinance, you may also need to post required local ordinances and provide additional notices to employees at the time of hire.

2. Use the *Termination Checklist* to make sure you fill out all the required paperwork for every employee who leaves your company (for a description of this form, see Table 94 on page 330).

3. Use the *Termination Decision Checklist* to alert you to possible negative repercussions that could follow a termination decision (for a description of this form, see Table 94 on page 330).

4. Provide the employee's final paycheck in the correct amount and within the required time period (see "Final Paycheck Time Requirement" on page 323).

Forms and Checklists

The following tables describe required and recommended forms and checklists associated with the termination process.

 TIP You can find these forms in your forms download, described in detail in "Online Forms" on page 9

Table 94. Forms and Checklists

Notice or Form	What Do I Use It For?	When Do I Use It?	Who Fills It Out?	Where Does It Go?
Authorization to Release Personnel Records	To authorize your company to release various information regarding an employee or former employee's employment.	Upon termination.	An employee or former employee should sign this form.	Maintain in employee's personnel file.
Cal-COBRA – Notice to Carrier	Required for **all** types of separation if your insurance plan covers between two and 19 participants.	Within 31 days of the time of the qualifying events of either separation or reduction in hours.	The employer.	Send the original form to your insurance carrier within 31 days of the qualifying event. Keep a copy of the form in your personnel records.

Table 94. Forms and Checklists *(continued)*

Notice or Form	What Do I Use It For?	When Do I Use It?	Who Fills It Out?	Where Does It Go?
Cal-COBRA – Notice to Employee	Required if you change health plans and Cal-COBRA protects former employees.	At least 30 days before a change in group plans.	The employer.	Send the original form to each individual who chose Cal-COBRA coverage. Also, send information about the new group benefit plan(s), premiums, enrollment forms, instructions and anything else necessary to allow the individuals to continue coverage. Keep a copy of the form in your personnel records.
COBRA Continuation Coverage Election Notice - California Employees	Required for **all** types of separation for employers with 20 or more employees, provide an employee health plan and self-administer COBRA.	Within 44 days of a qualifying event if you administer COBRA.	Employee fills it out.	Send via certified mail to the California employee and the employee's spouse.

Table 94. Forms and Checklists *(continued)*

Notice or Form	What Do I Use It For?	When Do I Use It?	Who Fills It Out?	Where Does It Go?
COBRA Continuation Coverage Election Notice - Outside California	Required for **all** types of separation for employers with 20 or more employees and some of whom are outside California, provide an employee health plan and self-administer COBRA.	Within 44 days of a qualifying event if you administer COBRA.	Employee fills it out.	Send via certified mail to the employee and the employee's spouse.
COBRA Notice to Plan Administrator	Required for **all** California employers with 20 or more employees and that outsource COBRA administration.	Within 30 days of a qualifying event if you do not administer COBRA.	The employer.	Send to the plan administrator.
COBRA Rights - Acknowledgment of Receipt of Notification	Required for **all** types of separation if your insurance plan covers 20 or more participants.	Within 14 days of the time you receive notification of a qualifying event.	Employee signs the notice.	Send via certified mail to the employee and the employee's spouse.

Table 94. Forms and Checklists *(continued)*

Notice or Form	What Do I Use It For?	When Do I Use It?	Who Fills It Out?	Where Does It Go?
Deceased Employee Compensation Collection Form	Provide this form to the surviving spouse, registered domestic partner, guardian or a conservator of an estate (affiant) to allow collection of the decedent's salary or other compensation. The maximum amount may not exceed $5,000.00 net.	After the death of an employee.	The surviving spouse, registered domestic partner, guardian or conservator of an estate.	Maintain in deceased employee's personnel file.
Employer Proof of Identity and Disbursement of Final Pay— Deceased Employee	Complete this form upon receipt of the *"Deceased Employee Compensation Collection Form."*	After the death of an employee when their survivor(s) request the employee's final pay.	The employer fills it out; the affiant signs it.	Place a copy of this completed form in the decedent's file and provide a copy to the affiant.
Exit Interview	Recommended for **all** types of separation.	On the final day of the employment, or ask the employee to return a paper form by mail.	Employee fills it out unless the interview is conducted orally; in that case, you may fill in the employee's answers.	Keep the exit interview in your personnel records.
Final Paycheck Acknowledgment	To ask an employee to certify receiving the final paycheck.	Upon termination of employment. Recommended for **all** types of separation.	The employer fills it out and the employee signs it.	In the employee's personnel file.

Table 94. Forms and Checklists *(continued)*

Notice or Form	What Do I Use It For?	When Do I Use It?	Who Fills It Out?	Where Does It Go?
Final Paycheck Acknowledgment - Spanish	To ask an employee to certify receiving the final paycheck.	Upon termination of employment. Recommended for **all** types of separation.	The employer fills it out and the employee signs it.	In the employee's personnel file.
Final Paycheck Worksheet	Recommended for **all** types of separation.	When preparing the employee's final paycheck. (For more information about how to calculate an employee's final paycheck, see "Calculating a Final Paycheck" on page 322.)	The employer.	Keep the worksheet in your personnel records.
For Your Benefit, California's Program for the Unemployed pamphlet (available in the ***2020 Required Notices Kit***)	Required for **all** types of separation.	Upon termination.	N/A	Give a copy to the employee. Use the *Termination Checklist* to document receipt.
HIPP Notice	Required for **all** types of separation.	Upon termination.	N/A	Give a copy to the employee. Use the *Termination Checklist* to document receipt.
HIPP Notice - Spanish	Required for **all** types of separation.	Upon termination.	N/A	Give a copy to the employee. Use the *Termination Checklist* to document receipt.

Table 94. Forms and Checklists (continued)

Notice or Form	What Do I Use It For?	When Do I Use It?	Who Fills It Out?	Where Does It Go?
Notice to Employee as to Change in Relationship	Required for: • Discharge • Layoff • Leave of absence Recommended for **all** types of separation. Written notice must be provided by: • Letter • Employer's own form • The form in your forms download	In your preparations to terminate an employee.	The employer. You should request the employee's signature, but the law doesn't require you to do so. The notice must include: • Employer name • Employee name • Employee Social Security number • Indication that the action was a discharge, layoff, leave of absence or a change in status • The date of the action	Give a copy to the employee. Keep a copy in the employee's personnel records.
Termination Checklist	Recommended for **all** types of separation.	During the separation.	The employer.	Keep the checklist in your personnel records.
Termination Decision Checklist	Recommended for **all** types of separation.	Before deciding to terminate an employee.	N/A	N/A

Table 94. Forms and Checklists *(continued)*

Notice or Form	What Do I Use It For?	When Do I Use It?	Who Fills It Out?	Where Does It Go?
Unemployment Insurance - Responding to a Claim Checklist	Recommended for **all** types of separation.	After the separation process.	The employer.	Keep the checklist in your personnel records.
Unemployment Insurance Claim - Appealing to an Administrative Law Judge (ALJ) Checklist	To help you prepare an appeal to an ALJ for a UI claim you want to protest.	During the appeal process.	The employer.	Keep a copy in the employee's personnel file.
Unemployment Insurance Claim - Appealing to the Appeals Board Checklist	To help you present your final case to the UI Appeals Board.	At the final stage of the appeal process, after an ALJ rejected your appeal.	The employer.	Keep a copy in the employee's personnel file.
Unemployment Insurance pamphlet (available in the **2020 Required Notices Kit***)*	Provide this pamphlet to any employee being terminated, laid off or given a leave of absence.	You must provide this pamphlet whenever you hire a new employee.	N/A	Give a copy to your workers and make sure they understand its contents.
Warning Letter Checklist and Sample	Review this letter and use the examples as a guide for how to draft your own letter of warning.	Before you prepare a warning letter for an employee.	The employer.	Keep a copy in your personnel records.

Where Do I Go for More Information?

CalChamber and federal and state government agencies offer a variety of resources to help prepare you for the separation process.

Table 95. Additional Resources

For Information On	Check Out These Resources
General	From CalChamber: • The **2020 California Labor Law Digest**, the most comprehensive, California-specific resource to help employers comply with complex federal and state labor laws and regulations • **Required Notices Kit**, available at **store.calchamber.com** • **HRCalifornia.com**
State Government	California's Employment Development Department at **www.edd.ca.gov**

CalChamber also provides many ongoing and comprehensive educational opportunities for small business owners, HR beginners and experienced HR professionals alike. These include online sexual harassment prevention training, special HR seminars and webinars. For more information, please visit our website at **store.calchamber.com**.

Glossary of Terms, Laws and Agencies

4/10 Workweek

A weekly schedule that allows the employee to work four 10-hour days each week; for exemption from overtime requirements, the schedule must be under an approved alternative workweek.

9/80 Workweek

A two-week schedule that allows an employee to work nine days and 80 hours — five days in one calendar week and four days the following week; for exemption from overtime requirements, the schedule must be under an approved alternative workweek.

Accrue

To accumulate or have due after a period of time.

ADA

Americans with Disabilities Act of 1990. Prohibits employers of 15 or more employees in the private sector, and state and local governments from discriminating against qualified individuals with disabilities. It requires employers to provide reasonable accommodation for individuals with disabilities, unless the accommodating measures would cause undue hardship. *See also* Reasonable Accommodation.

ADEA

Age Discrimination in Employment Act of 1967. Prohibits employers with 20 or more employees from discriminating against individuals 40 years of age and older.

Adverse Action

An employment decision that has a negative impact on hiring, promotion, termination, benefits or compensation.

Affirmative Action

An active effort to improve the employment or educational opportunities of members of protected classes.

ALJ

Administrative Law Judge. A judge appointed by an administrative agency for the purpose of conducting hearings and rendering decisions under the agency's unique jurisdiction. Typically, an ALJ's decisions are reviewed by the agency and by the courts.

Alternative Workweek

An alternative scheduling method that allows employees to work a standard workweek over less than a five-day period in one week or a 10-day period in two weeks without incurring overtime.

At-Will Employment

A legal concept, mandated by California law, assuring both employer and employee that either party can terminate the relationship at any time and for any reason or no reason.

Back Pay

A type of damages awarded in an employment lawsuit that represents the amount of money the employee would have earned if the employee was not fired or denied a promotion illegally.

Bereavement Leave

Time off for a funeral or for mourning when an employee's family member dies.

BFOQ

Bona fide occupational qualification. Qualifications and characteristics reasonably necessary to perform duties, tasks or processes required to conduct normal business operations.

California Labor Commissioner

Sets and enforces regulations for employee wages, paycheck deductions, breaks, vacation, jury/witness duty, or temporary military leave, the workweek, minors, employee access to personnel files, "lawful conduct" discrimination, exempt status, and independent contractor status. The commissioner also assesses fines and files charges with the District Attorney on behalf of underpaid employees, and investigates, holds hearings, takes action to recover wages, assesses penalties, and makes demands for compensation.

Cal-COBRA

California Continuation of Benefits Replacement Act. Requires insurance carriers and HMOs to provide COBRA-like coverage for employees of smaller employers (2–19 employees) not subject to COBRA.

Cal/OSHA

California Occupational Safety and Health Administration. Enforces California laws and regulations pertaining to workplace safety and health and provides assistance to employers and workers about workplace safety and health issues.

CFRA

California Family Rights Act. Provides employees 12 weeks of leave for bonding with a newborn or adopted child, caring for a family member with a serious health condition, and/or caring for the employee's own serious health condition. This law applies to companies with 50 or more employees.

Civil Rights Act of 1991

Amended Title VII, creating, among other things, the right to jury trials, and allowing those claiming intentional discrimination or harassment based on sex, race, religion, national origin or color under Title VII, or disability under the ADA or Rehabilitation Act, to obtain compensatory and punitive damages measured by the size of the employer's workforce, up to a maximum of $300,000.

Claimant

Individual making a claim for Unemployment Insurance, Workers' Compensation or other benefit.

COBRA

Consolidated Omnibus Budget Reconciliation Act of 1985. Requires employers with 20 or more employees to offer all employees covered by health care the option of continuing to be covered by the company's group health insurance plan at the worker's own expense for a specific period (often 18 months) after employment ends.

Collective Bargaining Agreement

An agreement resulting from "collective bargaining," or the negotiations between representatives of a union and employers. A collective bargaining agreement establishes employees' terms and conditions of employment, such as wages, hours of work, working conditions and grievance procedures.

Commission

Compensation paid to an employee based on a proportional amount of sales of the employer's property or services.

Compensation

Any monetary payment related to work, including wages, commissions and bonuses.

Compensatory Time Off (CTO)

Gives a nonexempt employee time off for extra hours worked instead of paying overtime; commonly referred to as "comp time" and almost always illegal for private sector employers.

Concurrent Leave

Two different types of leave (for example PDL and FMLA) that are used up simultaneously. Table 29 in Chapter 3, page 111 provides an overview of the ways PDL, FMLA/CFRA, Workers'

Compensation and disability leaves interact concurrently.

Conflict of Interest

A conflict between the private interests and the official responsibilities of a person in a position of trust.

Constructive Discharge

A wrongful termination claim that the working conditions were so intolerable that a reasonable person would be forced to resign.

CTD

Cumulative trauma disorder. *See also* RMI.

Deduction

An amount of money withheld from an employee's gross earnings for legally required or permitted purposes, such as taxes, garnishments, contributions to retirement plans or health plan premiums.

DFEH

California Department of Fair Employment and Housing. Enforces California's non-discrimination laws. DFEH has jurisdiction over private and public employment, housing, public accommodations, and public services. DFEH receives and investigates discrimination complaints, and provides technical assistance to employers regarding their responsibilities under the law.

DIR

California Department of Industrial Relations. Seeks to improve working conditions for California's wage earners and to advance opportunities for profitable employment in California.

DIR has these major areas of responsibility: labor law, workplace safety and health, apprenticeship training, Workers' Compensation, statistics and research, mediation, and conciliation.

Disability

In California, a physical or mental impairment that limits one or more of the major life activities.

Disability Insurance

A voluntary plan, for employers who do not want to participate in SDI, that provides short-term benefits for employees who are disabled by a non-work-related illness or injury.

Disparate (Unequal) Impact

Disparate impact refers to an employment practice that appears neutral but discriminates against a protected class in practice.

Disparate (Unequal) Treatment

Disparate treatment refers to an applicant or employee that belongs to a protected class receiving different treatment because of his or her membership in a protected class.

DLSE

California Division of Labor Standards Enforcement. Investigates wage claims and discrimination complaints and enforces California's labor laws and Wage Orders.

DOL

U.S. Department of Labor. Administers a variety of federal labor laws including those that guarantee workers' rights to safe and healthful working conditions, a

minimum hourly wage and overtime pay, freedom from employment discrimination, Unemployment Insurance, and other income support.

DOSH

California Division of Occupational Safety and Health. Enforces the state's occupational and public safety laws and provides information and consultative assistance to employers, workers and the public about workplace and public safety matters.

Double-Time

Two times an employee's regular rate of pay. *See also* Overtime.

EAP

Employee assistance program. A workplace program provided by the employer to assist employees in recovering from or dealing with personal issues or problems.

EDD

California Employment Development Department. Helps California employers meet their labor needs, job seekers obtain employment, and the disadvantaged and welfare-to-work recipients to become self-sufficient. It supports state activities and benefit programs by collecting and administering employment-related taxes (UI, SDI, employment training tax and personal income tax).

EEOC

Equal Employment Opportunity Commission. A federal agency that interprets discrimination law, collects employment data and handles employee complaints.

Employee

Any person rendering actual service in any business for an employer.

Employee Benefit Plans

Welfare and pension plans voluntarily established and maintained by an employer, an employee organization, or jointly by one or more such employers and an employee organization. Governed by ERISA.

Employer

Any person engaged in any business or enterprise in California with one or more persons in service. An employer can be an individual, association, organization, partnership, business trust, limited liability corporation or corporation.

Engineered Controls

Protective devices designed to reduce or eliminate the risk of workplace injury. Examples include machine guards, adjustable fixtures and tool redesign.

English-Only Policy

Prohibits the use of other languages in the workplace. It is illegal in California unless certain conditions are met, including business necessity and employee notice.

Equal Pay Act

Part of the federal Fair Labor Standards Act, which requires "equal pay for equal work." Employers are required to pay employees of the opposite sex in the same establishment equal wages for equal work without regard to an employee's gender. *See also* Fair Pay Act.

Ergonomics

The scientific study of the relationship between people and their work environments. The goal of the field is to minimize workplace injuries and illnesses through improved workplace design.

ERISA

Employee Retirement Income Security Act. Regulates employee benefit plans and the numerous persons (for example, employers and unions) involved in establishing and maintaining these plans. ERISA sets uniform minimum standards to assure that employee benefit plans are established and maintained in a fair and financially sound manner. In addition, employers have an obligation to provide promised benefits and satisfy ERISA's requirements for managing and administering private pension and welfare plans.

Essential Functions

Fundamental job requirements of the position, or the reason the job exists.

Exempt

An employee who is not subject to any of the laws pertaining to overtime, meal periods, and rest periods.

Fair Pay Act

The Fair Pay Act prohibits California employers from paying any employees less than employees of the opposite sex, or of different races or ethnicities, for substantially similar work.

Family Leave

Family and medical leave, typically called "family leave," is time off available to employees for specific reasons, as defined in federal and state statutes.

Family leave covers time off for bonding with a newborn or adopted child; caring for a family member with a serious health condition; caring for the employee's own serious health condition; and under federal law, caring for an ill or injured servicemember; and qualifying exigency related to a close family member's military service.

FCRA

Fair Credit Reporting Act. Requires specific disclosures in a specific format, in addition to any waiver that might be on an application, before checking the applicant's credit, and restricts an employer's ability to use credit reports for employment purposes.

FEHA

California's Fair Employment and Housing Act. Prohibits discrimination/ harassment on the basis of race/color, religious creed, national origin/ancestry, physical disability, mental disability, medical condition (including no genetic testing), marital status, sex, age, and sexual orientation. This law provides more protection than the ADA.

Fitness for Duty

A medical practitioner's certification releasing an individual under his/her care to assume or resume full or modified duties before hire or following a leave of absence due to illness or injury.

Flat Rate

Pay based on a job completed, not the number of hours spent completing it.

Flexible Schedule

An eight-hour work schedule where some employees begin the shift early in the day and others begin their work later in the day.

FLSA

The federal Fair Labor Standards Act. Regulates minimum wages, overtime, and working conditions for all employees of businesses that engage in interstate commerce and have an annual gross volume of sales of not less than $500,000, or an individual employee who is involved in interstate commerce, contracts to do work for a firm engaged in interstate commerce, or travels across state lines in the course of employment.

FMLA

Family and Medical Leave Act. Provides up to 12 weeks of job-protected, unpaid leave during a pre-defined 12-month period for employees who work for a public agency, a local education agency, or an employer in the private sector who has 50 or more employees each working day during at least 20 calendar weeks in the current or preceding calendar year.

Front Pay

A type of damages awarded in an employment lawsuit that represents the amount of money the employee would have earned if he or she was reinstated or hired into the higher-paying position from which he or she was illegally rejected.

Full Time

An employee who works the number of hours designated by the employer as "full time."

Garnishments

Money withheld by court order from an employee's check to pay for debt, back taxes or child support.

Good Faith and Fair Dealing

Employment decisions that are made fairly, treating similarly situated employees in the same manner.

Harassment

Behavior toward a person that a reasonable person would find unwelcome or hostile.

HAZCOM

Hazard Communication Program. Requires all employers to communicate workplace hazards to employees, particularly when employees handle or may be exposed to hazardous substances during normal work or foreseeable emergencies.

HIPP

Health Insurance Premium Payment program. A California program that requires all employers to provide departing employees with notice of a state program that pays COBRA payments under certain circumstances.

Hostile Work Environment

An unproductive work environment caused by unwelcome sexual comments, touches, or visual displays.

IIPP

Injury and Illness Prevention Program. A company's general plan for keeping its workforce free from work-related injuries and illness, mandated by California law.

Independent Contractor

A person or company that supplies goods or services to an individual or business. The independent contractor should not have any of the characteristics of an employee.

Intern

Student who performs work in the course of his/her studies, as part of the curriculum.

IRCA

Immigration Reform and Control Act. A federal law requiring employers to verify all employees' legal eligibility to live and work in the United States.

IRS

Internal Revenue Service. The nation's tax collection agency, which administers the Internal Revenue Code enacted by Congress.

IWC

Industrial Welfare Commission. A defunct California agency that monitored the hours and conditions of employment; was responsible for the content of the Wage Orders.

Just Cause

A fair and honest cause or reason, acted on in good faith by the employer.

Kin Care

Care of a sick child, spouse, parent, parent-in-law, sibling, registered domestic partner, child of a registered domestic partner, grandparent or grandchild, using up to half of an employee's annual accrual of paid sick leave.

Labor Commissioner

See **California Labor Commissioner**.

Lay Off

To cease to employ a worker, often temporarily, because of economic reasons.

Living Wage

A wage sufficient to provide the necessities and comforts essential to an acceptable standard of living. Generally mandated by local ordinances.

Log 300

A series of recordkeeping forms for recording workplace injuries and illnesses. Part of a Cal/OSHA record-keeping requirement.

Major Life Activities

Caring for oneself, sleeping, learning, walking, interacting with others, working, and other physical, mental, and social activities. Used to determine whether a worker is disabled.

Makeup Time

Allows nonexempt employees to request time off for a personal obligation and make up the time within the same workweek without receiving overtime pay.

Mass Layoff

The laying off of 50 or more employees, under WARN.

Meal Period

An unpaid, 30-minute block of time for nonexempt employees for every period of work that lasts for more than five hours; must begin no later than four hours and 59 minutes into the employee's work period.

Medical Certification

A statement from an employee's health care provider as to the necessity of time off from work. Usually required by an employer when an employee is off for a reason protected by law.

Minimum Salary

The smallest amount a salaried exempt employee can make, in order to be considered exempt.

Minimum Wage

The smallest hourly wage a nonexempt employee can make. *See also* **Regular Rate of Pay**.

Minor

Any person under the age of 18 who is required to attend school, or any person under the age of six.

Misdemeanor

A criminal offense that is more serious than an infraction, but less serious than a felony. A misdemeanor is punishable by fine, incarceration in county jail, or a combination of both.

MSD

Musculoskeletal disorder. See **RMI**.

NLRA

National Labor Relations Act. Prohibits employers from basing any employment action on employee participation in labor organization (union) activities. Such activities include attending union meetings, speaking with union representatives, and discussing union activities with other employees.

Negligence

A lack of prudent care (neglect).

Noncompete Agreements

An agreement between an employer and an employee which says that when an employee leaves the company, the employee will not work for a competitor for a certain amount of time. With few exceptions, noncompete agreements are illegal in California under most circumstances.

Nonexempt

An employee who is subject to the laws pertaining to overtime, minimum wage, meal periods and rest breaks.

Occupational Wage Order

Same as a Wage Order. Contains the instructions for payment of wages to nonexempt employees as well as specific rights and responsibilities of the employee and the employer. *See* Wage Orders.

Open-Door Policy

A policy encouraging employees to bring employment issues to the attention of the employer, rather than going outside the company.

Open Enrollment

A period of time during which employees can sign up for an employer's group health plan or benefit plan, such as a retirement fund.

OSHA

Occupational Safety and Health Administration. The federal agency that ensures safe and healthful workplaces by issuing standards, performing inspections, and levying penalties for violations.

Overtime

Hours worked beyond a "normal" amount of hours for a day or week. For nonexempt employees with a regular workweek, normal is eight hours per day and 40 hours per week. For employees with an alternative workweek, normal could be nine or 10 hours. For more information on alternative workweeks, see Chapter 5, "Paying Employees." *See also* Pyramiding of Overtime.

Parental Leave

California's New Parent Leave Act. Provides eligible employees 12 weeks of leave for bonding with a newborn, foster or adopted child. This law applies to companies with 20 or more employees.

Part Time

An employee who works less than the number of hours that qualify him/her as a full-time employee, according to your policy.

PDA

Pregnancy Discrimination Act of 1978. An amendment to Title VII, requires that employers treat a pregnant employee the same as any other employee, and that when a female employee becomes unable to work due to pregnancy, childbirth, or related medical conditions, the employer treat her disability the same as any other disability.

PDL

Pregnancy Disability Leave. California employers with five or more employees must provide as much as four months of leave for employees disabled by pregnancy and pregnancy-related conditions.

PFL

Paid Family Leave. A wage replacement program funded through employee contributions and administered by the Employment Development Department for employees unable to work when they are needed to care for a family member.

PPE

Personal protective equipment. Items such as gloves, masks, and special clothing used to protect against hazardous, toxic, or infectious material.

PTO

Paid time off. An informal term referring to an employer-defined combination of sick pay, holiday pay, and/or vacation.

Pension Plan

Provides retirement income or defers income until termination of covered employment or beyond. Governed by ERISA.

Personal Days

Time off associated with a particular event, such as an employee's birthday.

Piece Rate

An amount paid for completing a particular task or making a particular piece of goods.

Plant Closing

The shutting down of a facility or laying off 50 or more employees. *See also* WARN, *Mass Layoff.*

Proposition 65

Requires that employers with 10 or more employees warn any person (employees and others who may enter a laboratory) prior to their exposure to a chemical known to the state of California to cause cancer, birth defects, or other reproductive harm.

Protected Class

Different classes of individuals who receive specific legal protection against discrimination and harassment based on the individuals belonging to a protected class, including individuals over the age of 40.

Pyramiding of Overtime

Not required by California law, exists when an employee earns overtime on top of overtime already paid.

Qualifying Event

For benefits purposes, one of several defined events that permits a change of benefits enrollment status outside of open enrollment periods or that entitles an eligible beneficiary to COBRA or Cal-COBRA benefits.

Qualified Beneficiary

An employee covered under an employer's group health plan.

Quid Pro Quo

Latin, meaning "this for that." A type of sexual harassment that conditions job continuance, promotions, benefits, etc. in exchange for sexual favors.

Rate of Pay

A fixed amount of payment based on a unit of time or a piece of work performed.

Reasonable Accommodation

Any change in the work environment or in the way a job is performed that enables a person with a disability to enjoy equal employment opportunities. *See also* Disability.

Registered Domestic Partner

Either one of an unmarried heterosexual couple over the age of 62 or a same-sex couple registered with the California Secretary of State.

Regular Rate of Pay

The calculated amount of an employee's actual earnings, which may include an hourly rate, commission, bonuses, piece work, and the value of meals and lodging.

Religious Holidays

A day specified for religious observance. Employers must make reasonable accommodations for employee requests for time off for religious holidays.

Reporting Time Pay

Payment to a nonexempt employee who reports to work at his/her normal time and is not put to work, or is given less than half the hours for which he/she was scheduled.

Rest Period

A 10-minute, paid block of time for nonexempt employees for each four hours worked; should be scheduled near the middle of the work period.

Retaliation

California regards retaliation as any adverse employment action that results because an individual has opposed practices prohibited by the Fair

Employment and Housing Act, or has filed a complaint, testified, assisted or participated in any manner in an investigation, proceeding or hearing conducted by the Department of Fair Employment and Housing or its staff.

Retirement Plan

A fund that provides individuals with income after retirement. Employees and employers contribute money to a fund during an employee's term of employment, and employees receive a defined income from the fund upon retirement.

RMI

Repetitive motion injury. A problematic injury that builds over time, caused by overuse or overexertion of some part of the musculoskeletal system. Often referred to as cumulative trauma disorders (CMDs) or musculoskeletal disorders (MSDs).

Safety Data Sheets

An information sheet provided by the manufacturer of a product that describes the product's chemical properties, potential hazards, and instruction in safe handling (formerly called "material safety data sheets").

Salary

A fixed amount of money for each payroll period, whether weekly, bi-weekly, semi-monthly or monthly.

SDI

California State Disability Insurance. Provides temporary disability benefits for employees who are disabled by a non-work-related illness or injury. Benefits are paid by the Employment Development

Department from employee contributions in the form of a tax.

Seventh-Day Rule

Nonexempt employees who work on each day of your established seven-day workweek are entitled to overtime at the rate of time and one-half for the first eight hours worked and double time for any hours worked beyond that on that seventh day.

Severance Pay

Money paid to an employee at the time of termination or layoff, to compensate in part for the sudden job loss. Not required by law.

Sexual Harassment

Unwelcome verbal, visual or physical conduct of a sexual nature that is severe or pervasive and affects working conditions or creates a hostile work environment.

SIC

Standard Industry Code. System that classifies businesses by their primary activity. The SIC is used for a variety of statistical purposes.

Split Shift

Any two distinct work periods separated by more than a one-hour meal period.

Standby

Time the employee spends on call that cannot be used for his/her benefit. Depending on the limitations on the employee during this time, the standby time may be paid or unpaid.

Statute

A law enacted by the legislative branch of a government.

Telecommute

To work at home by the use of an electronic linkup with a central office. Employees may use an electronic linkup with a central office or other technology to work from a location away from their office.

TICP

Targeted Inspection and Consultation Program. A Cal/OSHA program that identifies certain high-hazard employers, and requires a fee paid to fund a special inspection unit.

Time-And-One-Half

The regular hourly rate for the job an employee is doing, plus one-half the regular rate of pay. *See also* **Double-Time**, **Overtime**.

Title VII, Civil Rights Act of 1964

Prohibits employers of 15 or more employees from discriminating on the basis of race, color, religion, sex, or national origin.

UI

Unemployment Insurance. An employer-paid tax, which is held in reserve for employees in case they become unemployed.

USCIS

U.S. Citizenship and Immigration Services. The USCIS enforces the laws regulating the admission of foreign-born persons to the United States, and administers various immigration benefits, including work visas and the naturalization of qualified applicants for U.S. citizenship.

USERRA

Uniformed Services Employment and Reemployment Rights Act. This act prohibits discrimination or reprisals against past and present members of the uniformed service. No employer may deny a person initial employment, retention in employment, promotion or any benefit of employment based on a person's membership, application for membership, performance of service, application to perform service or obligation for service in the uniformed services.

VETS

Veterans' Employment and Training Service. Federal agency that enforces the Uniformed Services Employment and Reemployment Rights Act.

Volunteer

A person who intends to give his/her time for public service, religious or humanitarian objectives without wanting pay.

Wage Orders

Contain the instructions for paying nonexempt employees their wages. There are currently 17 Wage Orders, organized according to industry, plus a Minimum Wage Order. The purpose of your business determines which Wage Order applies to you.

Wages

Money received by an employee for labor performed of every description, whether the amount is fixed or determined by the standard of time, task, piece,

commission or other methods of calculation.

WARN

Worker Adjustment and Retraining Notification Act. A federal law requiring employers to give employees advance notice of a plant closing or a mass layoff if the action involves a requisite number of employees. California has a similar law that provides more protection than that of federal law, therefore more employees are covered by state law.

Welfare Plan

Provides health benefits, disability benefits, death benefits, prepaid legal services, vacation benefits, day care centers, scholarship funds, apprenticeship and training benefits, or other similar benefits. Governed by ERISA.

Whistleblowing

Any report made by an employee or an employee's family member of suspected illegal activity on the part of an employer.

Workday

Any consecutive 24-hour period starting at the same time each calendar day. If an employer doesn't define the workday, the California Labor Commission will presume a workday of 12:01 a.m. to midnight.

Workweek

Any seven consecutive 24-hour periods, starting on the same calendar day and at the same time each week. If an employer doesn't define the workweek, the California Labor Commissioner will presume a workweek of Sunday through Saturday.

Work Permit

A document establishing the maximum number of days and hours a minor may legally work during the workweek. The permit may also impose other limitations on the scope of the minor's work.

Workers' Compensation

A mandatory "no-fault" insurance program, paid for by employers, to cover medical treatment and wage replacement for an employee who suffers a work-related illness or injury.

Index

(DHS)

DIR. *See* Department of Industrial Relations (DIR)

Direct Deposit Authorization 66

Direct deposit of wages 196

Disabilities 264, 277–278
    alcohol abuse as 278
    discrimination 277–280
    drug abuse as 278
    reasonable accommodation 278–279

Disability Insurance Provisions pamphlet 29

Disability leave 109–110
    reasonable accommodation 109

Discharge. *See* Termination

Discrimination 257–280
    age 263
    AIDS status 263
    claims
        investigating 281
        witnesses 307
    compliance 283
    consumer reports 41
    disabilities 264, 277–280
    employee handbook 293–295
    forms 284–285
    gender 20, 264
    genetic characteristics and information 266–267
    height 267
    hiring process 63–64
    HIV status 263
    immigration status 267–269
    jury/witness duty 119
    language 269
    lawful conduct 270
    liability 281–282
    marital status 270
    medical conditions 271
    national origin 271
    penalties 281–282
    poster requirements 283, 311
    pregnancy 272
    protected classes and activities 261–276
    religion 274

sex 274
sexual orientation 275
veteran status 275
wages 165
weight 267
whistleblowers 276

Discrimination and Harassment in Employment are Prohibited by Law poster 5

Division of Occupational Safety and Health (DOSH) 215

Doctors. *See* Physicians

Document abuse 48

DOL. *See* Department of Labor (DOL)

Domestic employees, paying 193

domestic partner 270

Domestic partners of employees 149
    Cal-COBRA 152
    CFRA 87–89
    COBRA 151–152
    crime victims' leave 114
    family and medical leaves 87
    health insurance 151
    paid sick leave 103

Domestic violence leave 117–119

DOSH. *See* Division of Occupational Safety and Health (DOSH)

Double-time 187

Drivers' licenses 49

Drug abuse
    and workers' compensation claims 143
    disability 278

Drug tests 32, 42

E

EDD. *See* Employment Development Department (EDD)

Education verification, hiring process and 32

eLaws Advisor 134

Emancipated minors, employing 59

Emergency Action Plan 250

choice of 146–147

minimum wage 171

Piece rates 172–173

Policies

bereavement leave 127

discipline 328

discrimination 293–295

harassment 293–295

holidays 107

marijuana 217

minimum wage 166

personal leave 127

use it or lose it 107

Posters 4–9

Pre-Hire Checklist 12, 75

Pre-Adverse Action Disclosure 75

Pregnancy Disability Leave 93

Pregnancy Disability Leave (PDL) 93–98

employers subject to requirements of 3

other leaves and 111

sick leave 105

Pregnancy Disability Leave Notice poster 6

Pregnancy, discrimination 272

Prior salary 20, 43

Privacy

background checks 25

checking references 43

protected activities 329

providing references 324

Privacy, invasion of 22

Private Attorneys General Act of 2004 (PAGA) 208–209

Probationary period 30

Process Safety Management (PSM) of Acutely Hazardous Materials standard 236

Professional exemptions 168–169

Profit-sharing plans 154

Property Return Agreement 75

Protected activities 329

PTO. *See* Paid time off (PTO)

Public policy violation, wrongful termination

lawsuits and 325

Q

Qualifying exigency 87, 138

Quit. *See* Voluntary quit

R

race

hairstyles 262

protections 262

Reasonable accommodation. *See* Accommodation, reasonable

Reasonable victim standard 289

Record keeping

and interview notes 25

disciplinary process 327

employee orientation 30

harassment investigations 304

hiring 26, 28–29

Injury and Illness Prevention Program standard 219, 220, 221, 222, 223, 224, 226

Log 300 240

occupational injury and illness 240–242

paid sick leave 104

payroll 198

training 30

Recovery periods from heat 230

Recruiting Checklist 75

References, employee 324–325

checking 22, 32, 43

Refusal to accept available work 320

Registered domestic partners of employees. *See* Domestic partners of employees

Regular employees 15

Regular rate of pay 185

determining 185–186

multiple hourly rates 187

piece rate employees 172

Regular workweek 164

314

CalChamber®